The Karbala Story and Early Shiʿite Identity

Edinburgh Studies in Classical Islamic History and Culture
Series Editor: Carole Hillenbrand

A particular feature of medieval Islamic civilization was its wide horizons. The Muslims fell heir not only to the Graeco-Roman world of the Mediterranean, but also to that of the ancient Near East, to the empires of Assyria, Babylon and the Persians; and beyond that, they were in frequent contact with India and China to the east and with black Africa to the south. This intellectual openness can be sensed in many inter-related fields of Muslim thought, and it impacted powerfully on trade and on the networks that made it possible. Books in this series reflect this openness and cover a wide range of topics, periods and geographical areas.

Titles in the series include:

The Body in Arabic Love Poetry: The 'Udhri Tradition
Jokha Alharthi

Owning Books and Preserving Documents in Medieval Jerusalem: The Library of Burhan al-Din
Said Aljoumani and Konrad Hirschler

Arabian Drugs in Early Medieval Mediterranean Medicine
Zohar Amar and Efraim Lev

The Abbasid Caliphate of Cairo, 1261–1517: Out of the Shadows
Mustafa Banister

Christian Monastic Life in Early Islam
Bradley Bowman

Queens, Concubines and Eunuchs in Medieval Islam
Taef El-Azhari

Islamic Political Thought in the Mamluk Period
Mohamad El Merheb

The Kharijites in Early Islamic Historical Tradition: Heroes and Villains
Hannah-Lena Hagemann

Between Rebels and Rulers in the Early Islamicate World: Power, Contention and Identity
Edited by Hannah-Lena Hagemann and Alasdair Grant

Classical Islam: Collected Essays
Carole Hillenbrand

Islam and the Crusades: Collected Essays
Carole Hillenbrand

The Medieval Turks: Collected Essays
Carole Hillenbrand

Medieval Damascus: Plurality and Diversity in an Arabic Library – The Ashrafiya Library Catalogue
Konrad Hirschler

A Monument to Medieval Syrian Book Culture: The Library of Ibn 'Abd al-Hādī
Konrad Hirschler

The Popularisation of Sufism in Ayyubid and Mamluk Egypt: State and Society, 1173–1325
Nathan Hofer

Defining Anthropomorphism: The Challenge of Islamic Traditionalism
Livnat Holtzman

The Karbala Story and Early Shi'ite Identity
Torsten Hylén

Making Mongol History: Rashid al-Din and the Jami' al-Tawarikh
Stefan Kamola

Lyrics of Life: Sa'di on Love, Cosmopolitanism and Care of the Self
Fatemeh Keshavarz

Art, Allegory and The Rise of Shiism In Iran, 1487–1565
Chad Kia

The Administration of Justice in Medieval Egypt: From the 7th to the 12th Century
Yaacov Lev

Zoroastrians in Early Islamic History: Accommodation and Memory
Andrew D. Magnusson

A History of Herat: Fro Chingiz Khan to Tamerlane
Shivan Mahendrarajah

The Queen of Sheba's Gift: A History of the True Balsam of Matarea
Marcus Milwright

Islam, Christianity and the Realms of the Miraculous: A Comparative Exploration
Ian Richard Netton

The Poetics of Spiritual Instruction: Farid al-Din 'Attar and Persian Sufi Didacticism
Austin O'Malley

Sacred Place and Sacred Time in the Medieval Islamic Middle East: An Historical Perspective
Daniella Talmon-Heller

Conquered Populations in Early Islam: Non-Arabs, Slaves and the Sons of Slave Mothers
Elizabeth Urban

Medieval Syria and the Onset of the Crusades: The Political World of Bilad al-Sham, 1050–1128
James Wilson

edinburghuniversitypress.com/series/escihc

The Karbala Story and Early Shiʿite Identity

Torsten Hylén

EDINBURGH
University Press

Edinburgh University Press is one of the leading university presses in the UK. Publishing new research in the arts and humanities, EUP connects people and ideas to inspire creative thinking, open new perspectives and shape the world we live in. For more information, visit www.edinburghuniversitypress.com.

We are committed to making research available to a wide audience and are pleased to be publishing Platinum Open Access editions of the ebooks in this series.

Edinburgh University Press Ltd
13 Infirmary Street, Edinburgh EH1 1LT

Typeset in 11/15 Adobe Garamond by
Cheshire Typesetting Ltd, Cuddington, Cheshire and
printed and bound by CPI Group (UK) Ltd, Croydon, CR0 4YY

A CIP record for this book is available from the British Library

ISBN 978 1 3995 2205 2 (hardback)
ISBN 978 1 3995 2206 9 (paperback)
ISBN 978 1 3995 2207 6 (webready PDF)
ISBN 978 1 3995 2208 3 (epub)

Contents

Part III From Skirmish to Cosmic Battle

Illustrations

Note on Conventions

When transliterating Arabic words, I have used the system employed in the *International Journal of Middle East Studies*. Words of Arabic origin that are found in English dictionaries, and place names commonly used in English, are rendered in their English form (for example hadith, Mahdi, Medina, Karbala). In an attempt to make the book readable to non-specialists as well as scholars in the field, I have used English plural forms of Arabic words (for example *isnād*s instead of *asānīd* and *khabar*s instead of *akhbār*). An exception to that rule is the use of Arabic plurals when referring to some groups such as the Tawwābūn and the Ghulāt, as these are the forms normally used in the literature of the field. In proper names, 'b.' stands for the word *ibn*, meaning 'son of'. Similarly, 'bt.' is a short form of *bint*, 'daughter of'.

I discuss my use of the terms 'Shiʿism', 'Shiʿites', etc. in Chapter 1.

The Arabic word *muʾminūn*, 'believers', has different connotations for Shiʿites and non-Shiʿites, and its meaning has moreover changed over time. Fred Donner argues that the earliest followers of Muḥammad's teachings, used 'believers' as a self-designation, and did not begin to talk of themselves as 'Muslims' until the end of the first/seventh century.[1] At the same time, Shiʿites have always distinguished between Muslims – non-Shiʿite followers of the teachings of Islam – and 'Believers' – those devoted to the family of the Prophet and the imams, that is, the true Shiʿites. In this book, I will often use 'believers' with a lower-case 'b' to denote the earliest non-Shiʿite community, and with a capital 'B' for the Shiʿite community. I have found it very difficult to be absolutely consistent on this matter, though.

[1] Donner, 'Believers to Muslims'; Donner, *Muhammad and the Believers*.

I have used Droge's translation of the Qur'an; minor changes are indicated. Translations from al-Ṭabarī's *Ta'rīkh* are taken from, or heavily dependent on, *History of al-Ṭabarī*, the SUNY translation of the entire work in forty volumes. Volumes XIX, XX and XXI, translated by I. K. A. Howard, Gerald Hawting and Michael Fishbein respectively, are particularly relevant for the present study. I have always checked the Arabic original, though, and have often amended the translations slightly. Throughout the book, dates are given according to both the Islamic '*hijrī*' and the Gregorian calendar, with a slash separating them (for example '61/680' or 'second to fourth/eighth to tenth centuries'). When I refer to an imam by number, for example the fifth or eighth imam, I am aware that it is an expression of an anachronistic, and in a sense a specific, religio-political standpoint. As we will see in Chapter 10, the Twelver list of imams was settled only in the late ninth or early tenth centuries (see also 'Genealogy of the imams' on p. xiv).

Note on the Cover Image

The cover image is a good illustration that the Karbala story has developed into something much more than just an ordinary battle account, and that it has ever since continued to grow, with characters and events constantly added. The image is a reverse painting on glass from the Qajar period (1796–1925; no precise date or artist are available), representing al-Ḥusayn on his horse with his baby son in his arms.[1] In the bottom left corner of the picture, his dead companions lie, decapitated. All of them are bloody and pierced with many arrows. These are features of the story that can be found in the early versions of the story analysed in Chapter 3. In the hadiths from the fourth/tenth-century collections discussed in Chapter 11, angels and jinn are prepared to support al-Ḥusayn in the battle, but he neglects their help. These figures can be seen at the top and bottom right corners of the picture. Much later, other elements were added to the story. The man standing to the left with a bowl in his hand is a nineteenth-century addition, the dervish of Kabul, who passed by the battle, heard the cry of the thirsty baby and appeared at the battle to offer water and ease the suffering of the child. Again, however, al-Ḥusayn refused to accept any help.[2] The image thus incorporates elements from several periods in the development of the story.

[1] The image is taken from Kazerouni and Salahshour, *Reverse Painting*, 108. I am grateful to Ms Salahshour for allowing me to use it, and to Ulrich Marzolph who alerted me to the picture and helped me interpret it.

[2] On the dervish of Kabul and other late additions to the Karbala story, see Deacon, 'Curious Addition'. Thanks to Lucy Deacon for sending me a copy of her article.

Preface and Acknowledgements

In September 1979, when I began my studies in religion at Uppsala University, the Iranian revolution had just taken place. The revolution had a huge impact on the Department of Theology, and in particular the Department of the History of Religions. For decades, in Sweden and elsewhere, religion had been seen as a private matter, of little or no interest in terms of influencing modern society. As a consequence, religious studies as an academic discipline had often been regarded as a rather obscure subject cultivated largely by nerds with little interest in what went on in society at large – and to some extent this had been true. The revolution in Iran took politicians, political scientists and scholars of religion by surprise. Suddenly it became obvious that religion can have a very forceful influence on contemporary society, and it became important to study religion as a factor in the development of political and social issues at national and even global levels. Many events in the past forty years have intensified this insight, and this has led the academic study of religion to reconsider some of its methods and objects of study. Hence, to its preoccupation with sacred beings, acts and beliefs religious studies has had to add a concern with the social powers that *create* these, that *make* such phenomena sacred and thus contribute to the formation of identities and societies.

One aspect of Twelver Shiʿism that was referred to again and again in the deluge of scholarly literature that materialised in the wake of the Iranian revolution was the remembrance of the killing of al-Ḥusayn b. ʿAlī, the grandson of the Prophet Muḥammad, at Karbala in 61/680. That story, and the rituals commemorating the event, became a pattern for the revolutionaries to follow, a paradigm which placed their struggle in a cosmic order. The regime and its security forces were regarded as an extension of al-Ḥusayn's enemies and the Shah as the evil caliph Yazīd; the revolutionaries who were killed by the forces of the Shah were regarded as martyrs, following the example of al-Ḥusayn. The story and the rituals connected with it have also been studied in numerous other contexts besides the Iranian revolution, and have been confirmed and reconfirmed as an example for emulation. Very little scholarship, however, has been devoted to the earliest development of the story. Through what processes was this account of a small battle in the early days of Islam transmuted into a prototype for emulation today? It is this gap in our knowledge that the present book attempts to fill.

I hope that the book will be of benefit both to specialists in early Islam and to non-specialists, such as advanced students in religious studies or the history of Late Antiquity, and I trust that readers who find parts of it too difficult or too easy will have the courage to skip these.

Needless to say, a book that has developed over the last thirty years is indebted to many people and institutions, and I want to thank all of these. Thus, I have been given much time to work on the project by my home institution, Dalarna University. I am also grateful for generous grants from Vetenskapsrådet (the Swedish Research Council): one that lasted from 2012 to 2014, and another, shared with five Nordic scholars, between 2013 and 2015. The writing of this book was made possible by a scholarship from Riksbankens Jubileumsfond (the Central Bank Tercentenary Foundation) between 2020 and 2022. The last of these grants fell under the spell of the coronavirus pandemic, so that despite the substantial allowance for international travel, most of the work had to be done in my home or at my university. In spite of this, several colleagues in Sweden and elsewhere have read and commented on various parts of the book. I want to express my sincere thanks to Mohammad Ali Amir-Moezzi, Mushegh Asatryan, Majid Daneshgar, Mohammad Fazlhashemi, David Thurfjell and George Warner. Some of these I have had the opportunity to meet and discuss with online. I am especially grateful to the anonymous reviewer of the publisher who read the first version of the complete manuscript and gave me invaluable input. My friends and colleagues at the Humanities Seminar here at Dalarna University have had to put up with texts on Karbala for a very long time. I am particularly grateful to Tomas Axelson, Therese Rodin and Gull Törnegren for their pertinent comments. Lovisa Berg and Nejood al-Rubaye from the Arabic department at Dalarna University assisted me in deciphering some cryptic Arabic texts.

Ulrich Marzolph helped me find the picture used for the cover image, and also managed to trace the contact information for Ms Ferial Salahshour, who owns the rights to the picture and has kindly allowed me to use it. My daughter Astrid Hylén made the map at the beginning of the book. My sometimes awkward 'Swenglish' has been rendered smooth and flowing by my excellent editor Lucy Seton-Watson. Some passages, however, have been added after her editing, and thus the reader may find phrases that sound strange. Lucy must not be blamed for them! I have probably forgotten to name some people who have helped me, but I am so thankful to all of you. The responsibility for any remaining errors is, of course, my own.

Genealogy of the Imams

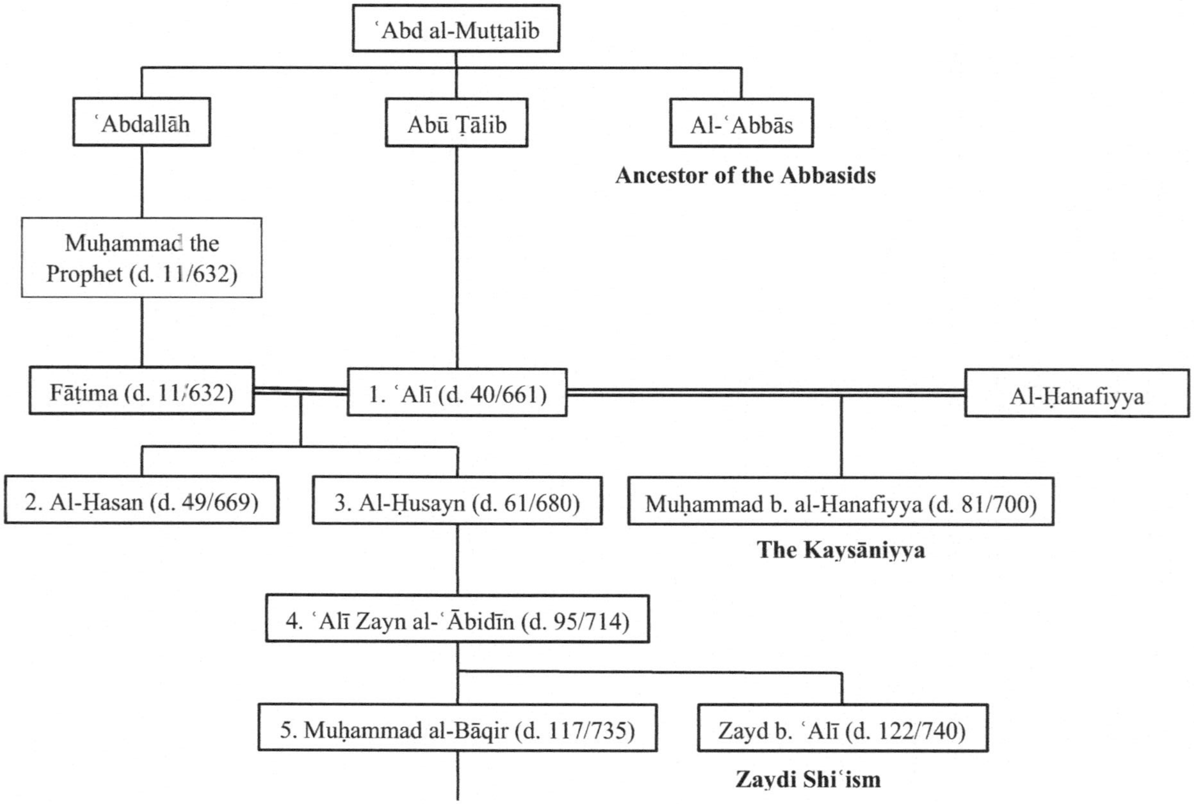

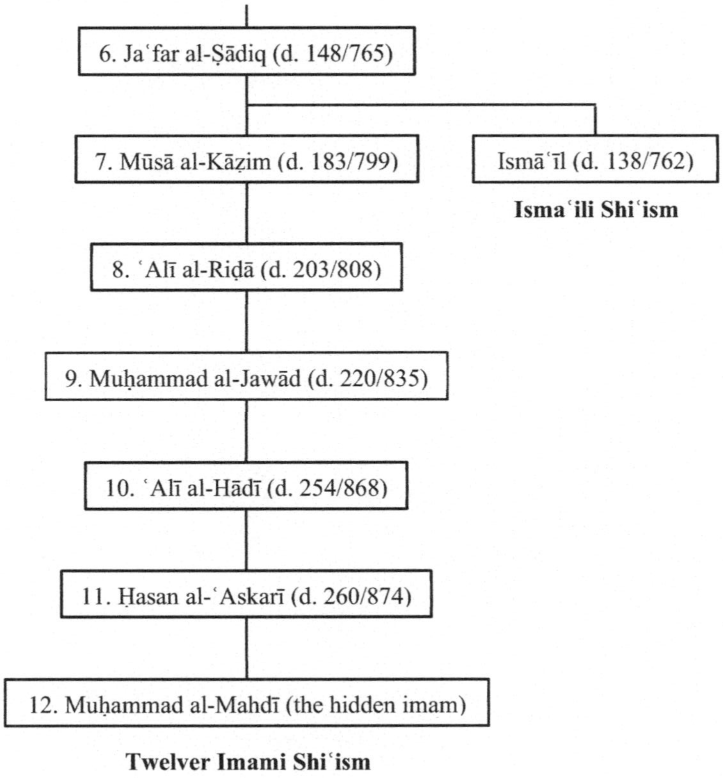

Genealogy of the Twelver imams. Dates of death are generally approximate.

Map of the Region

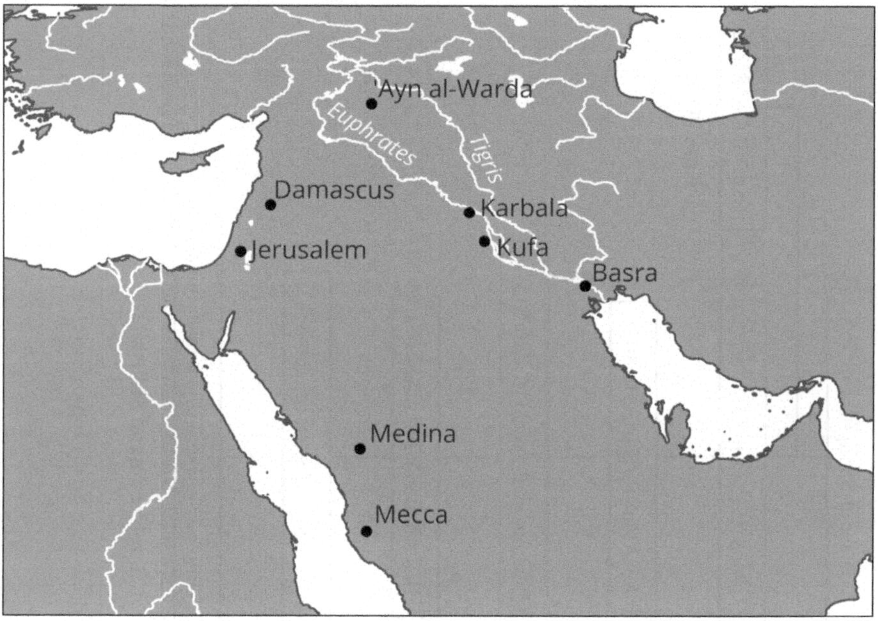

Map of the region discussed in the book. Courtesy of Astrid Hylén.

1

Introduction: The Karbala Story and Shiʿite Identity

Muḥarram Celebration in Pakistan

The taxi stops at Hathi Chowk, the Elephant Crossing, in Saddar Bazaar, Rawalpindi. At this place three narrow streets meet, and a small open place has been made between the houses. In the centre of the crossing, there is a small traffic island with a roof. I have always imagined that it was once made for a policeman to stand there and direct the traffic, but I have never seen it used. Now, a microphone is placed there, and loudspeakers are put on the roof. I step out of the car, and immediately see my friends who have placed their stand just where one of the streets opens up to the square. They greet me and offer me a chair to sit on. There is an atmosphere of expectancy, even tension, among the people gathered. A number of policemen, some of them heavily armed, are posted around the square, prepared to take action to uphold order.

I ask my friend Noman why he and his family, who are Sunni Muslims, have put up their stand to distribute drinks during the principal Shiʿite festival. He replies by telling me the story of imam al-Ḥusayn, the grandson of the Prophet Muḥammad, who was attacked and besieged by the forces of the caliph Yazīd in the desert at Karbala in Iraq. No one gave them water. It is sunna, a sacred tradition to follow, to make up for that sin by giving water to those who want to commemorate the death of al-Ḥusayn and his followers. Later I learnt that, especially in South Asia, al-Ḥusayn is highly revered also among Sunnis.

Today is 9 Muḥarram, and for the first time I am about to see this Shiʿite ritual that I have read about so many times during my studies in Uppsala. Some one hundred metres away, by the Shiʿite mosque, we see black and red standards raised, and behind them a procession is formed. We hear a rhythmic pounding sound, and Noman and I go towards it to find out what is going on. The sound comes from a large group of men who are beating their bare chests, following the rhythm of other men's chanting. Nearby a circle of people forms. The people around the circle are rhythmically shouting: 'Ya Ḥusayn! Ya Ḥusayn!' In the middle of the circle, we see two young boys – they cannot be more than ten to twelve years old – who are facing each other, holding whips made of chains that end with sharp blades in their hands. They wear no shirts. As the shouts from the people surrounding them increase in intensity, they begin to flagellate themselves with the chains, making the blood run on their backs. After half a minute or so they cannot endure it any longer, and cease while the shouts become less intense. After a little while the shouts, 'Ya Ḥusayn! Ya Ḥusayn!', grow stronger again, and the boys begin whipping themselves once again. They constantly keep mutual eye contact, as if to detect if the other one will give up first. Noman and I leave the place and return to the stand, where my friends are distributing water and lemonade in small bowls of clay to thirsty people passing by.

After a while the procession draws closer. At Hathi Chowk it stops. Many people sit down, and others come to our stand to get a drink. I see a number of men whose backs are nothing but blood from the whipping. Two or three have fainted from pain and loss of blood and are taken to a nearby hospital. Someone begins to speak in the microphone at the traffic island. After that, another person sings a song about the tragedy at Karbala, and then a mullah begins to preach. I don't understand what he is saying, but every now and then the whole crowd replies 'Ya ʿAlī!', or 'Ya Ḥusayn!'. At the periphery the women cry. The atmosphere is tense.

I can understand how easy it would be to mobilise people through the powerful symbolism that is found in this story. That was exactly what happened during the revolution in Iran in 1978–9, when the Shah was given the role of the evil caliph, Yazīd, with the people taking the role of al-Ḥusayn, so that martyrdom became a legitimate means in the struggle against the evil regime.

About half an hour later the sermon is over, and the crowd begins to dissolve. A part of the procession continues, but most of the people return to their homes. Suddenly I see, at the end of the procession, a beautifully adorned white horse. My friends explain to me that it symbolises Dhū al-Jināḥ, the horse that al-Ḥusayn was riding during the battle of Karbala. Many people, mostly women, gather around it. The horse is covered with a bloodstained white sheet and adorned with garlands and flowers. On the saddle a long stick is raised, at the top of which there is a metal hand. The five fingers of the hand symbolise the five members of the *ahl al-bayt*, the family of the Prophet: Muḥammad himself, ʿAlī, Fāṭima, al-Ḥasan and al-Ḥusayn. The women who crowd around the horse pray and cry, and many give money to the functionaries who stand around the horse. I am told that prayers uttered close to Dhū al-Jināḥ are answered by God more often than not. The procession and the horse move on, and we return to the stand, which is now disassembled for the night. Next day it will be put up there again, to cater for the people of the new, even larger processions to be held on the day of al-Ḥusayn's death.

This event, which I witnessed in Rawalpindi, Pakistan, in June 1993, made a strong impression on me. I was both fascinated by the frenzy and the devotion the people displayed and ill at ease at the blood and the pain.[1] What I experienced then in Pakistan, and even more so after the celebration of Muḥarram in 1993,[2] made me realise how deeply the story of al-Ḥusayn and his death at Karbala is rooted in the world-view of Shiʿite Islam and in the consciousness of Shiʿites. It constitutes the centre of a 'paradigm' that Shiʿites carry within themselves; a paradigm of symbols, stories, rituals, attitudes and values that relate not only to al-Ḥusayn and his martyrdom, but to

[1] The conclusion I drew when watching the flagellated bodies was that the ritual must be very painful. Actually, participants in the flagellation rituals often say that it is physically painless (Schubel, *Religious Performance*, 146).

[2] In South Asia, the processions commemorating the killing of al-Ḥusayn are often called Muḥarram after the month in which it takes place. In other parts of the Shiʿite world, other names are used, for example 'Āshūrā', after the day on which it occurred, or Taʿziya, connoting 'mourning'.

the whole of the family of the Prophet and their suffering. Thus, the celebrations described above have their background in the decades after the death of the Prophet Muḥammad in 11/632.[3] The Karbala story has been continually retold ever since among Muslims of different religious affiliation, though especially among Shiʿites, and it is written down in countless versions from the early centuries of Islam to today. In the following section, I will first give a brief historical background to the Karbala tragedy, then summarise the story and its immediate consequences as they are retold by the Muslim historian al-Ṭabarī, the main source of this study.

The Karbala Story and its Context

The Setting

Shiʿism is not, and has never been, a uniform movement. What eventually coalesced into the three main branches of Shiʿism, Zaydism, Ismailism and Twelver Shiʿism, was from the earliest years an amorphous movement consisting of numerous groups with varying religious and political agendas. The issue that united all who called themselves Shiʿites was the idea that ʿAlī b. Abi Ṭālib, the cousin and son-in-law of the Prophet Muḥammad, was the rightful successor, the legatee (*waṣī*) of the Prophet. They were known as adherents of *shīʿat ʿAlī*, 'the party of ʿAlī', one of several religio-political groups that emerged after the death of the Prophet.[4] The Shiʿites were in unceasing opposition to other contestants for political power. The first rulers, who were regarded as usurpers, were the three caliphs who followed the death of Muḥammad: Abū Bakr, ʿUmar and ʿUthmān, who ruled from Medina. ʿAlī became the fourth caliph, but his rule was contested by several non-Shiʿite groups, among them the Umayyad family, who after the murder of ʿAlī in 40/661 gained the upper hand in the struggle and set up their rule in Damascus.[5]

[3] The year of the Prophet's death has been contested in some modern research. See Crone and Cook, *Hagarism*; Shoemaker, *Death of a Prophet*.

[4] Crone, *Political Thought*, 20; Amir-Moezzi and Jambet, *Shiʿi Islam*, 11. On the use of this name for the sprawling and amorphous movement, see below in this chapter.

[5] Other groups such as the Kharijites were also fierce enemies of the Shiʿites, and, as we are told, it was in fact a Kharijite who killed ʿAlī. On the Kharijites, see Hagemann, *The Khārijtes*.

It seems that ʿAlī was very early – probably already in his lifetime – held in considerably higher esteem than as a mere political leader by some Shiʿite groups, in that they regarded him as 'a semilegendary figure of heroic and even sacred dimensions'.[6] This veneration of ʿAlī was often referred to as *dīn ʿAlī*, 'the religion of ʿAlī'.[7] Furthermore, immediately after his murder, some Shiʿites, in particular the group that came to be called the Sabaʾiyya, either denied that he had died or expected him to return from death to set things right in the world.[8] In fact, the preaching of the Prophet Muḥammad was already eschatological in character, and up to the beginning of the eighth century apocalyptic ideas flourished in this part of the world.[9] In some groups, notably those that held ʿAlī in high regard, such ideas were very prominent. So, for example, Sean Anthony has demonstrated that among the Sabaʾiyya, the idea of ʿAlī's return from death – his *rajʿa* – had obvious messianic overtones.[10] Many of these apocalyptic ideas were also common in Jewish, Christian and other apocalyptic thought at the time, and had been appropriated and adapted by the Sabaʾiyya movement. Anthony maintains that several themes can be historically verified as belonging to this group: the denial of the death of ʿAlī and the belief in his return, his messianic victory over the enemies of God while carrying the lost staff of Moses, and the identification of him with the apocalyptic beast (*dābba min al-arḍ*) mentioned in Qur. 27:82.[11] But, Anthony further argues,

6 Amir-Moezzi, '*Dīn ʿAlī*', 44.

7 Amir-Moezzi, '*Dīn ʿAlī*'. See also Madelung, *Succession*, 178–9. The view that ʿAlī had a special position in the minds of many of his followers from a very early stage is advanced by several scholars; see e.g. al-Qadi, 'The Term *Ghulāt*', 295–301; Kohlberg, 'Ṣaḥāba', 145–6; Dakake, *Charismatic Community*, 33–69; Anthony, *The Caliph, passim*.

8 Al-Qadi, 'The Term *Ghulāt*', 300–1; Anthony, *The Caliph*, 313–17; Amir-Moezzi, 'Muḥammad le paraclet', 44–5.

9 See e.g. Arjomand, 'Apocalypticism', 238–57; Crone, *Political Thought*, 75–80; Donner, *Muhammad and the Believers*, 78–82; Anthony, *The Caliph*, 224–5; Shoemaker, *Death of a Prophet*, 118–96. By 'apocalyptic' I mean ideas about the imminent end of the world and the signs preceding it.

10 Anthony, *The Caliph*, 195–225. Throughout this book, I use the terms 'Messiah' and 'messianic' in an eschatological sense for the redeemer who will return in the end times to set the world right. I do not include Judaeo-Christian notions of an anointed king.

11 Anthony, *The Caliph*, 218. The notion of the beast is probably an influence from apocalyptic texts in the Bible (Dan. 7:1–8; Rev. 13). Unlike the beast in Christian tradition, however, the Islamic *dābba* is often regarded as benevolent; see Arjomand, 'Apocalypticism', 239–40. Hence it was possible to identify it with ʿAlī.

> the full extent of Jewish influence (or Christian, Zoroastrian and Manichaean for that matter) on early Islam cannot be localized or limited within the confines of a singular sectarian trend ... These sorts of influences were, rather, pervasive and much more mutual and dialectic than has, until very recently, been appreciated ... These symbols, mythemes, prophesies, etc. were 'in the wind' and somehow – the fog of historical distance hinders our ability to find these intermediaries – they came to be attached to the person of ʿAlī and the hopes and ambitions of his partisans.[12]

Thus, ideas that can be called 'messianic' were associated with ʿAlī from a very early period, and although many Shiʿites objected to them, at least in their more extreme forms, as can be seen from the sources, they were quite widespread.[13]

After the murder of ʿAlī, many Shiʿites regarded his eldest son, al-Ḥasan, as the new leader of the community, the imam. The political power, however, at this time belonged to the Umayyad caliph Muʿāwiya, who made a deal with al-Ḥasan that he would not meddle in politics. On the death of al-Ḥasan (around 49/669–70), ʿAlī's second son, al-Ḥusayn, at first stuck to his brother's treaty with Muʿāwiya.

The Karbala Story

Following the death of Muʿāwiya in 60/680, al-Ḥusayn, who resided in Medina at the time, refused to pledge his allegiance to Muʿāwiya's son Yazīd and slipped away to Mecca. While he was in Mecca, the people of Kufa sent him letters and envoys, imploring him to come and lead them in an insurrection against the governor. Al-Ḥusayn replied by sending his cousin Muslim b. ʿAqīl as his representative to find out if the situation was as they described. When Muslim arrived in Kufa, a great number of people declared their allegiance to al-Ḥusayn. Muslim informed al-Ḥusayn that he had massive support and that it was safe for him to come to Kufa.

In the meantime, the ruthless ʿUbaydallāh b. Ziyād was installed as the new governor in Kufa. He infiltrated the Shiʿite community and was informed about Muslim's whereabouts. He caught and threatened to kill Hāniʾ b. ʿUrwa,

[12] Anthony, *The Caliph*, 224–5. But cf. Cameron, 'Late Antique Apocalyptic', for a more cautious approach to the phenomenon of apocalypticism in Late Antiquity.
[13] On this issue, see now also Amir-Moezzi, 'Muḥammad le paraclet'.

Muslim's host in Kufa. Upon hearing this, Muslim gathered his supporters and marched on the governor's palace in an attempt to release Hāniʾ, but his supporters gradually leached away. Muslim was arrested; both he and Hāniʾ were executed by Ibn Ziyād. Those who had pledged their allegiance to al-Ḥusayn were bribed or intimidated into withholding their support from him.

Al-Ḥusayn, however, had already left for Kufa, unaware of developments there. Since the people of the town were notorious for abruptly switching allegiance, he was warned several times against going to Kufa, both before his departure and on the journey; but al-Ḥusayn went on. Even when information about the true situation in Kufa and the death of Muslim reached him, he decided to continue.

As al-Ḥusayn and his group (perhaps a hundred persons, including men, women and children) approached Kufa, they were stopped by a vanguard of the governor's army, about one thousand men.[14] The commander of the force was al-Ḥurr b. Yazīd al-Tamīmī. Al-Ḥurr asked al-Ḥusayn to come with him to Kufa and submit to the governor, but al-Ḥusayn refused. The two groups faced off against each other, but occasionally gathered and prayed together, with al-Ḥusayn leading the prayer. Al-Ḥusayn also gave several speeches to the people of the Kufan army and to his own followers. Finally, al-Ḥusayn began to move with his group, and al-Ḥurr and his force followed them closely. Al-Ḥurr was clearly distressed at the situation he was in, since his esteem for al-Ḥusayn as the grandson of the Prophet was very high. Al-Ḥurr then received a letter from the governor, commanding him to stop al-Ḥusayn's group and cut them off from all access to water. They were brought to a halt at Karbala close to the Euphrates, but were prevented from reaching the water.

Eventually, the main army of 4,000 men, headed by ʿUmar b. Saʿd, joined al-Ḥurr's force. Al-Ḥusayn tried to negotiate with ʿUmar to settle the matter peacefully. The latter was prepared to accept al-Ḥusayn's offer to pledge his allegiance to the caliph Yazīd in Damascus, to return to Mecca, or to go somewhere else, but the governor, Ibn Ziyād, demanded that al-Ḥusayn must come to Kufa and give his pledge of allegiance to Yazīd there, before

[14] Numbers of participants in armies or other groups are impossible to verify and must be regarded with suspicion. Very often they were greatly exaggerated. The point here is to show that al-Ḥusayn's group was greatly outnumbered by the enemy.

the governor. When al-Ḥusayn refused to do that, ʿUmar was forced to fight him. As the army was set in motion against al-Ḥusayn, al-Ḥurr deserted and joined al-Ḥusayn.

The battle began. At first it proceeded through several duels, which are related in great detail, but the Kufan commanders realised that al-Ḥusayn's fighters were killing at least as many as were killed of their own group, and prohibited any further single combat. The Kufans then attacked on a larger scale. The bravery of al-Ḥusayn and his relatives and followers, their fierce defence, their thirst and desperation, but also their faith and determination to do God's will, are vividly described. Likewise, the cowardliness and wickedness of the enemy, who did not refrain from attacking and killing the family of the Prophet – including al-Ḥusayn's infant son – and their followers is related in great detail. Finally, al-Ḥusayn himself was killed, and his head was cut off. The head, together with the survivors from the family, was brought before Ibn Ziyād in Kufa and then sent to the caliph in Damascus. Finally, al-Ḥusayn's family were released and allowed to return to Medina.

The Immediate Aftermath

Immediately after the death of al-Ḥusayn, many of those who had pledged to support him but had failed to come to his aid felt a deep sense of guilt for their betrayal. One of the first expressions of this guilt is seen in the movement of the Tawwābūn, 'the Penitents'. Some of the men who had failed to support him gathered and decided that they would take up arms and go against the Umayyad army: to kill those who had killed al-Ḥusayn, or to be killed themselves in the attempt to avenge him. The Tawwābūn were well aware that this act would in all probability lead to their own deaths, but they regarded it as an act of martyrdom in the cause of loyalty to the Prophet and his family, and believed it would cleanse them of their sin. They set out in 65/684 and made a short stop at al-Ḥusayn's grave at Karbala. Eventually they met the Umayyad forces at ʿAyn al-Warda in northern Iraq, and were defeated. Among the few survivors, some felt great shame that they had not died in the campaign.

On the wider political arena, things became increasingly disturbed at this time. Soon after the death of the Umayyad caliph Yazīd b. Muʿāwiya in 64/683, the Meccan aristocrat ʿAbdallāh b. al-Zubayr conquered all of the

Hijāz, Southern Iraq and the Western areas of Iran. From Mecca he claimed the caliphate for himself and installed governors in the important towns of his empire, including Kufa. Thus, for about a decade (64–73/683–692), there were two caliphates competing for power over the entire region: one in the south with Ibn al-Zubayr as caliph in Mecca, and one in the north where members of the Umayyad family in Damascus claimed the authority for themselves.[15]

At this time, the Shiʿite leader al-Mukhtār b. Abī ʿUbayd rose up and set off a rebellion against Ibn al-Zubayr's governor in Kufa. He claimed to act on behalf of a third son of ʿAlī, Muḥammad b. al-Ḥanafiyya (see figure, 'Genealogy of the imams'). Al-Mukhtār and his followers exacted a terrible revenge on those Kufans who had taken part in the Karbala battle against al-Ḥusayn, even managing to kill the former Umayyad governor of Kufa, ʿUbaydallāh b. Ziyād, who had been responsible for the campaign against al-Ḥusayn. The rebellion was thus directed against both the competing caliphates: that in Mecca and that in Damascus. Finally, in 67/687, Ibn al-Zubayr's troops were able to quench the insurrection, kill al-Mukhtār and regain Kufa. The vengeance of al-Mukhtār has often been regarded as a kind of conclusion to the whole Karbala affair. As we will see, however, the story about Karbala continued to live and grow.

Previous Research on Early Shiʿism and the Karbala Story

The development of early Shiʿism has been the subject of a large number of studies, and I therefore confine the brief survey that follows to a few important works in order to display the variation in approaches to this fascinating subject and to position the present book in relation to previous scholarship. The footnotes throughout the book as well as the bibliography, however, reveal that I am also indebted to many other scholars and their studies.

On a general level, the relevant parts of Patricia Crone's *Medieval Islamic Political Thought* are very useful regarding the development of Shiʿism in the setting of emerging Islam. As the title of her book indicates, its emphasis is on the religio-political ideas that were formed in the early centuries, and thus discussion of the role and function of the imam in relation to non-Shiʿite

[15] Hawting, *First Dynasty*, pp. 46–57; Robinson, *Abd al-Malik*, pp. 35–39.

political ideas is in the foreground. More focused on Shiʿism in particular are Hossein Modarressi's *Crisis and Consolidation*, Andrew Newman's *Twelver Shiism* and Najam Haider's *Shīʿī Islam*. Though large parts of their books discuss the emergence of Shiʿism up to the fourth/tenth century, the authors treat this subject from slightly different angles. Modarressi and Newman are mainly interested in the emergence of Twelver Shiʿism, but while Modarressi focuses on the development of the rational imamology up to the 'consolidation' of Twelver Shiʿism in the fourth/tenth century, Newman's description is formed by political and legal aspects of the same era and extends further forward in time. Haider's book is unique in that he discusses the three main branches of Shiʿism that have survived until today – Zaydism, Ismailism and Twelver Shiʿism – including, but not confined to, their interlaced beginnings.

The earliest forms of Shiʿism in the first/seventh century are discussed by Wilferd Madelung, Mohammad Ali Amir-Moezzi and Sean Anthony from quite different perspectives. Madelung's *The Succession to Muḥammad* is a reinterpretation of relevant texts in the Qurʾan and in the historiography from about the time of the Prophet and the first four caliphs. Madelung discusses the early caliphate and the questions of succession much in line with the Shiʿite view, namely that the family of the Prophet should have inherited his political authority and his right to give spiritual guidance. Amir-Moezzi in some articles focuses on the cult of ʿAlī in early Shiʿism. Sean Anthony's book, *The Caliph and the Heretic*, deals with the 'extreme' Shiʿite group, the Sabaʾiyya. My description of early Shiʿism in the previous section is largely based on the latter two scholars' works. Anthony furthermore shows that many of the beliefs of the Sabaʾiyya continued to thrive and develop in the ensuing movement of the Kaysāniyya, beliefs which later came to influence various other Shiʿite groups including the Imamiyya. Some of these ideas can also be found in the slightly later texts studied by Mushegh Asatryan in *Controversies in Formative Shīʿism*, a study of the theology and cosmology expressed in early texts from *ghulāt* ('extremist') groups. Maria Massi Dakake's book, *The Charismatic Community*, is a penetrating study on the concept of *walāya*, an important and semantically rich concept in Shiʿite theology that can be translated as 'loyalty and love' for the Prophet and his family. Other works on early Shiʿite theology mainly discuss its rational aspects, for example the relevant parts of

Josef van Ess's magisterial *Theologie und Gesellschaft*,[16] as well as articles by Tamima Bayhom-Daou,[17] besides the already mentioned work of Modarressi.

Amir-Moezzi has also written several books and articles on the esoteric Imami Shiʿite theology, which developed in the second to fourth/eighth to tenth centuries. His sources for these studies are hadiths, the legal traditions that purportedly originate with the imams. His most important studies are *The Divine Guide in Early Shiʿism* and *The Spirituality of Shiʿi Islam*, the latter a collection of a number of previously published articles on the subject. In his *The Silent Qurʾan and the Speaking Qurʾan*, he studies early Shiʿite conceptions of the Qurʾan and its interpretation. Another work on early Shiʿite Qurʾanic exegesis is Meir Bar-Asher's *Scripture and Exegesis in Early Imāmī Shiism*.

The legal development in second/eighth century Shiʿism has been discussed by Najam Haider in his *The Origins of the Shīʿa*, where he analyses early hadiths and compares various groups' attitudes to some legal problems. The sources that he uses – the early hadiths – also show that at least by the turn of the second/eighth century, we can definitely speak of a Shiʿite identity. Roy Vilozny's *Constructing a Worldview* is a close study of the earliest extant collection of Shiʿite hadiths from the end of the third/ninth century. This and slightly later collections of hadiths have been investigated by Andrew Newman in *The Formative Period of Twelver Shīʿism*, where he traces the development of theological and legal matters in these collections according to changes in society in the fourth/tenth century. Like Newman, Edmund Hayes also works from a sociohistorical perspective in his book *Agents of the Hidden Imam*, in that he considers the institution of the middlemen between the Shiʿite believers and the increasingly inaccessible imams in the third/ninth and fourth/tenth centuries.

Some of the studies mentioned above contain sections on the Karbala event and its consequences,[18] but very few lengthy studies of the Karbala story

[16] van Ess, *Theologie*, vol. I, 233–403.

[17] Bayhom-Daou, 'The imām's knowledge'; 'Hishām b. al-Ḥakam'.

[18] So, for example, Dakake, *Charismatic Community*, 81–90. Haider's introduction to Shiʿism is, to my knowledge, the only study which compares the attitude to and significance of the Karbala story in the three main branches of Shiʿism (*Shīʿī Islam*, 66–81).

and the rituals associated with it could be added to the list.[19] The majority of earlier studies give a more or less detailed, usually quite uncritical paraphrase of the story, and then go on to comment on it from the various perspectives of the authors. Thus, more than a hundred years ago, Julius Wellhausen wrote a chapter on al-Ḥusayn and the battle of Karbala in his book *The Religio-Political Factions in Early Islam*.[20] After summarising Abū Mikhnaf's account in al-Ṭabarī's version, he went on to comment on Abū Mikhnaf's style and use of his sources, before discussing the personalities and sentiments of the characters involved. Here, Wellhausen's interest in hard power politics is clearly manifested. In his eyes, al-Ḥusayn was a selfish weakling, a dreamer who accomplished nothing through his futile attempt to grab the power: 'Like a child he stretches out his hands to the moon.'[21] Wellhausen's sympathies were all with the Iraqi governor, 'Ubaydallāh b. Ziyād, the official who was immediately responsible for al-Ḥusayn's death. 'With few means but with clear intent and firm hand, [the governor] understands the solution to the difficult problem ... He did his duty and in no wise exceeded the limits.'[22] In the meeting between these two antagonists, then, what happened was only to be expected: 'Like a clay pot [al-Ḥusayn] clashed against the iron 'Ubaydalla.'[23]

This unsympathetic attitude towards al-Ḥusayn is unusual among later writers.[24] A comprehensive summary of the story is that written by Laura Veccia Vaglieri in her article on al-Ḥusayn in the second edition of the *Encyclopedia of Islam*.[25] Veccia Vaglieri first relates the story of the battle of Karbala, before discussing 'The legend of Ḥusayn', that is, the ascription of marvels and miracles to him.[26] At the end of the article the author repudiates the views of Wellhausen and others with similar views. Referring to the speeches of al-Ḥusayn reported by the sources, she concludes that he was 'a man impelled by an ideology (the institution of a régime which would fulfil

[19] See also Hussain, 'Developmental Analysis', 1–6.
[20] Wellhausen, *Religio-Political Factions*, 105–20.
[21] Wellhausen, *Religio-Political Factions*, 116.
[22] Wellhausen, *Religio-Political Factions*, 115.
[23] Wellhausen, *Religio-Political Factions*, 116.
[24] But see Lammens, 'Al-Husain', published slightly later than Wellhausen's work.
[25] Veccia Vaglieri, 'Ḥusayn'.
[26] Veccia Vaglieri, 'Ḥusayn', 612–14.

the demands of true Islam)', albeit 'stubbornly determined to achieve his ends, as in general are all religious fanatics'.[27]

Mahmoud Ayoub's book, *Redemptive Suffering in Islām*, has become a classic and has probably been one of the most influential sources for a Western understanding of the Shiʿite sentiment. While the central purpose of Ayoub's book is to describe and discuss the devotional aspects of the 'Ashūrā' ritual (that is, the later interpretations of the Karbala drama), the author also deals with the 'historical' aspects of the person of al-Ḥusayn and the events at Karbala. Ayoub dismisses the less sympathetic interpretations of al-Ḥusayn and describes him as 'a man of piety, idealism, nobility of character and ascetic detachment from the world'.[28] He maintains that a careful study of the sources confirms the view that al-Ḥusayn had the right to rebel against 'the illegitimate usurpation of power by ... Yazīd' since it violated the ideals of Islam.[29] Although Ayoub is careful to state in his book that political factors were also involved in the event, he argues that these alone cannot explain the behaviour of al-Ḥusayn. In addition to these external factors, he identifies three internal motives for al-Ḥusayn's martyrdom: 'His idealism, the belief that his fate was predetermined and the certainty he seems to have had that he either had to submit or be killed'.[30] Here, like the previously mentioned scholars, Ayoub attempts to understand al-Ḥusayn as a person and his emotions, rather than regarding the sources as later generations' interpretations of an earlier event.[31] In other parts of the book, however, Ayoub makes a masterly study of the later, devotional interpretations of the Karbala story.

Boaz Shoshan dedicates a chapter of his monograph, *Poetics of Islamic Historiography*, to the Karbala story.[32] He investigates the story as an example of how the historian al-Ṭabarī (d. 301/923) used his material in his large historiographical compilation *Taʾrīkh al-rusul wa-l-mulūk*. Shoshan's interest, then, is not so much the Karbala story as such, but al-Ṭabarī's rendering of it. To Shoshan, al-Ḥusayn's death in al-Ṭabarī's rendering is a tragedy through

[27] Veccia Vaglieri, 'Ḥusayn', 614.
[28] Ayoub, *Redemptive Suffering*, 93.
[29] Ayoub, *Redemptive Suffering*, 93.
[30] Ayoub, *Redemptive Suffering*, 103.
[31] This is no less true of Syed Husain Mohammad Jafri's depiction of Ḥusayn and the Karbala Drama in *Origins*, 174–221.
[32] Shoshan, *Poetics*, 233–52.

and through. It contains two different strands that, in a complex manner, work together to convey a tragic effect: on the one hand al-Ḥusayn's determination to follow God's will and go to Kufa against the advice of his friends, and on the other his attempt to escape his destiny when he realises that he is threatened by death.[33] In this way, Shoshan concludes, the Karbala story 'comes pretty close to the classical definition of tragedy, save for the element of *hubris*'.[34]

My own PhD thesis was a structural analysis of the Karbala story, using a method inspired by the French structuralist Claude Lévi-Strauss.[35] My conclusion was that al-Ḥusayn is portrayed as a mediator in the structuralist sense of the word. In his attempt to save the emerging movement of believers from destruction, he must have recourse to violence and rebellion. Thus on the one hand he sunders the community of believers, but on the other, he does so in order to save it. Like Shoshan, I work with al-Ṭabarī's rendering of the story without analysing its components.

A study that is closer to the one I present in this book is the doctoral thesis of Ali J. Hussain.[36] The intention of his thesis, he writes, is to

> trace the development of depictions of the battle of Karbala' through the centuries, and to study through critical analysis of the earliest sources how later Shīʿīs developed elaborate rituals commemorating Husayn's martyrdom and his final battle, and how the literate class of Shīʿī *ʿulamā'* scholars added to and institutionalized these rituals as an integral part of Shīʿī cultural and religious identity.[37]

Hussain's work is interesting in that it lists and uses a large number of sources for the Karbala story, it takes into consideration the emergence of rituals in the history of the Karbala story, and, unlike the present study, it also analyses the Umayyads' propaganda, which foregrounds their view of the matter. In my opinion, however, considering the nature of early Islamic historiography as it is preserved for us, there are two methodological problems

33 Shoshan, *Poetics*, 235–6, 245.
34 Shoshan, *Poetics*, 252.
35 Hylén, 'Ḥusayn, the Mediator'.
36 Hussain, 'Developmental Analysis'. Unfortunately, I became aware of this work too late to make much use of it in the present study.
37 Hussain, 'Developmental Analysis', 3.

with Hussain's thesis. To simplify matters, this corpus consists of three 'levels' of historiography, which correspond to three phases of development (see Chapter 2): (1) short anecdotes, *khabars*, that were normally transmitted orally and were assembled and arranged into (2) 'monographs', coherent narratives on specific subjects (such as the Karbala event), which were in their turn compiled in (3) large historiographical works that are partly still extant.[38] The first problem with Hussain's thesis is that his analyses are based on the chains of authorities, *isnāds*, that precede the *khabars*, and he seems to generally accept the historicity of these chains of transmission.[39] As I will argue in Chapter 2, I find such a method untenable, at least without a much closer scrutiny of each of the elements of the *isnāds*.[40] Second, Hussain disregards the 'second level' of the corpus, the monographs, and goes straight to the large historiographical compilations by historians like Ibn Saʿd (d. 230/845) and al-Ṭabarī (d. 310/923). The monographs were certainly in a more or less edited state at the stage when they were incorporated in the larger works, but since the same monographs were used in several of the larger compilations, it is possible to compare the different versions and get a fairly good understanding of what the originals looked like.[41] Therefore, in my view, Hussain is overlooking almost a century of development of the Karbala story in claiming that the earliest extant narrative of the Karbala event is Ibn Saʿd's *Kitāb al-Tabaqāt*, rather than going back about a century to the monographs analysed in Chapter 3 of this book.[42]

In the analysis of the Karbala story in Chapter 3, two articles are of particular importance: I. K. A. Howard's 'Husayn the Martyr' and Antoine Borrut's 'Remembering Karbalā''. As I will discuss these studies thoroughly in that chapter, I leave them for now, as I also set aside discussion of the extremely few studies that exist about the movement of the Tawwābūn for analysis in Chapters 5–8.

[38] Robinson, *Islamic Historiography*, 18–38.

[39] An example of Hussain's method is found on pp. 46–56 of his thesis.

[40] As I will show in Chapter 2, Harald Motzki developed a method for analysing *isnāds* that has been used with some success, not least by Haider in his *Origins*. The method has been criticised, however, and if accepted, its application demands a much more detailed study of each *isnad* and *matn* than that given by Hussain.

[41] On the problem of using the term 'original' in this context, see Chapter 2, n. 35.

[42] Hussain, 'Developmental Analysis', 18.

Purpose and Outline of the Present Study

This book attempts to discuss how and why Shiʿites in the first centuries after the death of the Prophet Muḥammad came to perceive themselves as a community distinguished from others who also regarded themselves as believers.[43] As we have seen, this not only was a question of religious belief, but also involved various political, social and economic matters. While there are a number of studies on this process regarding the formation of Islam and its various sub-groupings, similar developments have been much more closely observed in other contexts, in particular Christianity. In a study of the emergence of Christian communities in the first centuries CE, the biblical scholar Burton Mack uses the concept *social formation* to refer to the behavioural aspects of the creation of group identities. Closely related to social formation, Mack suggests, is an intellectual process in which the group creates a discourse about its own position in society and the world at large. This intellectual process Mack calls *mythmaking*, and he continues:

> Social formation and mythmaking are group activities that go together, each stimulating the other in a kind of dynamic feedback system. Both speed up when new groups form in times of social disintegration and cultural change ... Social formation and mythmaking fit together like hand and glove.[44]

The above survey of previous scholarship shows that many other historians have discussed the social formation and mythmaking of Shiʿism in its many appearances from various angles (though none of them has used these terms). In this book, I will focus on a specific aspect of Imami/Twelver Shiʿite mythmaking which has hitherto been largely neglected: the Karbala story with its concomitant rituals. By focusing on this story, I do not mean to downplay other factors. Political, social and ideological issues other than the Karbala story are of course also crucial in the formation of Shiʿite identity. Yet the story did play an important role in the formation of Shiʿism, and its function in this process will be the main focus of this study.

[43] An earlier and now classical attempt in the same vein is Hodgson, 'Early Shīʿa'.
[44] Mack, *Who Wrote the New Testament?*, 11; and see also Mack, 'Redescribing', 255. For a historical overview of the concept of social formation, see Mack, 'Social Formation', 283–8.

Modern historians have described the Karbala battle as little more than a skirmish. Gerald Hawting writes: 'It seems unlikely that at the time itself the affair had very much importance for the Umayyads. Husayn's force had been small and was suppressed with relative ease.'[45] According to Donner, 'the snuffing out of this little insurrection had been an easy task for 'Ubayd Allah's much larger force'.[46] M. A. Shaban even talks of the Karbala affair as 'a routine police operation'.[47] Yet, among Shi'ites, the Karbala story within a short time had developed into an account of a cosmic battle between the good and the evil powers of the universe. It was an important factor in giving the (Twelver) Shi'ites, in the midst of their social and political vicissitudes, a place not only in this temporal world, but in a divinely ordered cosmos, and thus legitimated the formation of their self-identity vis-à-vis other Muslims. How come, then, that the story of this particular battle, which was similar to innumerable battle stories from early Islam, developed into a myth of universal significance? This is the main problem on which I wish to concentrate in this book.

Social formation and mythmaking are never-ending processes. As circumstances change, so do the ways in which a group constitutes and regards itself: it may consolidate its borders, it may split or totally dissolve, it may emphasise different aspects of its mythology and thus vary in the way it thinks of itself in relation to the changing surroundings.[48] This is as true of Shi'ism as of any other religious or social movement, of course, and necessitates a short discussion of the use of the label 'Shi'ism' in the present work. Here, I will use Madelung's wide definition and use 'Shi'ism' and 'Shi'ite' to denote any group or individual that is 'upholding a privileged position of the Family of the Prophet (*ahl al-bayt*)'.[49] The ideas of who were included in this family, and what 'a privileged position' involved, varied considerably in early times and gave rise to different, often mutually antagonistic groups within the larger community of Shi'ites. The name seems to stem from the phrase *shīʿat ʿAlī*, 'the party of 'Alī', which is apparently recorded for the first time in connection

[45] Hawting, *First Dynasty*, 50.
[46] Donner, *Muhammad and the Believers*, 179.
[47] Shaban, *Islamic History*, vol. I, 91.
[48] Assmann, *Cultural Memory*, 124–41.
[49] Madelung, 'Shīʿa'.

with the battle of Ṣiffīn in 37/657 to refer to the supporters of ʿAlī, though the love and loyalty – the *walāya* – for the family of the Prophet and for ʿAlī goes back to the lifetime of Muḥammad.[50] At Ṣiffīn, the expression *shīʿat ʿAlī* was used to distinguish the adherents of ʿAlī from their opponents, the *shīʿat ʿUthmān*, that is the supporters of the murdered caliph ʿUthmān. The word *shīʿa*, 'party' or 'sect', is thus neutral and does not in itself denote adherence to a certain doctrine or belief. In some of the early texts about the Tawwābūn or 'Penitents' that will be discussed in Part II of this book, the word is used without reference to ʿAlī. In the speeches and letters analysed in Chapter 6, the Tawwābūn use the expression *shīʿatunā* ('our party'), *hādha al-shīʿa* ('this party') and *shīʿat āl nabiyyukum* (the party of your prophet's family),[51] without referring to ʿAlī.

As we will see throughout the book, this *walāya* came to be expressed in many very different and often contradictory and contentious ways, until they finally crystallised into the three branches of Shiʿism that are extant today. Though we often can see a continuation of tenets and ideas from earliest history – particularly of course the *walāya* for the family of the Prophet – early forms were thus very different from the Shiʿism that we see today. This has caused several scholars use the term 'proto-Shiʿism' for the early varieties of the movement.[52] I prefer not to use this term, however, first because I want to emphasise the continuity in the development; second because the term *shīʿa* and its derivates are often employed in the sources as a name for the various groups claiming to be loyal to the family of the Prophet. I therefore advise the reader to remember that Shiʿism in the first centuries was normally very different from Shiʿism today.[53]

As historians, we cannot freeze a moment when a group is supposed to have reached its 'true' potential and regard everything that follows as decline or deviation from its essence.[54] Even though the present work finishes with the 'consolidation' of Twelver Shiʿite identity in the fourth/tenth century, I do

[50] See n. 7 above.

[51] al-Ṭabarī, *Taʾrīkh*, II, 498–500.

[52] So e.g. Marsham, *Rituals*, 186–7; Baker, *Sectarianism*, 6–12.

[53] The expression 'proto-Sunni' (e.g. Baker, *Sectarianism*, 7) is more apt, in my opinion, as it took several centuries before 'Sunni' was used as a label for a group with a specific identity. See also Chapter 10.

[54] Hylén, 'Closed and Open'.

not mean to say that the Karbala story (or Twelver Shiʿism at large) stopped evolving at this point. As many scholars have demonstrated – and as, indeed, the cover image of this book illustrates perfectly – the story and its interpretation grew in various directions depending on the material and social circumstances, in what Mack calls 'the process of experimenting with better and less better ways to do things and think about them'.[55]

In Chapter 2, I will further elaborate the concept of mythmaking and how it is used throughout this book. And since ritualisation is one of the most important ways of making a myth out of a story, I will also say something about how I regard the relationship between myth and ritual, arguing that it is through rituals that emotions become attached to a myth. I will furthermore discuss the sources for this study and their place in the context of early Islamic historiography, and I will say a few words about the methods I have used to analyse the sources.

Part I of the book is dedicated to studies of the three earliest versions of the Karbala story that are extant, all of which originated in the second/eighth century. In Chapter 3, I make a comparative analysis of these versions, demonstrating that in the few decades that passed between the two shorter accounts on the one hand – one of which was compiled by al-Ḥuṣayn b. ʿAbd al-Raḥmān, and the other of which is ascribed to Abū Jaʿfar al-Bāqir (the fifth imam) – and the much longer version of Abū Mikhnaf on the other, the mythmaking process had already made significant progress. I also forward the hypothesis that what is now a single story may once have been transmitted as two separate narratives: one about the affair of Muslim b. ʿAqīl in Kufa, and the other about the battle of al-Ḥusayn at Karbala. Chapter 4 is a more detailed analysis of the version of Abū Mikhnaf. There, I argue that Abū Mikhnaf views the Karbala event from the perspective of the covenant of God with humanity. He argues, I claim, that loyalty to al-Ḥusayn means adhering to the divine covenant, and enmity towards him is breaking it.

The four chapters of Part II deal with the story of the Tawwābūn, the movement that arose among those Kufans who regretted not having

[55] Mack, 'Social Formation', 289. On later interpretations of the Karbala story, see Aghaie, *Martyrs of Karbala*.

supported al-Ḥusayn at Karbala and made a futile attempt to exact revenge for him by fighting the Umayyad army in 65/685. In these chapters, I argue that it is possible to identify several layers of the story: an early one, in which al-Ḥusayn's descent from the Prophet via his mother Fāṭima is more visible than his connection to his father ʿAlī, and later additions, in which ʿAlī is more prominent and in which we see, in embryonic form, Shiʿite ideas that later came to be noticeable. I argue that the earliest layer can be dated at least as early as the end of the first/beginning of the eighth century.

While the first two parts are primarily based on my own research, and at times consist of quite dense analyses of the texts in question, the chapters in Part III are more of an overview of the developments in the following centuries and largely build on previous research. In Chapter 9, I discuss the rebellion of al-Mukhtār in Kufa in 65–7/685–7. Unlike the Tawwābūn, al-Mukhtār and his movement, in the name of ʿAlī's third son Ibn al-Ḥanafiyya, were able to avenge the death of al-Ḥusayn by killing those responsible for it. Eventually, al-Mukhtār was defeated, but the intensely apocalyptic movement of the Kaysāniyya continued to revere Ibn al-Ḥanafiyya as the Mahdi. Several of the doctrines of this group later developed and were incorporated into the teaching of other Shiʿite communities, including the Twelvers. Chapter 10 is a survey of the development of Shiʿite religio-political and doctrinal disputes between the second/eighth and fourth/tenth centuries. This chapter, which builds entirely on previous scholarship, provides the context for Chapter 11, where the development of the Karbala story into a myth and the elevation of the image of al-Ḥusayn during these centuries are further discussed. I argue that two factors are particularly significant in this process: the placing of the Karbala event in a cosmological context, and the rituals that emerged to commemorate the event. Chapter 12 is a short summary of the results from the previous chapters of the book in the light of the theoretical framework.

I hope that the book will be read both by specialists on early Islam and by non-specialists, such as scholars or advanced students in other fields of religious studies or in history other than the Late Antique Middle East. Various categories of readers will undoubtedly find particular parts of the book more interesting than others. Thus, some of the analyses in Parts I and II are quite technical, and readers not interested in the detailed arguments may skip the formal analyses without losing too much of the argument. Chapter 10, on the other hand, is an overview that is wholly based on the research of other scholars. Thus, readers acquainted with this scholarship are likely to find little that is new to them in that chapter.

2

Studying the Karbala Story as Myth

Myth, Mythmaking and Ritual

Several scholars have remarked that the concept of myth has rarely been used as an analytical tool in the academic study of Islam.[1] There are, I reckon, at least two reasons for the reluctance to use this concept in connection with Islam. First, despite the great variation in scholarly approaches to myth,[2] there is a traditional tendency to talk about myth as a literary *genre* in contradistinction to other genres of folklore such as legend and folktale.[3] Though it is true that this distinction is hardly employed today in my own discipline, religious studies, it has been very influential, and the criteria used to distinguish myth from other kinds of folk narratives are often used, consciously or not, in definitions within other academic fields. To distinguish between different categories of such genres, criteria of form and content and of the attitude held towards the story have normally been used. An often-cited example is the table of criteria made by William Bascom, whose classification is based on these criteria (see Table 2.1).[4]

1 E.g. Hylén, 'Ḥusayn, the Mediator', 20–4, 32–7; Vilozny, *Constructing a World View*, 60; Ebstein, 'In Truth', 362; Inloes, 'Joseph Campbell', 1–3. An attempt to remedy this lack of studies on myth in Islam was the symposium 'The Mythic Dimension of Islam: Examining the Sources through the Lens of Myth' at the Van Leer Jerusalem Institute in December 2015, several of the papers from which were published in a special issue of *Intellectual History of the Islamicate World* (vol. 6, no. 3, 2018).

2 For surveys of various approaches, see e.g. McCutcheon, 'Myth', 193–8, and, more comprehensively, Csapo, *Theories of Mythology*.

3 Other terms are often used for the category of 'folktale', and a large amount of confusion seems to underlie this class of tales with its sub-classes. See Bascom, 'Forms of Folklore', 7.

4 Bascom, 'Forms of Folklore', 9. For a similar though less detailed categorisation of Islamic narratives, see Neuwirth, 'Myths', 477.

Table 2.1 Three forms of prose narrative, according to Bascom

Form	Belief	Time	Place	Attitude	Principal characters
Myth	Fact	Remote past	Different world: other or earlier	Sacred	Non-human
Legend	Fact	Recent past	World of today	Secular or sacred	Human
Folktale	Fiction	Any time	Any place	Secular	Human or non-human

Several of the criteria for myth mentioned in Table 2.1 exclude the Karbala story, as well as other narratives from early Islam, from being counted within this category. Although the battle at Karbala is held to be fact, it is held to be *historical* fact and not placed in a remote past or a different world. Furthermore, the principal characters are human, although God is certainly thought to be active in the background. Thus, this way of classifying 'prose narratives' would determine the Karbala story to be a legend, not a myth – which is actually what a professor of religious studies told me as a PhD student in Uppsala when I suggested that we should treat this story as a myth. Most scholars of Islam, when talking of myth, do so using criteria similar to those in Table 2.1, that is, as dealing with events in prehistory or at the end of the world, or as describing divine intervention in history, and so on.[5]

The second reason for the exclusion of the foundational Islamic narratives from the category of myth is the popular view of myth as false stories. The clear-cut distinction between *mythos* (false stories) and *logos* (true, reasoned words or stories) goes back to Plato and has prevailed ever since in Western society.[6] This categorisation has become an instrument for distinguishing truth from falsehood in general in the West, and is commonly applied to distinguish between science (logic) and other concepts such as superstition

[5] For some examples, see Neuwirth, 'Myths'; Stetkevych, *Muḥammad*; Humphreys, 'Qur'ānic Myth'; and, particularly concerning Shiʿism, Amir-Moezzi, 'Cosmogony'; Dakake, *Charismatic Community*, 143–51; Vilozny, *Constructing a World View*, 57–109. The only Islamicists I have found who diverge from this approach to myth are Claude Gilliot ('Mythe'), who is influenced by Lévi-Straussian structuralism, and Amina Inloes ('Joseph Campbell'), who uses Joseph Campbell's Jungian approach to myth on Islam and particularly on the Karbala story.

[6] Lincoln, *Theorizing Myth*, 37–42; McCutcheon, 'Myth', 191. As both Lincoln and McCutcheon show, however, the distinction was not at all as definite in Greek society before Plato.

or religion (myth). As history belongs to the category of science, it is set in opposition to myth – a distinction that has consequences for the classification of Islamic historiography. During much of the nineteenth century, the majority of Western scholars of Islam accepted the Muslim view that the works of history written by Muslim historians (including such works as the biographies of the Prophet Muḥammad, many of the hadith, and the great historical compilations of historians like al-Balādhurī and al-Ṭabarī) conveyed basic facts about events that really happened in the formative period of Islam.[7] Since this textual corpus was *history* (although, admittedly in many cases, biased history), it could not be *myth*.[8]

A crucial notion in most traditional approaches to myth, including Bascom's criteria in Table 2.1, is that myth is a *sacred* story. The concept 'sacred' as an analytical category in the study of religion has recently been severely criticised.[9] According to the critics, the term, which originally denoted something set apart or dedicated – in other words, the result of a social process, an act or a technique – has become reified so that, since the mid-eighteenth century, it denotes a quality that exists in and by itself. Aaron Hughes and Russell McCutcheon write:

> What is curious is that the quality claimed to result from *setting* something apart, and thereby *marking* it as sanctified ... eventually comes to be so closely associated with this term 'sacred' that the supposed quality is eventually taken to be an autonomous and self-evident feature of the item. Once signified in this manner, we tend to lose sight of the practical, social procedures that led to the appearance or institution of the trait in the first place.[10]

Scholars working in the tradition of Émile Durkheim, who emphasised the human processes of sanctifying rather than the inherent quality of objects, stories, rituals, times and groups of people, avoid using the term 'sacred' without defining it. Rather than using the term as a vague adjective, they try to

[7] Of course, there were exceptions to this view, at least from the beginning of the twentieth century.
[8] This is, of course, mirrored by the Islamic perception of its history as based partly on revelation, the very opposite of false stories.
[9] E.g. Hughes and McCutcheon, *50 Words*, 263–9; Mack, 'Social Formation'; Paden, 'Before "The Sacred"'.
[10] Hughes and McCutcheon, *50 Words*, 264–5, italics in original.

investigate how and by what means the phenomenon in question has become set apart or sanctified. From this point of view, nothing is sacred in itself, but is made and kept so by people's acts and discourses. In other words, sacrality is a social construction.[11] Hence, rather than working with myth as a literary genre, McCutcheon argues that it is better regarded as 'a class of *social argumentation* found in all human cultures'. Myths, according to him, 'are not special (or "sacred") but ordinary human means of fashioning and authorizing their lived-in and believed-in "worlds"'. Myth as an 'ordinary rhetorical device in social construction and maintenance makes *this* rather than *that* social identity possible in the first place' and it 'reflects, expresses and legitimizes [a people's] own self-image'.[12] Therefore, following Mack's approach (see Chapter 1), McCutcheon prefers to talk of 'mythmaking' instead of the more static 'myth'. Thus, he continues towards the end of his article,

> myths are the product and the means of creating authority by removing a claim, behavior, artifact or institution from human history and hence from the realm of human doings. A rectified study of myths thus turns out to be a study of mythmaking.[13]

I find the approach of Mack and McCutcheon fruitful and will attempt to follow it in this book. Elsewhere, I have defined myth as *a narrative that is foundational to the world view and identity of a group of people*.[14] While I think it is impossible to define 'myth' in a way that will be acceptable to all, I will stick to this provisional definition throughout this work. In doing so, however, I must emphasise that I regard myth as I have defined it here as the result of a social process. Perhaps it would be better to change the verb 'is' in the definition to the phrase 'has been made'. The present work, then, is an attempt to study the development of the Karbala story as a process of removing the battle

[11] McCutcheon, 'Myth', 199–201.

[12] McCutcheon, 'Myth', 200. Italics original. Omitted from this quotation is a clause in which McCutcheon seems to argue that people use the 'label "myth"' for their own such process. On this point I disagree, as I have never heard of any person or group that uses the term 'myth' for their own stories. 'Myth' as used by McCutcheon and others, in my opinion, can only be regarded as an analytical concept.

[13] McCutcheon, 'Myth', 207. On 'mythmaking' as an analytical tool, see also Sinding Jensen, 'Modern Myths'.

[14] Hylén, 'Ḥusayn, the Mediator', 15.

at Karbala from human history, and hence, of making the story about it into a myth that is foundational to the world-view and identity of the Shiʿites.

An obvious advantage of working with mythmaking as a social process is that it includes all kinds of stories that are of such importance to people that they can be labelled 'foundational' to their identity and world-view. It does not matter whether a story is 'historically correct' (in the sense that the events it relates can be verified by scholarly research) or not. The dichotomy between myth and history loses its importance; history can function as myth and myth as history. Jan Assmann writes that

> foundational stories are called 'myth', and the term is usually used in contrast to history. There are two pairs of opposites involved here: fiction (myth) as opposed to reality (history), and purpose-oriented evaluation (using the past for an argument – myth) as opposed to pure objectivity (studying the past for the past's sake – history). These conceptual pairs, however, have long been due for the scrap heap ... The forms of the remembered past entail myth and history without any distinction between them. The past that is fixed and internalized as foundational is myth, regardless of whether it is fact or fiction.[15]

In my opinion, Assmann goes too far in equating myth and history in this passage. They certainly overlap (as in the case of the Karbala story), but there is of course history, in the sense of what is written in history books, that is not foundational and thus cannot be called myth. On the other hand, there are stories which are not necessarily believed to be factual, but which convey important values and for that sake are foundational to a group of people (that is, myths). For example, the biblical creation story may be very important to Jews or Christians even though they do not believe in its factuality.

This brings us to a further point: when a story is foundational, it is always so *to* someone. Accordingly, when I use myth as an analytical category, I always try to do so in relation to a group of people and their context. The Karbala story may function as a myth for most Shiʿites, but for many Sunnis it does not, and it certainly does not for most non-Muslims; to them it is perhaps a tragic story, but it is not foundational to their world-view and identity.

[15] Assmann, *Cultural Memory*, 59; see also McCutcheon, 'Myth', 204.

For Mack, as we have seen, mythmaking is the intellectual aspect of social formation. McCutcheon seems to have a wider notion of the concept of mythmaking, and sees it 'as a discourse involving acts and institutions as well as narratives'.[16] In my view, McCutcheon's broader use blurs the distinction between 'social formation' and 'mythmaking'. It seems to me that by enlarging 'mythmaking' to encompass that much, he makes the concept of 'social formation' superfluous. In this book, the making of a story into a myth and its role within the larger process of the formation of a Shi'ite identity are at the centre of my attention. Hence, I will distinguish between the two concepts and stick to Mack's more limited use of mythmaking as an aspect of, or one of several factors within, the larger process of social formation.

Curiously, however, neither of the two scholars places any emphasis on ritual, which, within the Durkheimian tradition that both profess to be inspired by, is said to be the main factor in creating and keeping group identity and solidarity.[17] Ritualisation of a story, according to this tradition, is one of the main factors in making it a myth, because ritual is what attaches emotions to a narrative. Following the tradition of the sociologists Émile Durkheim and Erving Goffman, Randall Collins argues that the reason for the efficacy of rituals for social formation is that they create emotions that function as 'glue' for the group.[18] Durkheim argued that people acting together also share emotions; they not only *do* things together, but they *feel* things together. Everyone who has been to a football match or a rock concert, or has sung in a choir, has experienced this. Durkheim called this state of common emotionality, especially when the emotions are strong, 'collective effervescence'.[19] These common emotions result in symbols which 'act as markers of group identity' as they 'represent the group and its attendant solidarity'.[20] Another result of

[16] McCutcheon, 'Myth', 204.

[17] Mack mentions ritual here and there in 'Social Formation' and touches on the relation between myth and ritual in *Who Wrote the New Testament?*, 300–1; he also has a short discussion in 'Redescribing', 255–6. Probably McCutcheon includes rituals in the 'acts and institutions' mentioned in the previous quotation, but he does not elaborate on its function in relation to myth.

[18] Collins, *Interaction Ritual Chains*, 103. See also summaries of his argument in Rossner and Meher, 'Emotions' and Summers-Effler, 'Ritual Theory'. Collins argues that not only Durkheim but several of the 'classical' sociological theories point to emotions as the uniting factor of groups, often without using the term, however (*Interaction Ritual Chains*, 102–3).

[19] Durkheim, *Elementary Forms*, 216–20 and *passim*.

[20] Rossner and Meher, 'Emotions', 203.

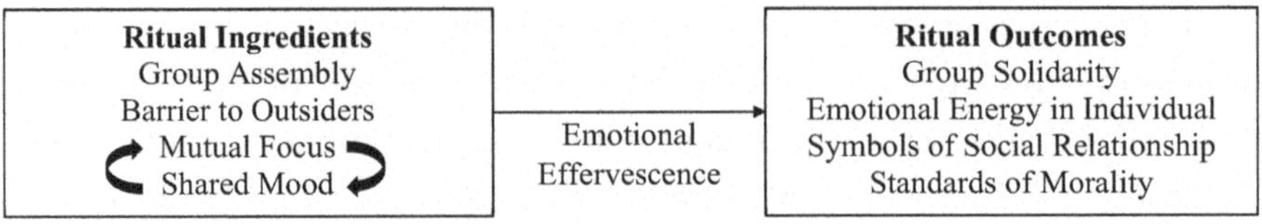

Figure 2.1 Interaction ritual chains, after Collins, *Interaction Ritual Chains*, p. 48.

the collective effervescence is a common morality, a 'collective sense that the group's actions and belief are right, and that violations of the group norms are wrong'.[21] On the basis of Durkheim's ideas, Collins developed a theory of ritual which he calls 'interaction ritual chains'. An interaction ritual, according to him, is any encounter between two or more people where they mutually focus their attention on something, thereby making it sacred (see Figure 2.1).[22] Gathering like this creates boundaries against outsiders. The focus on a common object or activity and the communication of this mutually shared focus create a shared mood or emotional experience.

The ingredients of the ritual, especially the mutual focus and the shared mood, feed back on and reinforce each other:

> As the persons become more tightly focused on their common activity, more aware of what each other is doing and feeling, and more aware of each other's awareness, they experience their shared emotion more intensely, as it comes to dominate their awareness. Members of a cheering crowd become more enthusiastic, just as participants of a religious service become more respectful and solemn, or at a funeral become more sorrowful, than before they began.[23]

This feedback becomes even stronger when a ritual is repeated, leading to a collective consciousness or collective effervescence, which in turn results in *solidarity* with the group – a feeling of belonging together, of group identity. Another important outcome of the ritual is the emergence of *symbolic representations* of the group and the solidarity between its members which function as markers of group identity. 'These symbols remind us of the powerful

[21] Rossner and Meher, 'Emotions', 203.
[22] Collins, *Interaction Ritual Chains*, 49–50. In this, Collins follows Erving Goffman.
[23] Collins, *Interaction Ritual Chains*, 48.

feeling we felt during the ritual. We charge up objects with symbolic meaning as a shortcut to representing the intense feeling of collective effervescence.'[24] Symbols can, for example, be artefacts (as, in the case of Shiʿism, the soil from the grave of al-Ḥusayn), people (the imams) or words (the Karbala story). A further result of the collective effervescence is certain standards of *morality* specific to the group. Finally, emotions raised through ritual, according to Collins, can be not only dramatic and short-term (for example, enthusiasm during the ritual itself), but also long-term heightened moods which extend beyond the ritual in time (such as heightened self-esteem and feelings of attachment to the group). These durable feelings Collins calls *emotional energy*, and they are reactivated and reinforced each time a person takes part in the ritual.[25] Thus, 'the "charge" of short term emotional energy can be translated into a long-term emotional state ... In this way, interaction rituals develop from separate encounters into a series of ritual chains.'[26] Rossner and Meher further argue that physical meetings between people are not necessary in order to bring about emotional energy. In solitary rituals, such as solitary prayers, the imagined presence and mutual communication with another person (for example, unworldly or non-human characters) is sufficient to produce similar results to a ritual at which other humans are bodily present.[27]

While the study of Shiʿite rituals plays a relatively minor role in the present work, I think that they are of the utmost importance for the development of the Karbala story into a myth. As we will see in Chapter 11, various rituals, such as the formal narration of the story in various gatherings, weeping over the injustice and suffering that befell the family of the Prophet, and particularly over the death of al-Ḥusayn, and visiting his grave, all contributed to raising the story into something more than an ordinary battle account.

On Sources and Methods

The Karbala story as it is analysed here had been retold in various versions in historiographical works dating from the second to fourth/eighth to tenth

[24] Rossner and Meher, 'Emotions', 203. See also Summers-Effler, 'Ritual Theory', 141–6.
[25] Collins, *Interaction Ritual Chains*, 102–40. Collins demonstrates here that this is physiologically confirmed.
[26] Rossner and Meher, 'Emotions', 208. See also Assmann, *Religion*, 42.
[27] Rossner and Meher, 'Emotions', 216.

centuries. The historical reliability of the sources for early Islam has been a matter of constant debate among scholars for the last hundred and fifty years; and though much of the discussion has centred on the life and activity of the Prophet Muḥammad himself, the sources for the centuries after his death have also been widely disputed.[28] In this section, I discuss the sources I have used for this study and my assessment of them. They can be divided into two main categories: historiographical works and poetry. I will also say a few words about Shiʿite hadiths, because although I have made only a very limited use of these, some of the scholars I refer to base much of their research on them, and they are thus indirectly relevant for the present study.

Historiographical Works

Historiography as a literary genre grew rather quickly in the first centuries of Islam. Chase Robinson speaks of three phases in its development, roughly corresponding to each of the first three centuries, and for the present study I find it convenient to follow his model.[29] The historiographical material used in this book is to various degrees related to all three phases.

The first phase, approximately up to the end of the first century after the death of the Prophet, is difficult to reconstruct, because very few texts remain from this time. The period was characterised by oral transmission, and only towards its end do we see the emergence of written material. It seems that among the earliest forms of historical texts were lists of people who were active in various important events, such as the battles of the Prophet. The oldest extant biographical material about the Prophet is also said to have appeared towards the end of the first/seventh century, but this is debated by modern scholars.[30] As I will argue throughout the following chapters, the narratives

[28] Only a few examples of overviews of the sources and the debates about them can be given here: see e.g. Donner, *Narratives*, 5–25; Kennedy, *Prophet*, 345–75; Noth and Conrad, *Early Arabic Historical Tradition*; Robinson, *Islamic Historiography*; and particularly, on the life of Prophet, Schoeler, *Biography*, 3–13.

[29] Robinson, *Islamic Historiography*, 18–38. Some other works on the emergence of Islamic historiography are Roberts, 'Early Islamic Historiography'; Humphreys, *Islamic History*; Noth and Conrad, *Early Arabic Historical Tradition*; Donner, *Narratives*. This list is far from complete.

[30] On the various opinions about the biographical material ascribed to ʿUrwa b. al-Zubayr, see e.g. Robinson, *Islamic Historiography*, 23–4; Görke and Schoeler, 'Reconstructing'; *Die ältesten Berichte*; Shoemaker, "Urwa's Sīra'; Anthony, *Muhammad*, 102–5.

about the Karbala battle and the subsequent events are to some extent probably based on oral traditions from this period.

The second phase occurred during the following century, up to c. 215/830. Here, Islamic historiography was arranged in chronological patterns. At this time, we see the emergence both of smaller monographs – such as accounts of the Karbala event and the Tawwābūn, which will be studied in the following chapters – and of more comprehensive biographies of the Prophet, including Ibn Isḥāq's (d. c. 150/767) enormous world history, culminating in the life and work of the Prophet.[31] An important reason for the flowering of historiography in this period was the Abbasid sponsorship of all kinds of learning, including such historiography as legitimised the dynasty's own position. Few of the 'relatively brief and single-topic "monographs"' written in this period have survived, except as edited versions incorporated into larger historiographical compilations from the following century,[32] when the third phase in historiographical writing took place. This phase continued up to roughly the beginning of the fourth/tenth century. This, then, is the time when many previous works were edited and compiled into large biographical, prosopographical and chronographical works,[33] such as the biography of the Prophet, *Sīrat rasūl Allāh*, by Ibn Hishām (d. 220/835), a chronologically arranged biographical album of early Muslims called *Kitāb al-Tabaqāt al-Kabīr* by Ibn Sa'd (d. 230/845), al-Balādhurī's (d. 279/892) large genealogical work *Ansāb al-Ashrāf*, and al-Ṭabarī's (d. 310/923) huge world history *Ta'rīkh al-rusul wa-l-mulūk*. All the texts I study in the following chapters are found within large works like these. In particular, while I have at times referred to other versions for comparative purposes, I have based my analyses on the versions incorporated in al-Ṭabarī's *Ta'rīkh*, as these are the most comprehensive.

Although al-Ṭabarī uses several sources when he narrates the group of stories that relate to the Karbala affair (the events leading up to the battle and the battle itself, the subsequent story of the Tawwābūn, and finally the revenge of al-Mukhtār),[34] the historian Lūt b. Yahyā al-Azdī, better known as Abū Mikhnaf, stands out for his ubiquity, and for that reason we need to look a

31 On Ibn Isḥāq and his *Kitāb al-Maghāzī*, see Anthony, *Muhammad*, 150–71.

32 Robinson, *Islamic Historiography*, 34.

33 On these categories, see Robinson, *Islamic Historiography*, 55–79.

34 On this cycle of stories, see the introduction to Chapter 9.

bit closer at this author and his work. More than 90 per cent of Al-Ṭabarī's account of the Karbala story is a reproduction of passages from Abū Mikhnaf's 'book' *Kitāb maqtal al-Ḥusayn*.[35] For the story of the Tawwābūn, al-Ṭabarī is still more dependent on Abū Mikhnaf: almost the whole of his account seems to consist of Abū Mikhnaf's 'book' *Kitāb Sulaymān b. Ṣurad wa-'Ayn al-Warda*. Abū Mikhnaf is also one of al-Ṭabarī's most important sources for the story of al-Mukhtār, though here he refers to other sources as well.

Abū Mikhnaf was a truly prolific author; it is not known exactly how many works he produced, but between thirty and forty works are normally ascribed to him.[36] Al-Ṭabarī apparently did not have access to Abū Mikhnaf's books at first hand, but reproduced them in the version given by Hishām b. al-Kalbī (d. 204/819), another productive writer, historian and genealogist, who apparently faithfully quoted long passages from Abū Mikhnaf's works. Ibn al-Kalbī also included material from other authorities, which means that his rendering of the texts of Abū Mikhnaf might to a certain extent have been processed and edited. Although his long quotations from Abū Mikhnaf seem to have been accurately reproduced, they could have been moved around so as to fit his own version of the story. The same, of course, is true of al-Ṭabarī's rendering of Ibn al-Kalbī. But a comparison of al-Ṭabarī's version with those of other historians who also based their accounts on Abū Mikhnaf reveals more or less the same order of related events, so it appears that al-Ṭabarī's text is much the same as Abū Mikhnaf's original.[37]

Very little is known about Abū Mikhnaf's life. He was born in Kufa, and considering that his writings mostly covered events in Iraq, he probably spent most of his life there. Several scholars hold that the historical writings of Abū Mikhnaf are to a large extent stories about his own family (the Mikhnaf family) or tribe (al-Azd), who were deeply involved in the politics of Iraq, often on

35 I have put the word 'book' in quotation marks in order to show that by this I do not mean a published book in the modern sense. For a discussion of the question of oral and written material, see Schoeler, *The Oral and the Written*, 28–44.

36 See Sezgin, *Geschichte*, vol. I, 308. Ursula Sezgin mentions 39 titles (*Abū Miḫnaf*, 99–116), and Bahramian 37 ('Abū Mikhnaf').

37 Even the 'original' authors of Arabic historiography often produced several variant versions of a text. For this reason, it is hardly correct to talk of an original version in the Western sense of the word (Schoeler, *The Oral and the Written*, 62–86).

the side of the Shiʿites.[38] The question about Abū Mikhnaf's religio-political position is unsettled, and there are differing opinions among both Muslim and Western scholars on this matter.[39] Several modern scholars ascribe various positions to him without argument. Thus, Fuat Sezgin makes him an Imami, while Josef van Ess and Patricia Crone just state that he was a 'soft Shiʿite', that is, that he held the view that authority over the Muslim community should have belonged to the family of the Prophet, but he could still accept a non-Shiʿite ruler.[40] Others are more hesitant to ascribe a Shiʿite inclination to him.[41] The year of Abū Mikhnaf's death is usually given as 157/774, but as Bahramian demonstrates, there is only one source for this. Other sources give a death date about a decade later.[42] To be safe, I will specify his year of death as before 170/786–7.

Abū Mikhnaf's historical writing, like most Arabic historiography from the first centuries of Islam, is anecdotal to a large degree.[43] In general, longer accounts, such as Abū Mikhnaf's version of the Karbala story, are built from many independent reports (*khabar*s), varying in length from one line to several pages. A *khabar* consists of two parts. The main text (*matn*) is the anecdote itself, the historical information that is provided, while the *matn* is introduced by the *isnād*, the chain of authorities who have transmitted it, beginning with the immediate authority of the compiler of the work and leading back to an eyewitness of the event or a famous authority of some kind (legal hadiths are structured in the same way; the main difference between hadiths and *khabar*s is their content).[44] Normally, the *khabar*s are lined up to drive the narrative forwards, but sometimes (and especially in al-Ṭabarī's work) a number of slightly different traditions on the same event are placed together so as to give a complementary view, and at times traditions with completely opposite opinions of what happened are put together. The constant

[38] Athamina, 'Abū Mikhnaf'. See also Sezgin, *Geschichte*, vol. I, 308; Bahramian et al., 'Abū Mikhnaf'; Borrut, 'Remembering Karbalā'".

[39] On Muslim scholars, see Bahramian et al., 'Abū Mikhnaf'.

[40] Sezgin, *Geschichte*, vol. I, 308; van Ess, *Theologie*, vol. I, 311; Crone, *Political Thought*, 117–18. On 'soft Shiʿism', see Chapter 10.

[41] So, for example, Bahramian et al., 'Abū Mikhnaf', and Athamina, 'Abū Mikhnaf'.

[42] Bahramian et al., 'Abū Mikhnaf'.

[43] This paragraph is based on Leder, '*Khabar*' and Robinson, *Islamic Historiography*, 15–17.

[44] For examples of *khabar*s, including their chains of transmission, see Chapter 7.

use of the *isnād* in the *khabar* form has often led scholars from the Western academic tradition to characterise Islamic historiography as traditionalistic and conservative, playing down the role of the individual author.[45] Ulrika Mårtensson, however, argues that *isnād*s in historiographical works have a role similar to that of footnotes in present-day academic tradition. When al-Ṭabarī provides differing reports of the same event, he merely wants to show that various eyewitnesses perceived the same event differently and to expose the contribution of individual transmitters.[46] As every modern historian knows, however, references in footnotes are not always accurate, and the *isnād*s of the Arabic historians are even less accurate. They are no guarantee of the historical reliability of their accounts. First, *isnād*s are often incomplete or even missing, and are sometimes demonstrably fabricated. Second, even though the author supports his accounts with *isnād*s,

> the *khabar*-form ... also conveys the personal opinions of the historian who is writing. Studies of Ṭabarī's sections on specific historical events, e.g. the second *fitna*, the murder of ʿUthmān b. ʿAffān, and the Battle of the Camel, show that his views come through in his arrangement and evaluation of reports, and his interspersed comments.[47]

The modern debate on the historical reliability of the *khabar*s has often focused on the trustworthiness of the *isnād*s. Since the 1990s, some scholars, mainly from a German background, have developed a method for analysing legal hadiths. Harald Motzki gave the most systematic description of this method, which he called *isnād-cum-matn* analysis.[48] In brief, the scholar following this method tries to correlate the variations of the *matn*s with the *isnād*s to see if a specific variant of the *matn* corresponds to a particular transmission history. In this way, the analyst should be able to discern whether or not two or more versions of traditions are transmitted independently of one another. Motzki himself mainly used this method on the study of legal hadiths, and

[45] Robinson, *Islamic Historiography*, 35; Mårtensson, 'Discourse', 292–3.
[46] Mårtensson, 'Discourse', 296–7.
[47] Mårtensson, 'Discourse', 297.
[48] Several of his most important articles on methodology have been translated into English and are published in Motzki et al., *Analysing Muslim Traditions*; a brief overview of the *isnād-cum-matn* method is found on pp. 146–7 of that work.

it has also been successfully used by Najam Haider on early Shiʿite hadiths.[49] Andreas Görke and Gregor Schoeler have applied it to historical traditions about Muḥammad as well, but their studies have been criticised.[50]

While the *isnād-cum-matn* method can at times give positive results, especially with sources that originate after the turn of the second/eighth century, it is hardly applicable in the present study. The method is primarily designed for, and tested on, hadiths that have been widely disseminated and exist in many versions. The historiographical texts that I work with often lack the *isnād*s that are found in hadiths with a legal content or in *khabar*s relating the life of the Prophet Muḥammad. Furthermore, most of the accounts I analyse exist in a few versions only, and thus the comparison of numerous versions – so important for a Motzkean analysis – is impossible. My analysis of the historical texts follows more traditional lines, which will be further described in connection with each analysis.

Two basic criteria keep recurring throughout the analyses in the book, however. One, the criterion of multiple independent sources, says that the larger the number of sources that independently of one another indicate the same thing, the more probable it is that the indication (for example, that a certain event has occurred, or that a tradition originated at a certain time) is correct.[51] The problem with this criterion is often not so much finding a number of sources as determining whether they are mutually independent. An example in this book is Chapter 3, where I have attempted to establish the independence of three versions of the Karbala story.

The second general criterion is what has sometimes been called 'the criterion of embarrassment'. This says that words, actions and ideas that would cause embarrassment for, or go against the interests of, the later community are probably early.[52] At a stage later in the history of a group, once a mythology and

[49] Haider, *Origins*: his method is described in Chapter 2 of that work.

[50] Görke and Schoeler, 'Reconstructing'; Görke and Schoeler, *Die ältesten Berichte*. Their attempts have been seriously criticised by Stephen J. Shoemaker ("Urwa's Sīra'), whose main argument is that 'Urwa's letters are attested only (or almost only) in al-Ṭabarī's works, and that several of the *isnād*s are suspicious and might well be inventions by al-Ṭabarī or one of his sources. Görke, Schoeler and Motzki have responded in 'First-Century Sources'.

[51] Meier, *A Marginal Jew*, vol. I, 174–5. For a critique of this criterion in the study of the historical Jesus, see Allison, 'How to Marginalize', and the response by Meier, *A Marginal Jew*, vol. V, 27, n. 28.

[52] Meier, *A Marginal Jew*, vol. I, 168–71.

ideology have already developed, the group is unlikely to create traditions that contradict this. This criterion has often been used in studies on Islamic history. One of the most famous examples is the episode of the so-called Satanic verses, in which the Prophet Muḥammad is said to have referred to pre-Islamic divinities. Modern scholars deem this episode authentic because it casts the Prophet in an unfavourable light and thus is unlikely to have been invented later.[53] One of several comparable examples in this book is to be found in Chapter 9 in the discussion about the 'chair of ʿAlī'. As references in the footnotes to this paragraph reveal, both these criteria have their caveats. The biblical scholar John P. Meier has written that 'no criterion can be used mechanically and in isolation; a convergence of different criteria is the best indicator of historicity'.[54] Used with care, however, these criteria have often yielded important results in various fields of historical research.

Poetry

Meier further writes of the criterion of multiple independent attestations that 'the force of this criterion is increased if a given motif or theme is found both in different literary sources and different literary forms'.[55] The idea behind this statement is that a single author is less likely to produce material in different literary genres, such as historiographic narratives, official letters, hadiths and poetry. The Karbala story is of course narrated in various historiographical writings, but it is also alluded to in poetry, some of which is purportedly much older than the earliest historiography (see Chapter 11). The same is true of the story of the Tawwābūn. As we will see in Chapter 5, the only narrative we have of this suicidal mission is that of Abū Mikhnaf; all other accounts are based on his. To my knowledge, there is only one source which is probably independent of Abū Mikhnaf: a poem written by the famous poet Aʿshā Hamdān (d. 82 or 83/701 or 702).[56] Also in al-Ṭabarī's rendering of the story of al-Mukhtār, poems reflecting the events are interspersed (see Chapter 7). Thus it would

53 Shoemaker, "Urwa's Sīra', 322–4, answering a critique of this criterion in Hoyland, 'Writing the Biography'.

54 Meier, *A Marginal Jew*, vol. I, 175. It is not unusual, for example, that unfavourable traditions were forged by opponents of a group with the sole purpose of embarrassing them.

55 Meier, *A Marginal Jew*, vol. I, 174.

56 See below, Chapters 5 and 8.

seem that we have a number of independent sources confirming the basic outlines of the historiographical narratives, and, what is more, sources belonging to different genres.

Arabic poetry as a source for the early history of Islam is tricky, however. First, the authenticity of the poems, in the sense that they are composed by the person they are ascribed to, can seldom be verified. Just because al-Ṭabarī says that Aʿshā Hamdān wrote the poem about the Tawwābūn, we cannot know if he actually did. Someone who lived later and had read Abū Mikhnaf's account might have written it and ascribed it to the famous Aʿshā. In this case, furthermore, it seems that the only source for this particular poem is al-Ṭabarī. He appended it to Abū Mikhnaf's account of the Tawwābūn, but to my knowledge it is not found anywhere independently of al-Ṭabarī.[57]

A second problem is that as poems were transmitted and related in various political and religious contexts, the content was often modified. Verses were sometimes forgotten with the passage of time, and replaced by other verses; in other cases, a compiler might have found the poem too long and included only the verses he thought important; sometimes verses thought to be scandalous and upsetting were removed or modified. A case in this book is the poem by al-Zāhī (d. 352/963) quoted in Chapter 11. The last line, in which al-Ḥusayn is called 'he through whom all existence subsists' and which could be interpreted as a violation of the Islamic doctrine of monotheism, is missing in one version.[58]

This said, it seems that most modern historians are prepared to accept poetry as an auxiliary source at least.[59] My position in this book is that poems ascribed to famous and well-established poets are less likely to be forged, and thus I will accept them, at least in the main, as genuine. As such they can be used to complement, and at times to verify, the historiographical narratives.

Hadiths

Finally, a few words must be said about the hadiths ascribed to the imams as historical sources. I will refer to these now and then, in particular when

[57] El-Achèche, *La poésie šiʿite*, 197–9.
[58] See e.g. al-Majlisī, *Biḥār*, vol. XLV, 248, where also the first line is modified. I am grateful to Lovisa Berg and Nejood al-Rubaye for this reference.
[59] So e.g. Crone and Hinds, *God's Caliph*, *passim*; Donner, *Narratives*, 207; Robinson, *Islamic Historiography*, 52; Webb, 'Poetry'.

describing the esoteric theology of early Shiʿism. These descriptions are based on the work of other scholars, in particular that of Mohammad Ali Amir-Moezzi, and here I have adopted his view on the hadiths from the imams.

A hadith, like a *khabar*, consists of two parts: (1) the main text, the information given (*matn*), and (2) the chain of transmitters (*isnād*) preceding it. Amir-Moezzi argues that we cannot accept the *isnād*s of these hadiths.[60] It is impossible to trace a particular hadith to the imam from which it is said to have originated. But the hadiths from the pre-Buyid collections are nevertheless very old, and 'characterized by teachings of an esoteric, initiatic, mystical even magical type and intense messianic coloration'.[61] Thus they express ideas that were later discarded (see Chapter 10). My position, then, is that while the attribution to a specific imam cannot be taken for granted, the ideas expressed normally belong to the period between the second/eighth and fourth/tenth centuries.

[60] The following paragraph is based on Amir-Moezzi, 'On Spirituality', but he argues similarly throughout much of his authorship.

[61] Amir-Moezzi, 'On Spirituality', 111. See also Newman, *Formative Period*, 97–8. Similar ideas are also found in the old texts studied by Asatryan in his *Controversies*.

PART I

THE KARBALA STORY

3

Three Times Karbala: Early Accounts of the Killing of al-Ḥusayn

Introduction

The story of the killing of al-Ḥusayn b. ʿAlī at Karbala in 61/680 has reached us in several versions, but, as previously mentioned, it has been subjected to little investigation despite its importance throughout history.[1] Two important studies have compared the various early versions of the Karbala story. In his survey of early Arabic accounts of the martyrdom of al-Ḥusayn in 1984, I. K. A. Howard claims to list all early 'monographs or lengthy accounts on the martyrdom of al-Ḥusayn which we have some record of or which we can surmise' – nine accounts in all.[2] Howard did an important job in tracing, collecting and describing early versions of the Karbala tradition, and the present study is deeply indebted to his article, in spite of my frequent disagreements with his conclusions. Howard's purpose, even if not explicitly stated, is clearly to assess the value of the various early versions of the story as historical sources; I will argue below that, on this point, his study is often problematic.

I have also benefited greatly from a more recent comparative study of 2015 of the Karbala narrative by Antoine Borrut, who has investigated two Muslim, as well as the extant Syriac Christian, versions of the story.

1 See Hussain, 'Developmental Analysis', 1–8.

2 Howard, 'Husayn the Martyr', 124. A notable omission in Howard's study is the version of Ibn Saʿd (*Ṭabaqāt*, vol. VI, 421–60). Sachau's edition from 1904–40, which was the only one available to Howard when he worked on his article, does not include the biography of al-Ḥusayn (see Lucas, 'Ibn Saʿd'). Ibn Saʿd's account largely depends on Abū Mikhnaf, though he has some interesting additional material. I was made aware of the new edition of *Tabaqāt* late in my work, so I will only occasionally refer to it.

He discusses the problem of the almost total absence of the story from Umayyad historiography, and its return in Abbasid times. Borrut concludes that the two Muslim versions on which he focuses were 'local and familial memories'.[3] Thus, the 'long version' by Abū Mikhnaf is written from a Kufan perspective, to preserve the memory of the Karbala event from the perspective of his own family, as his ancestors were active adherents of Shiʿism. The 'short version', on the other hand, was transmitted by al-Ḥusayn's grandson, the fifth imam, Abū Jaʿfar al-Bāqir, who lived in Medina. Hence, according to Borrut, this version preserved the memory of the event from the perspective of the ʿAlid family in Medina.

This chapter will analyse and compare the three earliest complete recensions of the Karbala story that are available to us. I will explain below what I mean by 'complete' versions; although some earlier accounts seem to have existed, only fragments of these are still extant.[4] The three versions studied here are ascribed to or were compiled by the fifth Shiʿite imam, Abū Jaʿfar al-Bāqir (d. 114/732–3), the Kufan traditionist al-Ḥuṣayn b. ʿAbd al-Raḥmān (d. 136/753–4),[5] and the Kufan historian Abū Mikhnaf (d. before 170/786–7).[6] All three versions are reproduced in the *Taʾrīkh al-rusul wa-ʾl-mulūk*[7] of al-Ṭabarī (d. 311/923), and I will use his rendering as my point of departure, although I will make comparisons with other sources when necessary.[8]

An important question is, of course, whether the three versions analysed here are interdependent in any way. Did any of these authors, in other words, use one of the other accounts as a source, and abbreviate it, expand it, or in other ways use parts of it when composing a new version? In what follows, I will argue that, although there are several close similarities between the three versions, the differences are far too significant to hypothesise the direct

[3] Borrut, 'Remembering Karbalā'', 271.
[4] Howard, 'Husayn the Martyr', 124–7.
[5] In order not to confuse him with al-Ḥusayn b. ʿAlī, I will henceforth use his patronymic Ibn ʿAbd al-Raḥmān, though it is a bit clumsy.
[6] On Abū Mikhnaf's death date, see Chapter 2.
[7] Al-Ṭabarī, *Taʾrīkh*, II, 216–390; English translation by Howard in al-Ṭabarī, *History*, vol. XIX, 1–183.
[8] According to Ali J. Hussain there is a source on the Karbala story by a certain al-Fadīl b. al-Zubayr (d. 110–145/728–62), which has not been available to me. This seems to be more a list of names of the people killed with al-Ḥusayn than a narrative of the battle, however ('Developmental Analysis', 17–18).

dependence of one of the texts upon the other. Apart from certain differences in structure and content which will be discussed below, the wording and phrasing of the three texts are divergent enough to preclude one of the versions having been used as a model for the others. When various compilers base their accounts on, for example, Abū Mikhnaf's version – as, in part, did al-Balādhurī, al-Ṭabarī and al-Ya'qūbī – long passages are almost word for word identical. When a section is abbreviated in one version, often what remains is not just summarised in the compiler's own words, but, even when parts have been left out, the very phrasing of the original is frequently used. To take only one example: when al-Balādhurī's and al-Ṭabarī's rendering of the first meeting between al-Ḥusayn and al-Ḥurr and their followers are compared, we see that, although al-Balādhurī's version is much shorter and structured somewhat differently from al-Ṭabarī's, the words and phrases used are almost the same.[9] Though al-Balādhurī does not give an *isnād* at this point in his account, it is clear that both historians base their accounts of this episode on the same text. According to al-Ṭabarī, this is Abū Mikhnaf.[10] When the three versions discussed in the present study are compared, on the other hand, we see very few verbatim correspondences of this kind. Only in a few places, where the words of a person or a poem are quoted, is such an agreement in words and phrasing to be seen in the versions of al-Bāqir and Abū Mikhnaf. In Ibn 'Abd al-Raḥmān's version, there are no such close resemblances with the other two. This paucity of correspondence, in my opinion, clearly argues against any one version being dependent on any of the others. Rather, I believe that the three versions emerged independently of one another. Where there are close correspondences between two versions, these are based on common reports and earlier traditions.

I stated above that the three versions of the Karbala story that I will study here are the earliest complete versions available to us. By complete, I mean that they include all or most of the following sections:[11]

[9] Al-Balādhurī, *Ansāb*, vol. III, 380; al-Ṭabarī, *Ta'rīkh*, II, 295–6.

[10] Al-Balādhurī gives an *isnād* reaching back to Abū Mikhnaf at the beginning of his account, while al-Ṭabarī provides *isnād*s for each *khabar*.

[11] Comprehensive and readable, though uncritical summaries of the story, based mainly on Abū Mikhnaf's version, are found in Jafri, *Origins*, 174–221 and Veccia Vaglieri, 'Ḥusayn'.

Section 1. The Succession to Muʿāwiya

At the death of the caliph Muʿāwiya in Damascus, al-Ḥusayn, who has been living in Medina, is commanded to give his pledge of allegiance, his *bayʿa*, to Muʿāwiya's son Yazīd in the presence of the governor in Medina. Al-Ḥusayn manages to leave for Mecca without giving his *bayʿa*.

Section 2. The Call of the Kufans, Muslim b. ʿAqīl's Journey to Kufa and the Appointment of Ibn Ziyād as New Governor

While in Mecca, al-Ḥusayn receives letters from the Shiʿites in Kufa, asking him to come and lead them in an insurrection against the governor there, the lenient al-Nuʿmān b. Bashīr. Al-Ḥusayn sends his cousin, Muslim b. ʿAqīl, to Kufa to gather information. On his way through the desert, Muslim gets lost and almost dies of thirst. When he arrives, a large number of Shiʿites secretly pledge their alliance to al-Ḥusayn. The new caliph Yazīd learns of this and replaces al-Nuʿmān with the ruthless ʿUbaydallāh b. Ziyād as governor.

Section 3. Muslim's Mission in Kufa and his Death

Muslim stays with Hāniʾ b. ʿUrwa, and Ibn Ziyād learns of this. He arrests Hāniʾ and tries to force him to hand Muslim over, but Hāniʾ refuses. On hearing this, Muslim gathers the Shiʿites and marches on the governor's palace with several thousand men. However, the people desert him little by little, and eventually Muslim is left alone. He is captured at the house of a woman, where he is trying to hide. He and Hāniʾ are executed.

Section 4. Al-Ḥusayn's Journey to Iraq, his Interception and Negotiations with ʿUmar b. Saʿd

Ignorant of the latest developments, al-Ḥusayn sets out from Mecca towards Kufa. On the way he is told of the killing of Muslim, but decides to continue. He is intercepted by a vanguard of the governor's army and forced to stop in the desert. When the main army arrives, al-Ḥusayn tries to negotiate with the commander, ʿUmar b. Saʿd, but to no avail.

Section 5. The Battle and the Killing of al-Ḥusayn

The Kufan army engages in battle with al-Ḥusayn and his followers. Al-Ḥusayn's baby son is killed, together with almost all male relatives in his group. Finally, al-Ḥusayn himself is killed and decapitated.

Section 6. The Aftermath of the Battle

The survivors of al-Ḥusayn's family are brought before the governor Ibn Ziyād, then sent to Yazīd in Damascus. From there, Yazīd allows them to return to Medina.

This outline is what Najam Haider calls the 'core structure' of the story, the elements shared by all or most of the versions.[12] This core has been fleshed out by the development and addition of 'narrative elements' which are 'crafted by historians in a process of rhetorical elaboration and embellishment'.[13] Historians may have different motives for transmitting a story, and may thus use various rhetorical devices to make sense of a core structure in the context in which they are active. This context Haider calls the 'narrative framework' of the historian. He proposes a three-step method for analysis of stories in Islamic historiography. The first step is to identify the core structure, the second to compare and categorise the various narrative elements, and the third to establish the narrative framework.[14] Although I began working on the present study before reading Haider's book, I realise that this is more or less the same method as the one I use, though in a less detailed and systematic manner than he employs it.

Of the three versions, that composed by Abū Mikhnaf is definitely the longest and most detailed. It takes up around 80 to 85 per cent of al-Ṭabarī's compilation of sources for the Karbala drama, while al-Bāqir's version represents about 5 per cent of the text, and that of Ibn 'Abd al-Raḥmān is even shorter. Abū Mikhnaf's account deals with each of the sections at length; al-Bāqir's account has something on each of the sections, but at times as little

[12] Haider, *Rebel*, 6–7, 15–16.
[13] Haider, *Rebel*, 7.
[14] Haider, *Rebel*, 6–9.

as a sentence or two. Ibn ʿAbd al-Raḥmān omits Section 1 completely, but has material on all the other sections.

The Three Versions Compared

The story falls naturally into two parts, the first relating the events up to the execution of Muslim b ʿAqīl in Kufa (Sections 1–3), and the second recounting al-Ḥusayn's journey from Mecca, the battle at Karbala, and its aftermath (Sections 4–6). The analysis that follows will point to some of the most significant differences and similarities between the three versions by, first, comparing Sections 1–3 in Abū Mikhnaf and al-Bāqir section by section, then going on to compare these with the same sections in the version of Ibn ʿAbd al-Raḥmān. I will then proceed in the same way with Sections 3–6 in Abū Mikhnaf's and al-Bāqir's versions, before comparing these with Ibn ʿAbd al-Raḥmān's.

Section 1. The Succession to Muʿāwiya

Al-Bāqir's version has a few sentences about Muʿāwiya's death, al-Ḥusayn's refusal to give his pledge of allegiance to Yazīd, and his escape by night to Mecca.[15] Abū Mikhnaf's account of these events is several pages long, and thus much more detailed. He relates how not only al-Ḥusayn but also ʿAbdallāh b. al-Zubayr refuse to give their *bayʿa* to Yazīd and take refuge in Mecca.[16]

Section 2. The Call of the Kufans, Muslim b. ʿAqīl's Journey and the Appointment of Ibn Ziyād as New Governor

Al-Bāqir's and Abū Mikhnaf's versions follow the same basic structure:

1. The Kufans send messages to al-Ḥusayn, telling him that they support him and reject the Umayyad governor al-Nuʿmān b. Bashīr. They ask him to come.
2. Al-Ḥusayn sends Muslim b. ʿAqīl to Kufa. Muslim gets lost in the desert and almost dies of thirst.

[15] Al-Ṭabarī, *Taʾrīkh*, II, 227–8
[16] Al-Ṭabarī, *Taʾrīkh*, II, 216–23.

3. Muslim stays with one of the inhabitants of Kufa for a while (the two versions differ as to whom), and the Shiʿites of Kufa begin to visit him in large numbers.
4. Al-Nuʿmān b. Bashīr is accused of taking too lenient an attitude towards the Shiʿites, and messages are sent to Yazīd.
5. Yazīd appoints ʿUbaydallāh b. Ziyād as governor of Kufa (for this passage in Abū Mikhnaf, see discussion below, and note 24).
6. Ibn Ziyād travels from Basra to Kufa and enters the city veiled. The people think it is al-Ḥusayn who has arrived.

Although the narrative structure of the two versions is similar, there are considerable differences in detail. Abū Mikhnaf's version is of course much longer and more detailed than al-Bāqir's.[17] In addition to elements that are not extant in al-Bāqir's text (such as dialogues in direct speech and names of persons involved), Abū Mikhnaf's text also includes several longer passages that are not found in al-Bāqir's account. The most obvious of these are a letter sent by al-Ḥusayn in reply to the Kufans,[18] a passage about the Basran Shiʿites recounting how one of them decides to go to join al-Ḥusayn,[19] and a letter written by al-Ḥusayn to the Basrans asking them to join him.[20]

The two versions disagree on where Muslim first stayed when he arrived in Kufa. Whereas al-Bāqir says that he stayed with Muslim b. ʿAwsaja, who later fought and died with al-Ḥusayn at Karbala,[21] Abū Mikhnaf has it that he stayed with al-Mukhtār b. Abī ʿUbayd, known as the leader of a Shiʿite insurrection in Kufa a few years later.[22] Al-Bāqir also relates an episode not mentioned by Abū Mikhnaf. He writes that, when the caliph Yazīd is informed about the governor Ibn Bashīr's mildness towards the Shiʿites in Kufa, he asks for the counsel of his *mawlā* Sarjūn, who advises Yazīd to make Ibn Ziyād the new governor in Kufa.[23] This event is not related by Abū Mikhnaf, although a report with this

[17] In the Leiden edition, al-Bāqir's account is only about one page long (al-Ṭabarī, *Taʾrīkh*, II, 228–9), whereas Abū Mikhnaf's covers almost nine pages (al-Ṭabarī, *Taʾrīkh*, II, 233–9, 240–2).
[18] Al-Ṭabarī, *Taʾrīkh*, II, 235.
[19] Al-Ṭabarī, *Taʾrīkh*, II, 235–6.
[20] Al-Ṭabarī, *Taʾrīkh*, II, 240–1.
[21] Al-Ṭabarī, *Taʾrīkh*, II, 228.
[22] Al-Ṭabarī, *Taʾrīkh*, II, 237. On al-Mukhtār, see Chapter 9.
[23] Al-Ṭabarī, *Taʾrīkh*, II, 228.

content from another authority, ʿAwāna b. al-Ḥakam al-Kalbī, is inserted into Abū Mikhnaf's account as transmitted by Ṭabarī.[24]

Finally, as mentioned above, the phrasing of the texts is mostly divergent enough to preclude a close interdependence. Only one sentence in this section is almost word for word the same: the answer by al-Nuʿmān b. Bashīr to those who accuse him of being too lenient towards Muslim and the Shiʿites. In both versions, he replies almost verbatim, 'I would prefer to be weak in obedience to God than strong in disobedience of God.'[25]

Section 3. Muslim's Mission in Kufa and his Death

As in the previous sections, al-Bāqir's and Abū Mikhnaf's accounts are structurally similar:

1. Muslim moves to live in the house of Hāniʾ b. ʿUrwa (in al-Bāqir's account this is narrated after the event, at a later stage in the narrative).
2. Ibn Ziyād sends a spy with 3,000 dirhams to infiltrate the Shiʿites. One of the leading Shiʿites takes the spy to Muslim. The infiltrator reports Muslim's location to Ibn Ziyād.
3. Ibn Ziyād asks his nobles why Hāniʾ has not come to visit him. The governor sends Ibn al-Ashʿath, a Kufan nobleman, and some other men to go and fetch him.
4. Ibn Ziyād asks Hāniʾ where Muslim is, and reveals the spy.
5. Hāniʾ refuses to hand Muslim over. Ibn Ziyād strikes Hāniʾ on his forehead, wounding him, and orders his execution.
6. Muslim learns of Hāniʾs death sentence and raises the battle cry. Four thousand men gather with him. They march on the governor's palace.

[24] Al-Ṭabarī, *Ta'rīkh*, II, 239. It looks as though ʿAwāna's report continues beyond the episode of Sarjūn, relating how Yazīd commands Muslim b. ʿAmr al-Bāhilī to go to Basra and hand over the letter of appointment to Ibn Ziyād. I do not think this is so, however. Al-Balādhurī – who apparently follows Abū Mikhnaf when relating this section – talks about Muslim b. ʿAmr's mission to Ibn Ziyād, but does not mention the episode with Sarjūn (al-Balādhurī, *Ansāb*, vol. II, 335). This makes me inclined to think that, in al-Ṭabarī's account, the first part of the report (about Sarjūn) is from ʿAwāna according to the *isnād*, whereas the second part (the one about Muslim b. ʿAmr) actually comes from Abū Mikhnaf, even though no *isnād* is provided.

[25] Al-Ṭabarī, *Ta'rīkh*, II, 228, 239.

7. Ibn Ziyād gathers the nobles of the town. They observe Muslim and his men from the palace and induce them to leave. Muslim's men gradually desert him.
8. Muslim wanders through the streets alone and reaches the house of a woman who gives him water to drink and takes him into her house.
9. Her son discloses Muslim's hiding place to Ibn al-Ashʿath, who informs Ibn Ziyād. The governor sends a group of men commanded by ʿAmr b. Ḥurayth to get Muslim. Muslim fights them. Finally, he gets a guarantee of safe conduct, and surrenders himself.
10. Muslim is brought to Ibn Ziyād, who has him executed on the palace roof, and his body thrown down. Hāniʾ too is executed.
11. A poem is quoted (al-Bāqir cites three of the eight verses quoted by Abū Mikhnaf).

The general structure of this section is very similar in both versions. Even many of the details, such as the names of some of the persons involved, the sum of money given to the spy, Hāniʾ's beating and injury at Ibn Ziyād's command, the number of people responding to Muslim's battle cry, the woman giving shelter to Muslim and her son revealing his whereabouts, as well as the final poem quoted, are the same in both accounts.

On the other hand, there are significant differences. Once again, al-Bāqir's text is considerably shorter than Abū Mikhnaf's.[26] As in Section 2, this is because Abū Mikhnaf not only elaborates on the events described, but also includes a couple of episodes that al-Bāqir does not narrate. Thus, Abū Mikhnaf relates how Hāniʾ and Sharīk b. Aʿwar fall ill, and that there is a plot to murder Ibn Ziyād when he pays the sick men visits.[27] Another event found in Abū Mikhnaf's version but not in that of al-Bāqir is Ibn Ziyād's gathering of his loyal supporters in the mosque after Muslim and his men have left the palace.[28]

Again, the divergent wordings and phrasings of the two versions rule out a direct dependence. In this section, literal correspondences are to be found in

[26] Al-Bāqir has about one and a half pages on this section (al-Ṭabarī, *Taʾrīkh*, II, 230–2), compared to the twenty-five pages of Abū Miknaf's version (al-Ṭabarī, *Taʾrīkh*, II, 246–71).

[27] Al-Ṭabarī, *Taʾrīkh*, II, 247–9.

[28] Al-Ṭabarī, *Taʾrīkh*, II, 259–61.

two places only. The first is a short proverb uttered by Ibn Ziyād to the *qāḍī* Shurayḥ when Hāniʾ arrives at the palace. He says, 'His own legs have brought you one who will be destroyed.'[29] The second is a poem quoted at the end of the section, lamenting the deaths of Hāniʾ and Muslim.[30] Abū Mikhnaf cites eight verses, al-Bāqir three.

Ibn ʿAbd al-Raḥmān on Sections 1–3

I will now examine Ibn ʿAbd al-Raḥmān's account of what befalls Hāniʾ and Muslim in Kufa in relation to al-Bāqir's and Abū Mikhnaf's versions, before moving on to the second part of the story. The three sections studied so far are even briefer in the version by Ibn ʿAbd al-Raḥmān than in that of al-Bāqir, and in some respects this account differs significantly from both the others. Thus, Ibn ʿAbd al-Raḥmān mentions nothing about the succession to Muʿāwiya, and the first part of Sections 2 and 3, up to the capture of Hāniʾ, is very short.[31] He does not account for such important events as the change of governor in Kufa. Nor does he mention Muslim's perilous journey to Kufa, during which he nearly dies of thirst, nor that he stays with someone else first before moving on to Hāniʾ on his arrival in Kufa; nor does he mention the spy sent by Ibn Ziyād to infiltrate the Shiʿites. All of these details, as we have seen, are to be found in al-Bāqir's slightly longer account, and of course in even more extended and detailed form in that of Abū Mikhnaf. Still, thus far, the three versions are structurally similar in the sense that the events are related in the same order. It is also interesting to note that, while Ibn ʿAbd al-Raḥmān consequently uses the patronymic Ibn Ziyād when referring to the governor, al-Bāqir refers to him by his given name, ʿUbaydallāh, throughout his entire narrative. The only exception in al-Bāqir's account is the first two times the (future) governor is mentioned, when his full name is given.[32] In Abū Mikhnaf's account,

[29] Al-Ṭabarī, *Taʾrīkh*, II, 229, 251. In Arabic, this proverb contains only three words: *'Atatka bi-ḥāʾinin rijlāhu'*.

[30] Al-Ṭabarī, *Taʾrīkh*, II, 232, 269–70.

[31] It is only about seven lines long in the Leiden edition (al-Ṭabarī, *Taʾrīkh*, II, 284), as compared to just over two pages in al-Bāqir's version (al-Ṭabarī, *Taʾrīkh*, II, 228–30), not counting the *isnāds*. Nor have I counted the two lines, which are added to Ibn ʿAbd al-Raḥmān's account from a report of al-Ḥusayn b. Naṣr, containing a sharp exchange of words between Hāniʾ and Ibn Yazīd. These lines are not found in al-Balādhurī's version (*Ansāb*, Vol. III, 422).

[32] Al-Ṭabarī, *Taʾrīkh*, II, 228.

the full name of the governor, his patronymic and his first name are used interchangeably.

In Section 3, however, the sequence of events in Ibn ʿAbd al-Raḥmān's version differs in important respects from the sequence in the other two.[33] Like al-Bāqir and Abū Mikhnaf, Ibn ʿAbd al-Raḥmān tells us that Muslim's followers are already beginning to desert him as they make their way to the governor's palace; but in contrast to the other two versions, in Ibn ʿAbd al-Raḥmān's account the remaining core of Muslim's people – about fifty men – enter the mosque when they reach the centre,[34] as does Ibn Ziyād (and, presumably, his companions). Some of the governor's people attack Muslim and his followers: they wound Muslim severely, but he manages to get away and reaches a house of the tribe of Kinda, where a woman kindles a fire for him. Later, he is captured at that house as he washes the blood from himself; no fight is mentioned at this stage. What is significant here, then, is that Muslim encounters the governor's men, and that the fight at which he is wounded is located at a different time and place than in al-Bāqir's and Abū Mikhnaf's versions. This, in fact, seems to be in line with a report from the traditionist ʿĪsā b. Yazīd al-Kinānī (d. c. 134/750),[35] and the account of Ibn Saʿd.[36] Thus, it appears that two versions of what happened during the insurrection led by Muslim were in circulation: one – transmitted by Ibn ʿAbd al-Raḥmān, ʿĪsā b. Yazīd and Ibn Saʿd – in which the battle between Muslim and Ibn Ziyād's men takes place in the main mosque, before Muslim's solitary wanderings along the lanes of Kufa, and the other – related by al-Bāqir and Abū Mikhnaf – in which the fight occurs later, at the house of the widow who takes him in.

Section 4. Al-Ḥusayn's Journey to Iraq, his Interception and Negotiations with ʿUmar

Returning now to al-Bāqir and Abū Mikhnaf, we notice that, with one notable exception, al-Ḥusayn's journey from Mecca to Iraq and the immediate prelude

[33] Al-Ṭabarī, *Ta'rīkh*, II, 284–5. This seems to be in line with a report from Hārūn b. Muslim (al-Ṭabarī, *Ta'rīkh*, II, 272) or more probably ʿUmar b. Shabba (see al-Ṭabarī, *History*, vol. XIX, 65, n. 224).

[34] Al-Balādhurī does not mention the mosque (*Ansāb*, vol. III, 422–3).

[35] Al-Ṭabarī, *Ta'rīkh*, II, 272. According to al-Dhahabī (*Mīzān*, vol. V, 395), ʿĪsā b. Yazīd died before Mālik b. Anas (d. 179/796). See also Ladewig Petersen, *ʿAlī and Muʿāwiya*, 28.

[36] Ibn Saʿd, *Ṭabaqāt*, vol. VI, 433.

to the battle at Karbala follow the same basic pattern. The exception is their accounts of the meeting between al-Ḥusayn and al-Ḥurr b. Yazīd al-Yarbūʿī, and of the role of al-Ḥurr in the Karbala tragedy. We will return to this below. The basic narrative of this section goes as follows:

1. Al-Ḥusayn sets out from Mecca.
2. He meets people who warn him against going to Kufa.
3. The brothers of Muslim b. ʿAqīl refuse to give up quietly, as they want vengeance for their brother,[37] and al-Ḥusayn moves on.
4. The vanguard of Ibn Ziyād's troops confront al-Ḥusayn and his followers, who turn aside to a location where they have their back to the reeds so that they can be attacked from one direction only. Al-Ḥusayn has his tents set up.
5. ʿUmar b. Saʿd, previously appointed governor of Rayy by Ibn Ziyād, is now commanded to lead the army against al-Ḥusayn. ʿUmar at first hesitates and then, the following day, accepts.
6. When ʿUmar arrives at the place where al-Ḥusayn has encamped, the latter asks for permission to return to Mecca, to go to Yazīd and pledge his loyalty directly to him, or to go into exile at one of the frontier posts. ʿUmar accepts, but Ibn Ziyād refuses and demands that al-Ḥusayn submit to him personally. Al-Ḥusayn refuses that option.

Despite the similarities, the differences here between the two versions are more substantial than in previous sections. First, while in the previous sections Abū Mikhnaf's version was longer than that of al-Bāqir, the difference in length between the two versions is much more pronounced here.[38] As before, Abū Mikhnaf has elaborated on the events described by both authors, and he furthermore includes a number of events not found in al-Bāqir's version. Among these are Qays b. Mushir's mission to Kufa and his killing there,[39] the long

[37] While in Abū Mikhnaf's version it is explicitly stated that al-Ḥusayn and his company have been informed about Muslim's death (al-Ṭabarī, *Taʾrīkh*, II, 292), in al-Bāqir's version this is only implied (al-Ṭabarī, *Taʾrīkh*, II, 281).

[38] More than fifty pages in Abū Mikhnaf's version (al-Ṭabarī, *Taʾrīkh*, II, 272–81, 288–309, 311–35), compared to about one page by al-Bāqir (al-Ṭabarī, *Taʾrīkh*, II, 281–2).

[39] Al-Ṭabarī, *Taʾrīkh*, II, 288–9.

episode in which al-Ḥurr intercepts al-Ḥusayn at Dhū Ḥusum and al-Ḥusayn gives several speeches,[40] and various preparations and negotiations before the battle.[41]

As mentioned above, one of the main divergences between the two versions is in their descriptions of the meeting between al-Ḥusayn and al-Ḥurr and the role and function of the latter in the story. According to al-Bāqir, al-Ḥusayn met al-Ḥurr, and him alone, outside Qādisiyya on his way to Kufa. Al-Ḥurr warned al-Ḥusayn against going to Kufa, but the latter decided to continue.[42] This is all we hear of al-Ḥurr in al-Bāqir's version – just a couple of lines. Abū Mikhnaf, on the other hand, has al-Ḥurr play a much more significant role.[43] There, we read nothing of the meeting at Qādisiyya. Instead, al-Ḥurr is depicted as commander of the Kufan vanguard that intercepts al-Ḥusayn and his followers. Abū Mikhnaf reports that al-Ḥurr was clearly uneasy about his task of arresting the grandson of the Prophet, and that he tried to get al-Ḥusayn to surrender peacefully and come with him to Kufa. Later, when the battle is about to begin, he deserts the Kufan army and joins with al-Ḥusayn. To Abū Mikhnaf, then, al-Ḥurr is one of the main protagonists of the Karbala story. Another difference between the two versions, although a much smaller detail, is that al-Bāqir mentions the number of al-Ḥusayn's followers: 45 horsemen and 100 foot soldiers.[44]

Section 5. The Battle and the Killing of al-Ḥusayn

The description of the battle itself is the part of the story where al-Bāqir's and Abū Mikhnaf's versions differ the most. The basic structure is similar in both accounts:

1. The fighting takes place.
2. Al-Ḥusayn's baby boy is killed in his lap.
3. Al-Ḥusayn is killed and his head is cut off.

[40] Al-Ṭabarī, *Ta'rīkh*, II, 295–302. These speeches are analysed in Chapter 4.
[41] Al-Ṭabarī, *Ta'rīkh*, II, 316–35.
[42] Al-Ṭabarī, *Ta'rīkh*, II, 281.
[43] Al-Ṭabarī, *Ta'rīkh*, II, 295–303, 332–5.
[44] Al-Ṭabarī, *Ta'rīkh*, II, 281.

Although the order of events is similar in both versions, al-Bāqir dedicates no more than five lines to this entire section,[45] whereas Abū Mikhnaf spends almost thirty pages elaborating on the details of the battle up to the death of al-Ḥusayn.[46] For example, in relating the actual killing of al-Ḥusayn, Abū Mikhnaf describes the fighting, the various blows and stabs he receives, the names of the people involved in killing him, how he is put to death, an abortive attempt to cut off his head before it is actually severed, and so forth.[47] Al-Bāqir's account of the same episode is extremely laconic: 'He fought until he was killed. A man of the tribe of Madhḥij killed him and cut off his head.'[48]

Both versions give an account of the killing of al-Ḥusayn's baby boy.[49] According to the *isnād*s this is, in fact, the only report in Abū Mikhnaf's entire account that he derives from al-Bāqir. Again, Abū Mikhnaf's version is slightly more elaborated, and the prayer that al-Ḥusayn utters when his son is killed is somewhat different. I will return to this incident below.

Section 6. The Aftermath of the Battle

Both versions narrate the events after the battle in more or less the same order:

1. Al-Ḥusayn's head is brought to Ibn Ziyād, who forwards it to Yazīd. According to al-Bāqir, Yazīd pokes his cane into the mouth of the severed head of al-Ḥusayn; according to Abū Mikhnaf, both Ibn Ziyād and Yazīd do so.
2. The survivors from al-Ḥusayn's family are brought before Ibn Ziyād.
3. A boy or young man[50] from among them, who was ill during the battle, is the only male survivor from al-Ḥusayn's family. Ibn Ziyād threatens to kill him, but al-Ḥusayn's sister Zaynab pleads for him, and the governor relents.

[45] Al-Ṭabarī, *Ta'rīkh*, II, 282.
[46] Al-Ṭabarī, *Ta'rīkh*, II, 335–60, 362–6.
[47] Al-Ṭabarī, *Ta'rīkh*, II, 365–6.
[48] Al-Ṭabarī, *Ta'rīkh*, II, 282.
[49] Al-Bāqir's version is found in al-Ṭabarī, *Ta'rīkh*, II, 282, and that of Abū Mikhnaf in al-Ṭabarī, *Ta'rīkh*, II, 360.
[50] On this, see the discussion below.

4. The family is taken to Yazīd in Damascus. There, a man from Syria asks the caliph to give him one of the women, but Yazīd turns down the request.
5. Yazīd takes them into his own family and equips them for the journey to Medina.
6. When the family arrives in Medina, a woman recites a poem of lamentation (slightly shorter in Abū Mikhnaf's version).

Again, the two accounts differ greatly in length.[51] Most of the differences are due to Abū Mikhnaf's more detailed rendering. Both versions, however, relate the incident of the young boy who had been too ill to fight during the battle and had thus survived. Ibn Ziyād wants to kill him, but when Zaynab pleads for his life, the governor relents and allows him to live. According to Abū Mikhnaf and all later tradition, this lad was ʿAlī b. al-Ḥusayn (the fourth Shiʿite imam, Zayn al-ʿĀbidīn).[52] In the account given by al-Bāqir, however, his name is not mentioned: it is merely stated that 'the only male member of the family of al-Ḥusayn b. ʿAlī who had survived was a young lad who had been sick and had rested with the women'.[53] It is curious that al-Bāqir (if the text originates from him or his milieu) does not mention the name of the person who is to become next imam, al-Bāqir's own father. I will discuss the possible implications of this omission below. Ibn ʿAbd al-Raḥmān does not mention this incident at all.

Ibn ʿAbd al-Raḥmān on Sections 4–6

Sections 4–6 in the version by Ibn ʿAbd al-Raḥmān are slightly shorter than in that of al-Bāqir. The account of the battle itself is as terse as in that of al-Bāqir, and in fact, Ibn ʿAbd al-Raḥmān only implies the killing of al-Ḥusayn: 'On his horse, [ʿUmar b. Saʿd] ordered the people to attack them, and they fought them. The head of al-Ḥusayn was taken to Ibn Ziyād.'[54] In other words, although they phrase their reports of the battle and the killing of al-Ḥusayn differently,

[51] In al-Bāqir's version, this section fills a little more than one page (al-Ṭabarī, *Taʾrīkh*, II, 282–3), and Abū Mikhnaf uses almost fifteen pages (al-Ṭabarī, *Taʾrīkh*, II, 366–9, 370–4, 376–9, 382–3, 384–5, 385).
[52] Al-Ṭabarī, *Taʾrīkh*, II, 372–3.
[53] Al-Ṭabarī, *Taʾrīkh*, II, 283. I discuss alternatives to Howard's translation below.
[54] Al-Ṭabarī, *Taʾrīkh*, II, 286.

al-Bāqir and Ibn ʿAbd al-Raḥmān have in common that their descriptions are as brief as can be, in stark contrast to the elaborated account of Abū Mikhnaf. A further shared characteristic is that they mention Karbala as the name of the site of the battle.[55] Abū Mikhnaf, by contrast, mentions this toponym only once in a scene at the very end of the story, when a certain ʿUbaydallāh b. al-Ḥurr visits the grave regretting that he did not join al-Ḥusayn.[56]

Although the general sequence of the elements in the story is the same, Ibn ʿAbd al-Raḥmān's version has some details exclusively in common with Abū Mikhnaf. As mentioned above, al-Ḥurr is given very different roles in al-Bāqir's and Abū Mikhnaf's accounts. Though Ibn ʿAbd al-Raḥmān's account is much briefer that that of Abū Mikhnaf, it relates that al-Ḥurr is commander of some cavalry and recounts how he deserts the Kufan army and joins al-Ḥusayn, fights for him, and kills two of the governor's followers.[57] Ibn ʿAbd al-Raḥmān does not mention that al-Ḥurr was the commander of the vanguard and intercepted al-Ḥusayn before the main army arrived, nor does he say anything either about al-Ḥusayn's speeches or al-Ḥurr's attempts to persuade him to surrender without a fight and follow him to Kufa. Still, Ibn ʿAbd al-Raḥmān and Abū Mikhnaf have much more in common regarding al-Ḥurr than either of these two has with al-Bāqir on this matter.

There are also other details preceding the battle that are shared in the accounts of Ibn ʿAbd al-Raḥmān and Abū Mikhnaf. Both, for instance, mention Zuhayr b. al-Qayn, one of al-Ḥusayn's most ardent followers. Both also mention a speech delivered by al-Ḥusayn (although Ibn ʿAbd al-Raḥmān says nothing about its content), and both also mention that the governor has to explicitly command ʿUmar b. Saʿd to attack al-Ḥusayn before he does so.[58] Al-Bāqir, by contrast, mentions none of these details. Furthermore, the authors' different appellations of the governor mentioned above continue throughout these sections.

[55] Al-Ṭabarī, *Ta'rīkh*, II, 281 and 285 respectively.

[56] Al-Ṭabarī, *Ta'rīkh*, II, 388–9. I will come back to Ibn al-Ḥurr's visit at Karbala in Chapter 11.

[57] Al-Ṭabarī, *Ta'rīkh*, II, 285–6.

[58] For all these details in Ibn ʿAbd al-Raḥmān's account, see al-Ṭabarī, *Ta'rīkh*, II, 286; in Abū Mikhnaf's account, Zuhayr b. al-Qayn is mentioned in several places, such as al-Ṭabarī, *Ta'rīkh*, II, 290–1, 301, 323, 331–2; al-Ḥusayn's speech al-Ṭabarī, *Ta'rīkh*, II, 328–30; and Ibn Ziyād's command to ʿUmar to attack, in al-Ṭabarī, *Ta'rīkh*, II, 315–17.

An element of the story which Ibn ʿAbd al-Raḥmān alone relates is a scene of a group of old men from Kufa standing on a hill (presumably overlooking the battlefield[59]), weeping and asking God to send His help. The narrator Saʿd b. ʿUbayda tells them to go down and help 'him' (the pronoun apparently refers to al-Ḥusayn, although this is not made explicit).[60]

The incident of the ruler poking his cane into the mouth of the severed head of al-Ḥusayn is related in all three versions, but the perpetrator is variously given as the caliph Yazīd and/or his governor in Kufa, Ibn Ziyād.[61] A comparison between the versions may reveal who it is that the author of each account ultimately blames for the atrocities committed against the grandson of the Prophet. In al-Bāqir's account, it is the caliph who pokes inside the mouth of the severed head; according to Ibn ʿAbd al-Raḥmān, it is Ibn Ziyād. Abū Mikhnaf gives two versions, one with each of the two desecrating the head.

In my view the four versions clearly stem from a single tradition which has been adapted to suit the needs of the originators of the three accounts. Although there are certainly differences between the four versions, the structural similarities are too numerous to allow for two similar incidents, one at Ibn Ziyād's palace in Kufa and another with Yazīd in Damascus (see Table 3.1).

The Interrelationship of the Three Versions

To summarise the analysis so far, I conclude that none of the three versions of the Karbala story is dependent on any of the others. While the narrative structure is similar (although not identical), the differences between them, as regards both phrasing and content, show clear signs of independent development. The wording of each of the three narratives diverges too far from the other two to allow hypothesising a common original text. A similar conclusion follows from the variations in content: each of the three versions lacks certain elements of the narrative found in the other two, while all three relate details unique only to them. Thus, although we have three versions of a story that

[59] So it is interpreted by Howard (al-Ṭabarī, *History*, vol. XIX, 80), and I see no reason to think otherwise.

[60] Al-Ṭabarī, *Ta'rīkh*, II, 286.

[61] The four versions of the incident are found in al-Ṭabarī, *Ta'rīkh*, II, 282–3, 286, 370–1, 382–3.

Table 3.1 The head of al-Ḥusayn before the ruler

	Al-Bāqir	**Ibn ʿAbd al-Raḥmān**	**Abū Mikhnaf I**	**Abū Mikhnaf II**
Ruler	Yazīd	Ibn Ziyād	Ibn Ziyād	Yazīd
Al-Ḥusayn's head is placed in front of the ruler, who pokes the head with his cane.	X	X	X	X
The ruler insults al-Ḥusayn verbally.	Poem: '[Swords] split the skulls …'	'Abū ʿAbdallāh's hair has grown grey'		Poem: '[Swords] split the skulls …'
A companion of the Prophet rebukes the ruler, saying that the Prophet kissed those lips.	Abū Barza		Zayd b. Arqam	Abū Barza

closely resemble one another, none of the versions appears to have functioned as a source or model for the others.

Nevertheless, we may be able to draw tentative conclusions about the origins of the accounts. An overarching structural feature is discernible in the analysis above regarding each of the two main parts of the story: from the succession to Muʿāwiya to the killing of Muslim b ʿAqīl (Sections 1–3), and from al-Ḥusayn's journey from Mecca to the return of the survivors of the family to Medina (Sections 4–6). Al-Bāqir and Abū Mikhnaf narrate the elements of the first part in the same order, and both cover many of the same elements; in Ibn ʿAbd al-Raḥmān's account, on the other hand, many elements are absent or related in a different order. Thus, there is no mention here of Muʿāwiya's death or of al-Ḥusayn's refusal to give his *bayʿa* to Yazīd, nor of Muslim's journey to Kufa, the change of governor in the town, nor is Ibn Ziyād's infiltration of the Shiʿites recounted. Furthermore, the uprising of Muslim and the Shīʿites against Ibn Ziyād is related in a very different way. A similar pattern of structural variation is found in the second part of the Karbala story, but here it is the versions of Ibn ʿAbd al-Raḥmān and Abū Mikhnaf that share a number of elements which are absent from or retold in a different way by al-Bāqir. Most obvious is the minor role given to al-Ḥurr in al-Bāqir's account, but there are also the details of the prelude to the battle mentioned above.

Although many of the omissions just described can be explained by the brevity of the shorter versions, the more salient variations – such as Muslim's insurrection in Kufa and al-Ḥurr's differing positions with regard to al-Ḥusayn – indicate that the two parts of the story might originally have been transmitted separately and related in different ways. Thus, it is not impossible that the story of Muslim b. ʿAqīl and that of the battle at Karbala were initially two separate traditions. In fact, as Ursula Sezgin has shown, an indication in al-Ṭabarī may suggest this.[62] After relating al-Bāqir's account of Muslim in Kufa, al-Ṭabarī writes:

> As for Abū Mikhnaf, he gives a fuller and more complete account of the story of Muslim b. ʿAqīl's visit to al-Kūfah and his death [*qiṣṣat Muslim*

[62] Sezgin, *Abū Miḫnaf*, 83–4.

> *b. ʿAqīl wa-shukhūṣihi ilā al-Kūfa wa-maqtalihi*] than the report of ʿAmmār al-Duhnī from al-Bāqir, which we have just mentioned.[63]

Sezgin says that we cannot be sure what the word *qiṣṣa* means in this context: is it just the coherent account concerning Muslim included in Abū Mikhnaf's 'book' *Maqtal al-Ḥusayn*, or is it a separate story that was later inserted into the appropriate point in the timeline in the story of the killing of al-Ḥusayn?[64] In my opinion, the latter is the more compelling alternative.

The Relative Dates of the Three Versions

The discussion that follows of the origins and dates of the three versions takes al-Bāqir's account as the point of departure, because the purported origin of this version is the only one that has been challenged in a published study. Howard rejects authorship by the fifth imam of the account ascribed to him by arguing that the account contradicts basic Shiʿite tenets about al-Ḥusayn. To support this hypothesis, Howard compares al-Bāqir's and Abū Mikhnaf's accounts of two events in the story. The first is when al-Ḥusayn, on his way to Kufa, is told of the death of Muslim b. ʿAqīl. According to al-Bāqir, when al-Ḥusayn hears of this, he is prepared to return to Mecca, but decides against it at the urging of Muslim's brothers.[65] In Abū Mikhnaf's version, however, nothing is said about al-Ḥusayn's wish to return.[66] The second event Howard discusses is al-Ḥusayn's negotiations with ʿUmar b. Saʿd just before the battle. Both al-Bāqir and Abū Mikhnaf relate that al-Ḥusayn asks ʿUmar to allow him to return to Mecca, or to hand himself over directly to the caliph Yazīd, or to go to one of the frontier posts (in other words, to go into exile on the periphery of the empire).[67] In Abū Mikhnaf's account, this report is countered by another, according to which a certain ʿUqba b. Simʿān says that he followed al-Ḥusayn everywhere and heard every word he spoke from Medina to his death in Iraq. ʿUqba furthermore states that he never heard al-Ḥusayn either surrender to Yazīd or promise to go to the frontier.[68] In al-Bāqir's version,

[63] Al-Ṭabarī, *Taʾrīkh*, II, 232.
[64] Sezgin, *Abū Miḫnaf*, 84.
[65] Al-Ṭabarī, *Taʾrīkh*, II, 281.
[66] Al-Ṭabarī, *Taʾrīkh*, II, 292–3.
[67] Al-Ṭabarī, *Taʾrīkh*, II, 282, 314.
[68] Al-Ṭabarī, *Taʾrīkh*, II, 314.

there is no such counter-tradition. Thus, according to al-Bāqir, al-Ḥusayn is prepared to compromise in both these situations. He is prepared to go back to Mecca, to go into exile, or even to hand himself over to the caliph (though not to Ibn Ziyād, the governor of Kufa).

Howard's main argument is that al-Bāqir's rendering of these two events, while making it clear that the death of al-Ḥusayn was a tragedy, still 'diminishes the stature of the Imam'.[69] Howard does not explicitly say why this is so, but presumably he is implying that the account contradicts the Shiʿite idea that al-Ḥusayn had foreknowledge of the fatal end of the affair and submitted willingly to his divinely ordained destiny. The assumption is that this image of al-Ḥusayn had always been consistent and unchanging among Shiʿites, and that for this reason the version of the story ascribed to al-Bāqir, al-Ḥusayn's grandson and himself the fifth Shiʿite imam, could not have originated with him.

Howard also gives a second argument for his rejection of al-Bāqir as the originator of this version. Thus, he maintains that the account's brevity and its omission of a number of details of the actual battle and the killing of al-Ḥusayn mean that it could not have been the version related by one of his close descendants. Commenting on al-Bāqir's terse description of the battle, he writes:

> This is supposed to be a vivid account of the death of the Imam al-Ḥusayn, as told by the Imam al-Bāqir to a Shīʿī adherent, ʿAmmār. It is clearly unacceptable. He does not know the exact number of the members of the Imam al-Ḥusayn' family who were killed.[70]

The purpose of this fabricated ascription, Howard surmises, is

> to confirm to those who oppose the Imamate the weakness of individual Imams and to do so by putting the interpretation into the mouth of the Imam ... It almost certainly did not come from the Imam al-Bāqir and seems unlikely to be the work of a Shīʿī such as ʿAmmār.[71]

[69] Howard, 'Husayn the Martyr', 129.
[70] Howard, 'Husayn the Martyr', 130.
[71] Howard, 'Husayn the Martyr', 129–31.

Antoine Borrut, unlike Howard, accepts the ascription of this version to al-Bāqir – or rather, perhaps, to the milieu around the Shiʿite imams in Medina.[72] He finds Howard's arguments 'unconvincing' and regards the brevity of the account as support for its early date. In stark contrast to Howard, he writes that 'it is, in fact, quite likely that this was an original "official version" of the episode, a memory of the imams not yet transformed into some kind of epic'.[73]

While I agree with Borrut about the early date of the version ascribed to al-Bāqir's account, it is necessary to distinguish the problem of the date of origin – or, rather, the relative order of origin of the versions – from that of authorship, although the two questions are of course interlaced. Howard does not address the date of al-Bāqir's version *per se*, but just argues that it could not have been authored by the grandson of al-Ḥusayn. His focus is of course quite logical, given his view that the Shiʿite conception of the Karbala event did not develop. Thus, Borrut, who focuses his argument on the early date of the text rather than on the authorship, slightly misses his goal when arguing against Howard; it could of course be that the *isnād* given is false, and that the text is early without originating from al-Bāqir or his environment. In the following, I will try to keep these two questions separate, beginning by concentrating on the question of the order of origin of the three versions.

The main problem with Howard's argument is his basic presupposition that Shiʿism, including the image of al-Ḥusayn, has developed little over time but has always been more or less the same as it is today. An extensive amount of scholarship on early Islam has demonstrated this to be an untenable approach.[74] It is nowadays taken as axiomatic that Shiʿism, like all religious movements, will have developed over time. It is thus necessary to employ methods for analysis of the Karbala story, as well as for analysing other narratives from the history of Islam, which take this fact into consideration. One such method is

[72] Borrut, 'Remembering Karbalā'', 264.

[73] Borrut, 'Remembering Karbalā'', 265.

[74] Although much research has been published in the last few decades, ample evidence for such a process had been brought to light before Howard's article became available in 1986, although scholars' opinions have always varied as to the extent and speed of this development. A few examples of studies published before Howard's article where such a development in Shiism is demonstrated will suffice: Buhl, 'Alidernes stilling'; Hodgson, 'Early Shīʿa'; Watt, 'Shiʿism'.

that developed by Haider, as described above; Borrut's approach, which takes the development of the memory of the event into consideration, is another.

When such a perspective is applied to al-Bāqir's version of the Karbala story, the facts behind Howard's arguments against the alleged authorship can be viewed differently. Thus, the passages about al-Ḥusayn's wish to go back to Mecca and his negotiations with ʿUmar do not argue for the non-Shiʿite origin of the text, as Howard supposed, but for its relatively early date, and consequently the possibility that it originated with al-Bāqir or the milieu in which he was active. In Chapter 2, I discussed the so-called 'criterion of embarrassment' used in historical studies. This criterion, to recapitulate, says that if an incident is likely to have caused embarrassment for the later community, it is unlikely to have been created by later tradition, but is probably very early or even authentic. Applied to both these episodes, the criterion of embarrassment would seem to indicate that al-Bāqir's version emerged before the image of al-Ḥusayn was refined to the point at which he was prescient of his own end, but consciously and bravely advanced into the hands of the enemy. Abū Mikhnaf's version, by contrast, shows clear traces of a development in such a direction. In particular, I am inclined to interpret his version of the negotiations between al-Ḥusayn and ʿUmar b. Saʿd, and the counter-report from ʿUqba b. Simʿān, in this way. In my view, this is an obvious case where the criterion of embarrassment must be applied. The idea that an imam was prepared to capitulate to the Umayyads was unbearable to later Shiʿites. Yet, the story about the negotiations was widespread (it is found in all three versions studied here), so could not be neglected. ʿUqba's tradition is therefore likely to have been created to undermine the credibility of the negotiation report. To put it differently, the report from ʿUqba suggests that the negotiation tradition is very early and was so well-known that it could not simply be ignored, but had to be neutralised by a counter-tradition.

From these arguments we might draw two conclusions at which I have previously hinted. First, the embarrassment associated with the negotiation tradition is an indication of its early date, perhaps even its historical veracity: the talks between al-Ḥusayn and ʿUmar might very well have occurred, and something like the suggestions ascribed to al-Ḥusayn in the tradition may have been discussed. Second, the absence of ʿUqba's counter-tradition in al-Bāqir's version is a clear indication that it was compiled at a point preceding the formation of the idea of al-Ḥusayn as an imam elevated above ordinary humanity. By the time of Abū Mikhnaf, however, this development was already under way.

Howard's second argument, then, is that the version ascribed to al-Bāqir is too brief and too terse to have originated from him. On this point, I agree with Borrut's contention that the brevity of the version ascribed to al-Bāqir indicates, rather, an early date. Generally, longer and more detailed accounts of a historical event tend to be elaborated on the basis of earlier, more concise versions. Of course, the opposite could also be the case: that a shorter version can be a distillation of a longer one, and thus post-date it. But, as my analysis above of the three versions has demonstrated, there are good reasons to think that all three of these versions developed independently of one another. In particular, the laconic account of the battle, with hardly any description of the fighting, no dialogue, and no display of bravery on the part of the heroes so abundant in later versions of the Karbala story (and in much of Islamic historiography at large), points to al-Bāqir's account as not having been abbreviated from a longer version, and thus argues for its early date. The same can, of course, be said of the version of Ibn ʿAbd al-Raḥmān.

Abū Mikhnaf's account, on the other hand, is much more elaborate. This is not to say that every part of it is a later embellishment or rhetorical device. Many reports are of course very old, such as that of al-Ḥusayn's nocturnal negotiation with ʿUmar b. Saʿd. The narrative as a whole, however, must be considered later than those of al-Bāqir and Ibn ʿAbd al-Raḥmān. It shows clear marks of development towards an epic in which bravery and cowardliness, the emotions of despair and triumph and expressions of piety and unbelief figure prominently. Boaz Shoshan has demonstrated that even al-Bāqir's short version does not lack features of *mimesis*,[75] but in comparison with Abū Mikhnaf's account, it is dull and poor in detail, as Howard correctly maintains. What Shoshan and later Haider demonstrate, however, is that such details are often rhetorical devices, elements designed to make the story livelier and more reliable and to convey the perspective of the author/compiler.[76]

[75] Shoshan, *Poetics*, 6–7.

[76] Shoshan, *Poetics*, 1–60, see also his analysis of the Karbala story, 233–52; Haider, *Rebel*, 10–13. In Chapter 4, I will give an example of such a 'rhetorical elaboration' (the expression is Haider's). There, I argue that Abū Mikhnaf's rendering of the Karbala tragedy is meant to show that, when

Table 3.2 The killing of al-Ḥusayn's baby boy according to al-Bāqir and Abū Mikhnaf

Al-Bāqir	**Abū Mikhnaf**
An arrow came and struck his son while he had him on his lap.	Al-Ḥusayn was brought his young child; he was on his lap. Then one of you, Banū Asad, shot an arrow that slaughtered the child.
He began to wipe the blood from him, saying,	Al-Husayn caught the blood. When the palm of his hand was full, he poured the blood onto the ground and said,
'O God! Judge between us and a people who summoned us so that they might help us and then killed us.'	'O Lord, if it be that You have kept the help of heaven from us, then let it be because Your purpose is better than [immediate] help. Take vengeance for us on these oppressors.'

This point is further illustrated when we compare the episode of the killing of al-Ḥusayn's baby boy in the versions of al-Bāqir and Abū Mikhnaf.[77] That this is the only *khabar* in the entire account of Abū Mikhnaf that is transmitted from al-Bāqir adds to its interest and significance. Here, as in many other places, al-Bāqir's version is short and terse, whereas that of Abū Mikhnaf is more elaborate, although the content is basically the same (see Table 3.2). What is so striking is the difference in the content of the supplication al-Ḥusayn offers to God. Whereas in Abū Mikhnaf's account this is similar to many utterances by al-Ḥusayn as given by him, and is in fact what one might expect from a pious Muslim, al-Bāqir's rendering is more focused on the guilt of the Kufans, who at first beg al-Ḥusayn to come, only to betray him as he approaches their town. As we will see in Part II, this notion of guilt parallels that expressed in the story of the Tawwābūn. In the analysis of that story below, I will argue that this is a very early theme which goes back at least to the beginning of the second/eighth century, if not earlier. I am inclined to think that the feelings of guilt for the failure to support al-Ḥusayn

the Kufans broke the truce with al-Ḥusayn, they broke the covenant that God has established with humanity.

[77] For al-Bāqir's version, see al-Ṭabarī, *Ta'rīkh*, II, 282, and for that of Abū Mikhnaf, al-Ṭabarī, *Ta'rīkh*, II, 360.

are indeed the most ancient motif in his developing image.[78] The same idea is also expressed several times in Abū Mikhnaf's version of the Karbala story, though not in connection with the killing of al-Ḥusayn's baby son. While it is not made explicit in the particular passage discussed here, al-Ḥusayn's prayer as related by al-Bāqir is uttered against that backdrop. As mentioned in the chapters about the Tawwābūn below, the motif of guilt is quite unusual in other strands of Islam, and less common in later Shiʿism than in the earliest decades. Although feelings of guilt are certainly to be found in later Shiʿism, the idea of trust in God's higher purposes fits much better with the general image of God in the later development. It is thus more likely, in my opinion, that the idea of the betrayal of al-Ḥusayn is the earlier motif (as expressed in the version of al-Bāqir), and the idea of God's omniscience and best purposes (as found in Abū Mikhnaf's version) is later.

A further argument in favour of an early date for the two shorter versions of the story is a detail previously touched on above in the analysis of al-Bāqir's text, to which I now return. It will be recalled that after the battle, when the surviving relatives of al-Ḥusayn are brought before the governor Ibn Ziyād, the name of the only surviving male descendant is not mentioned;[79] yet, according to all later tradition, this is al-Ḥusayn's son ʿAlī, the fourth imam, Zayn al-ʿĀbidīn. But this is not the only relative of al-Ḥusayn's who goes unnamed. In fact, both al-Bāqir's and Ibn ʿAbd al-Raḥmān's accounts mention very few of al-Ḥusayn's family members by name. Both, of course, use the name of the main protagonists, al-Ḥusayn and Muslim b. ʿAqīl, but the only other relative of al-Ḥusayn's whose name al-Bāqir reveals is Zaynab, his sister, who is active in protecting her family at the court of Ibn Ziyād and Yazīd after the battle. Ibn ʿAbd al-Raḥmān mentions only al-Ḥusayn and Muslim by name (though he writes that 'five sons of ʿAlī b. Abī Ṭālib' were among al-Ḥusayn's men[80]). As has often been pointed out, there is a general tendency for later tradition to provide unnamed personalities with names in order to personalise them and make the accounts livelier.[81] This feature is very clear in the Karbala story. Thus, in contrast to the versions of al-Bāqir

[78] See also Halm, *Shīʿa Islam*, 16–20.
[79] Al-Ṭabarī, *Taʾrīkh*, II, 283.
[80] Al-Ṭabarī, *Taʾrīkh*, II, 286.
[81] For examples from the Christian tradition, see e.g. Metzger, 'Names'.

and Ibn ʿAbd al-Raḥmān, Abū Mikhnaf's account is replete with names of family members of al-Ḥusayn. The only close relative of his whose name is not given is his baby boy, who was killed. Later tradition names the baby ʿAbdallāh b. al-Ḥusayn,[82] however, and in the much later version by al-Mufīd (d. 413/1022) – a verbatim rendering of the report in Abū Mikhnaf – the baby's name is added.[83]

A final argument in favour of an early date for the two short versions is the scarcity of quotations from the Qur'an, whereas in Abū Mikhnaf's text passages from or allusions to the Qur'an are found on almost every page. A development towards a more general use of the sacred text in the second/eighth century is in line with what many other studies have argued, that the Qur'an as we know it was increasingly referred to and used from the beginning of that century.[84]

To conclude the discussion so far about the relative order of origin of the three versions of the Karbala story: without taking into regard the attributions in the *isnād*s, I am convinced that the accounts of al-Bāqir and Ibn ʿAbd al-Raḥmān are earlier than that of Abū Mikhnaf. I do not, though, think it is possible to determine the order of origin of the two short versions. As I will argue below, they probably emerged at the turn of the second/first quarter of the eighth century, one in Medina and the other in Kufa. This may seem rather a meagre finding for an extended discussion, as some scholars might regard it as quite evident, but to my knowledge this view has never been supported by argument. At this stage in the analysis, it is, however, possible to say something about the proposed origins of the three accounts. This will also help us towards placing their approximate time of origin in absolute, rather than merely relative, terms.

The Question of Origins

I argued above that the two short versions ascribed to al-Bāqir and Ibn ʿAbd al-Raḥmān are older than Abū Mikhnaf's long account. It is much more

82 Al-Iṣfahānī, *Maqātil*, 94–5.

83 Al-Mufīd, *Book of Guidance*, 359. According to Howard, al-Mufīd has most probably used al-Ṭabarī's account (*Book of Guidance*, 558, n. 12).

84 See e.g. Halevi, *Muhammad's Grave*, 21–30; Lindstedt, 'Who is In?'. Cf. also Görke and Schoeler, *Die ältesten Berichte*, 264.

difficult to reach a conclusion about their dates in absolute terms, and any such attempt depends on the scholar's evaluation of the alleged originators given in the *isnāds*. None of the three texts exhibits characteristics that might reveal the identity of the originator. However, in my opinion there is hardly any reason to doubt the origins assumed in the chains of authority. If my arguments against Howard's doubts are valid, there is little that seems to contradict the information given in the *isnāds*, and moreover, there is external evidence that supports it.

The Account Ascribed to al-Bāqir

Abū Jaʿfar Muḥammad b. ʿAlī b. al-Ḥusayn, the fifth imam according to the Twelver Shiʿite tradition, is held by both Shiʿite and Sunni traditions to have been one of the most prominent scholars of his time both in hadith and in Islamic law; his erudition caused him to be called *Bāqir al-ʿilm* ('the one who splits knowledge open'), or just *al-Bāqir*. He and his son Jaʿfar al-Ṣādiq laid the foundation for what developed into Shiʿī law and doctrine, and modern scholars therefore regard him as one of the persons who was greatly instrumental in the forming of an early Shiʿite identity.[85]

Al-Ṭabarī is not the only historian who relates the version ascribed to al-Bāqir. It was also used by al-Masʿūdī (d. 345/956) in his *Murūj al-dhahab*.[86] I agree with Howard's unsubstantiated statement that al-Masʿūdī took his version from al-Ṭabarī.[87] Though al-Masʿūdī does not reveal his source, his use of al-Ṭabarī is clear from the fact that he not only follows al-Bāqir's text as given by al-Ṭabarī in certain passages, but also reproduces various other traditions about the Karbala event that are also related by al-Ṭabarī. Since this is the only known source outside of al-Ṭabarī's *Taʾrīkh* that relates parts of al-Bāqir's account, we have no independently transmitted version of his text with which to compare that given by al-Ṭabarī. On the other hand, Abū al-Faraj al-Iṣfahānī (d. after 360/971)[88] seems to be aware of al-Bāqir's version independently of al-Ṭabarī. In his *Maqātil al-Ṭālibiyyīn*, Abū al-Faraj introduces the Karbala

85 On him, see e.g. Amir-Moezzi and Jambet, *Le shīʿisme*, 61–3; Buckley, 'Muḥammad al-Bāqir'; Lalani, *Early Shīʿī Thought*.

86 Al-Masʿūdī, *Murūj*, vol. V, 127–47.

87 Howard, 'Husayn the Martyr', 128.

88 Günther, 'Abū l-Faraj'.

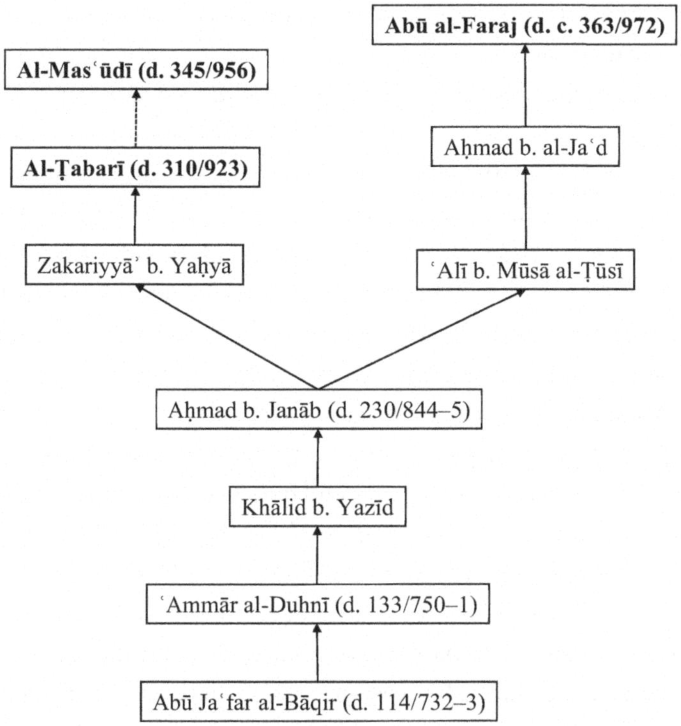

Figure 3.1 Tradition history of al-Bāqir's account. Names in bold indicate extant texts. Years of death are given whenever known. Dotted arrow signifies inferred transmission.

story with a collective *isnād* to sources for his account, saying that all these people relate more or less the same story about the killing of al-Ḥusayn.[89] One of these sources is al-Bāqir, by way of ʿAmmār al-Duhnī and two more intermediaries also found in al-Ṭabarī's rendering. Instead of the fifth and most recent transmitter in al-Ṭabarī's *isnād*, however, Abū al-Faraj gives two different authorities (see Figure 3.1).[90] It is thus probable that he received this account independently of al-Ṭabarī, though he does not reproduce it. This indicates that the purported origin of al-Bāqir's version was accepted as such

89 On al-Bāqir's use of collective *isnād*s, see Günther, '"... *nor have I learned it* ..."', 142–5.
90 Al-Iṣfahānī, *Maqātil*, 99; cf. al-Ṭabarī, *Taʾrīkh*, II, 227. Howard has also noted this ('Husayn the Martyr', 128).

among Shiʿites as late as Abū al-Faraj, two and a half centuries after the death of the fifth imam.[91]

According to the *isnād*, it was the Kufan traditionist ʿAmmār b. Muʿāwiya al-Duhnī (d. 133/750–1) who transmitted the story from al-Bāqir, who resided in Medina.[92] Of course, there is no way to check whether ʿAmmār actually heard al-Bāqir relate the story to him, but, as Borrut maintains, it is by no means impossible to imagine that ʿAmmār received the story from the Shiʿite milieu in Medina, whether directly from al-Bāqir or not.[93] Furthermore, the minuscule role played here by al-Ḥurr in comparison to the versions of Ibn ʿAbd al-Raḥmān and Abū Mikhnaf (see the analysis of Section 4 above) might indicate a Medinan rather than a Kufan provenance. If it is true that al-Ḥurr commanded a substantial part of the army, he must have belonged to the Kufan nobility.[94] As a nobleman, he would have been well known and remembered, and his character elaborated on in Kufa, especially if he had acted in a way that cost his own life in favour of al-Ḥusayn. In Medina, by contrast, he might have been less well-known, and his function in the Karbala drama not remembered correctly. Alternatively, of course, the account told by al-Bāqir could be correct, and the Kufan version entirely fictional. I consider this less likely, given that we have two mutually independent versions relating al-Ḥurr's active role in the battle. Furthermore, as we will see below, the Kufan Ibn ʿAbd al-Raḥmān seems to have been an adolescent at the time of the Karbala event and thus would have been quite well-informed about the nobility of the town. Finally, I am not convinced by Howard's attempt to harmonise the two versions, whereby he claims that al-Ḥurr first met al-Ḥusayn and then led the army out against al-Ḥusayn.[95]

There is one detail, however, that may speak against a Shiʿite origin of the version ascribed to al-Bāqir, an argument that Howard does not adduce even

[91] Abū al-Faraj, however, was a Zaydi, or at least a non-Imami Shiʿite (see Günther, 'Abū l-Faraj'; but cf. Su, *The Shiʿi Past*, 60–93), and thus probably did not regard the imams (al-Ḥusayn included) as infallible. For that reason, he might have been more prone to accept a description of al-Ḥusayn that was slightly less hagiographical than if he had belonged to the Twelver branch.

[92] On ʿAmmār al-Duhnī, see al-Mizzī, *Tahdhīb*, vol. XXI, 208–10.

[93] Borrut, 'Remembering Karbalā'', 265.

[94] This is how Howard describes him, though without adducing any sources or other arguments (al-Ṭabarī, *History*, vol. XIX, 74, n. 252).

[95] Al-Ṭabarī, *History*, vol. XIX, 74, n. 252.

though it supports his hypothesis. This is the omission of the name of the male relative of al-Ḥusayn who had been ill and had thus survived the battle (see the analysis of Section 6 above). According to other information, from Abū Mikhnaf and onwards, this was al-Ḥusayn's son ʿAlī, who, according to the Twelver tradition, later became the fourth imam, Zayn al-ʿĀbidīn, and who was the father of al-Bāqir. Why, then, is his name not mentioned in the version ascribed to the son of the fourth imam – or at least derived from the Shiʿite milieu of Medina of his time? As we have seen, the text does not even state that this person was the son of al-Ḥusayn, just that he was the only male survivor of the family.[96]

According to Abū Mikhnaf, who identifies him as ʿAlī b. al-Ḥusayn, the boy had just reached puberty; in fact, he was so young that Ibn Ziyād had his men uncover the boy's private parts, presumably to see whether his pubic hair had grown. The attendants confirmed that he had reached manhood, and Ibn Ziyād ordered him killed. At this threat, ʿAlī's aunt Zaynab intervened and pleaded for his life, and the governor let him live.[97] However, the age of ʿAlī b. al-Ḥusayn given by Abū Mikhnaf is not consistent with that given in other sources. According to most sources for his life, ʿAlī b. al-Ḥusayn was in his early twenties when his father was killed.[98] According to Ibn Saʿd, for example, ʿAlī was 23 at the time of the Karbala tragedy, and in his rendering of the confrontation with Ibn Ziyyād, nothing is mentioned about ʿAlī having just reached puberty.[99] This is supported by a tradition related by the Shiʿite historian al-Yaʿqūbī, where ʿAlī's son al-Bāqir says that he was four years old when al-Ḥusayn was killed, and that he remembered the occasion.[100] If this is correct, ʿAli b. al-Ḥusayn could hardly have just attained puberty at this time.

Al-Bāqir not only omits the boy's name but is also vague about his age. He uses the word *ghulām*, which often means 'a young boy' but can also

[96] Al-Ṭabarī, *Taʾrīkh*, II, 283.

[97] Al-Ṭabarī, *Taʾrīkh*, II, 372–3.

[98] See e.g. Kohlberg, 'Zayn al-ʿĀbidīn'; Madelung, "Alī b. Ḥosayn b. ʿAlī b. Abī Ṭaleb' and the references in these studies.

[99] Ibn Saʿd, *Ṭabaqāt*, vol. VII, 210.

[100] Al-Yaʿqūbī, *Tārīkh*, vol. II, 384. Contrary to what Lalani states, however (*Early Shīʿī Thought*, 196 n. 4), al-Bāqir does not say that he was present at the Karbala tragedy, only that he remembers it. There is a slight problem with al-Yaʿqūbī's chronology (*Works*, vol. III, 1,038 and n. 2,452), but it is hardly serious enough to challenge the information about al-Bāqir's age.

signify a young or even a middle-aged man.[101] Howard has translated this word as 'a young lad',[102] a translation which is perfectly all right in itself but does not convey the vagueness of the Arabic word. Here it seems that Howard was influenced by Abū Mikhnaf's rendering, and did not consider sources according to which 'Alī was older at the time.

Thus, there are several problems with this tradition. In the version ascribed to al-Bāqir, it is the omission of the name of the person who, according to all later tradition, is his own father, as well as the (possibly intentional) vagueness about this person's age; in Abū Mikhnaf's version, it is 'Alī b. al-Ḥusayn's young age, an age which contradicts other sources about him. The only explanation I can think of for these omissions, ambiguities and contradictions is that later Shiʿites were uneasy about the fact that the son of al-Ḥusayn, the fourth imam, now grown to adulthood, had survived without showing any resistance to the governor. Being imprecise about his identity and age – or alternatively, being clear about his identity but reducing his age by ten years or so – might represent attempts to evade this embarrassment.

To conclude. If its purported origin is accepted, al-Bāqir's version might well be what Sebastian Günther describes as one of the very early collections of reports on the death of al-Ḥusayn, collections that 'contributed to a considerable degree, to the development of a Shiʿite "self-awareness"', being 'recounted or recited as poems during mourning-assemblies, which were held in the houses of Kufan Shīʿites and at Karbala soon after this event'.[103] As related in al-Ṭabarī's *Ta'rīkh*, the story was transmitted orally to 'Ammār al-Duhnī by al-Bāqir.[104] Whether it was 'Ammār himself or one of those who forwarded it after him who put it into writing we cannot know. Günther dates these earliest *maqātil* works to the end of the first/seventh or the first half of the second/eighth century,[105] and that is in line with the date of al-Bāqir's death in 114/732–3 or 117/735. In summary, I would place the origin of the version ascribed to al-Bāqir in Medina at the turn of the second/the first decades of the eighth century.

101 Kazimirski, *Dictionnaire arabe-français*, s.v. ghulām; Lane, *Arabic–English Lexicon*, s.v. ghulām.
102 Al-Ṭabarī, *History*, vol. XIX, 76.
103 Günther, '*Maqātil* Literature', 194.
104 Al-Ṭabarī, *Ta'rīkh*, II, 227, 281.
105 Günther, '*Maqātil* Literature'.

Ibn ʿAbd al-Raḥmān's Version

In the introduction to this chapter, I mentioned that Howard claims to list 'all the early works [on the martyrdom of al-Ḥusayn] which we know at present'.[106] For that reason, it is all the more remarkable that he almost totally disregards the account given by al-Ḥuṣayn b. ʿAbd al-Raḥmān. This is one of the three complete versions of the story related by al-Ṭabarī,[107] and is also given in full by al-Balādhurī.[108] Howard does not mention this in the list of accounts he gives at the beginning of his article,[109] and he brings it up only in passing in a discussion of the sources used by al-Balādhurī and al-Ṭabarī. In relation to al-Balādhurī, he says that Ibn ʿAbd al-Raḥmān's account 'is brief and adds nothing to our knowledge of the historical tradition'.[110] As is clear from the discussion above, however, that version at times gives details that diverge from both al-Bāqir's and Abū Mikhnaf's accounts. Whether Ibn ʿAbd al-Raḥmān helps us know better what actually happened at Karbala is of course difficult, if not impossible, to say; but as we have seen, his account certainly helps us to trace the tradition history of the story.

According to al-Mizzī, al-Ḥuṣayn b. ʿAbd al-Raḥmān was a famous traditionist living in Kufa, and was considered trustworthy as transmitter of hadiths.[111] He died in 136/753–4 at the great age of ninety-three. More or less in passing, in a discussion of his age, al-Mizzī relates that Ibn ʿAbd al-Raḥmān transmitted material on the killing of al-Ḥusayn, and that he was married when the Karbala tragedy occurred, while Ibn Ḥajar tells us that he was an adolescent at the time,[112] in other words, that he would have been something like seventeen to eighteen when the Karbala tragedy occurred. Ibn ʿAbd al-Raḥmān does not seem to have had any particularly Shiʿite sympathies; at least, these cannot be inferred from al-Mizzī's entry about him, or from

[106] Howard, 'Husayn the Martyr', 125.

[107] Al-Ṭabarī, *Taʾrīkh*, II, 283–7.

[108] Al-Balādhurī, *Ansāb*, vol. III, 382–4, 422–5. Ibn Aʿtham also includes him in a collective *isnad* to the Karbala story; the *isnad* in which Ibn ʿAbd al- Raḥmān is included differs considerably from those given by al-Balādhurī and al-Ṭabarī, however (*Futūḥ*, vol IV, 209).

[109] Howard, 'Husayn the Martyr', 124–5.

[110] Howard, 'Husayn the Martyr', 138. Wellhausen (*Religio-Political Factions*, 112) has a similar statement.

[111] Al-Mizzī, *Tahdhīb*, vol. VI, 519–23.

[112] Al-Mizzī, *Tahdhīb*, vol. VI, 523; Ibn Ḥajar, *Tahdhīb*, vol. II, 382.

the authorities in his *isnād*s. Details in the text furthermore indicate that he was not a Shiʿite. Thus, according to Ibn ʿAbd al-Raḥmān's account, when al-Ḥusayn learnt about the situation in Kufa, he 'began to move toward the road to Syria, toward Yazīd'.[113] Furthermore, in his negotiations with ʿUmar b. Saʿd (and two of his associates), al-Ḥusayn asks only to be allowed to surrender to Yazīd; the other alternatives mentioned by al-Bāqir and Abū Mikhnaf are not recounted.[114] Finally, by making Ibn Ziyād in Kufa the ruler who desecrates the severed head of al-Ḥusayn by poking at it with his cane, Ibn ʿAbd al-Raḥmān diminishes the caliph's responsibility for the whole affair. Thus, his account is more sympathetic to the Umayyads than either al-Bāqir's or Abū Mikhnaf's, a fact which corroborates the impression that he was not a Shiʿite.

As mentioned above, Ibn ʿAbd al-Raḥmān's version is preserved in al-Balādhurī's *Ansāb al-Ashrāf* and in al-Ṭabarī's *Ta'rīkh*. Both have more or less the same material; often the wording is exactly the same. One difference is that al-Balādhurī has split Ibn ʿAbd al-Raḥmān's account and inserted it in two locations. The bulk of his material is given separately after his main account of the Karbala tragedy, which is chiefly based on Abū Mikhnaf.[115] However, the part where Ibn Ziyād's forces intercept al-Ḥusayn and al-Ḥurr decides to desert the governor's troops and join him is detached from the rest of the account and inserted in the middle of the main account immediately before al-Ḥusayn's meeting with the poet ʿUbaydallāh b. al-Ḥurr al-Juʿfī.[116] The reason for this is unclear. It might be that al-Balādhurī wanted to contrast the behaviour of two men with similar names: al-Ḥurr who joined al-Ḥusayn, and Ibn al-Ḥurr who did not. Furthermore, the *isnād* seems to be corrupt, as the main authority for this particular report is written not as Ḥuṣayn, but Ḥuḍayn,[117] and al-Balādhurī could have thought that this referred to another transmitter. Whatever the reason for al-Balādhurī's placing of portions of Ibn ʿAbd al-Raḥmān's version in two different sites in the

[113] Al-Ṭabarī, *Ta'rīkh*, II, 285.
[114] Al-Ṭabarī, *Ta'rīkh*, II, 285.
[115] Al-Balādhurī, *Ansāb*, vol. III, 422–5.
[116] Al-Balādhurī, *Ansāb*, vol. III, 383–4.
[117] In Arabic, the letters ṣ and ḍ are of course very similar, where the ḍ is distinguished only by a dot above the letter.

timeline, the separation signals that the account may not have been transmitted to him as a self-contained narrative. Thus, different versions of Ibn ʿAbd al-Raḥmān's rendering of the event could have been circulating in the time of al-Balādhurī.

Extensive passages of this version are not related at first hand by Ibn ʿAbd al-Raḥmān, as he in turn had received them from two earlier Kufan authorities: Hilāl b. Yasāf (written as Hilāl b. Isāf in al-Balādhurī) and Saʿd b. ʿUbayda. These two authorities were traditionists who probably lived in Kufa at the time of the Karbala tragedy.[118] This version is, thus, a collection of reports rather than a continuous narrative in the style of al-Bāqir's account.

While the attribution of al-Bāqir's version to the imam himself could have been an attempt to give it an 'official' seal of approval,[119] Ibn ʿAbd al-Raḥmān's account does not suffer from such bias. Hence, I see no reason to question its provenance. Given the date of death of Ibn ʿAbd al-Raḥmān, this version probably stems from the turn of the second/the first decades of the eighth century, just like that of al-Bāqir.

Abū Mikhnaf's Version

In Chapter 2, I have already mentioned the prolific historian Abū Mikhnaf and his motives for writing history. Ibn al-Nadīm, among others, attributes a 'book' with the title *Maqtal al-Ḥusayn* to Abū Mikhnaf.[120] This was probably his most influential work.[121] Besides al-Ṭabarī, many authors of historical narratives use it as a source for the Karbala event;[122] al-Ṭabarī himself does not quote directly from Abū Mikhnaf's *Maqtal al-Ḥusayn*, but uses the work with the same title by Hishām b. al-Kalbī (d. 204/819–20). Modern scholars argue

[118] Al-Mizzī describe them both as trustworthy. He says that Hilāl belonged to the class of Successors and met ʿAlī b. Abī Ṭālib. Thus, Hilāl probably died at the end of the first/seventh century (*Tahdhīb*, vol. XXX, 353–5). Saʿd died when ʿUmar b. Hubayra was governor in Iraq, i.e. between 101/720 and 105/724 (*Tahdhīb*, vol. X, 290–2).

[119] See Howard, 'Husayn the Martyr', 127; Borrut, 'Remembering Karbalā'', 265.

[120] Ibn al-Nadīm, *Fihrist*, vol. 1, 93. Others who mention this work are al-Tūsī and al-Najāshī; for references, see Günther, '*Maqātil* Literature', 201, n. 40.

[121] Bahramian et al., 'Abū Mikhnaf'.

[122] See e.g. al-Balādhurī, *Ansāb*, vol. II, 334–43 (on Muslim b. ʿAqīl); *Ansāb*, vol. III, 368–426 (on al-Ḥusayn); Ibn Saʿd, *Ṭabaqāt*; al-Iṣfahānī, *Maqātil*, 98–9; Ibn Aʿtham al-Kūfī, *Futūḥ*, vol. IV, 209 – vol. V, 251, though Ibn Aʿtham has greatly embellished his account with the help of a number of sources.

that comparison of al-Ṭabarī's/Ibn al-Kalbī's rendering of Abū Mikhnaf's text with other versions reveals that he has transmitted it very faithfully.[123]

Just like the rendering of Ibn ʿAbd al-Raḥmān, that of Abū Mikhnaf is not an unbroken narrative, but consists of *khabars* that are concatenated to form a continuous account. As we have seen in Chapter 2, many scholars point to Abū Mikhnaf's great interest in his family and tribe, al-Azd. Although some of his ancestors seems to have been allied with ʿAlī and to have supported the Shiʿites in Kufa up to the 60s/680s, it is uncertain whether Abū Mikhnaf considered himself a Shiʿite.[124] It seems clear that he takes the side of al-Ḥusayn and his family against the Kufan governor and the caliph, but this could be because of his aversion to the Umayyads, or a commitment to 'soft Shiʿite' ideas.[125] Still, his account of the Karbala event has functioned as model for many later versions. As Bahramian writes, 'it was the most important documentary source on the events of Karbala for later authors',[126] and, as Borrut maintains, 'it is difficult to overestimate Abū Mikhnaf's role in shaping Shiʿism's early image, to the point that it should be regarded as a major historiographical filter'.[127] That Abū Mikhnaf should be the author (or, more correctly perhaps, the compiler) of most of the long version in al-Ṭabarī's *Taʾrīkh* no one has questioned, and this is also my position. Bahramian argues that Abū Mikhnaf compiled most of his works in early Abbasid times. Thus, it is likely that this text as a whole originated in the decades before his death, that is, in the third quarter of the second/eighth century.

Summary and Final Reflections

To summarise the preceding analysis, I conclude that the three accounts originated independently of one another. While all three versions relate the same story, very few passages are identically worded. Furthermore, there are significant differences between all three accounts. The two short versions by al-Bāqir and Ibn ʿAbd al-Raḥmān are clearly the earliest ones. I see no reason

123 Bahramian et al., 'Abū Mikhnaf'; Veccia Vaglieri, 'Ḥusayn', 608; Howard, 'Translator's Foreword', x. On Ibn al-Kalbī's use of Abū Mikhnaf's writings, see also Sezgin, *Abū Miḫnaf*, 43–4.

124 Athamina, 'Abū Mikhnaf'; Bahramian et al., 'Abū Mikhnaf'.

125 Athamina, 'Abū Mikhnaf'; Howard, 'Husayn the Martyr', 133.

126 Bahramian et al., 'Abū Mikhnaf'. See also Veccia Vaglieri, 'Ḥusayn', 608.

127 Borrut, 'Remembering Karbalā'', 264.

to doubt that the version ascribed to al-Bāqir actually originated with him or at least with the Shiʿite milieu in Medina where he lived. Likewise, Ibn ʿAbd al-Raḥmān was probably the originator of the version that bears his name. This places both these versions in the decades following the turn of the second/beginning of the eighth century. While many of the traditions in Abū Mikhnaf's account are probably early, his version as it exists now was probably compiled and edited a few decades later, most likely in the third quarter of the second/eighth century. There are traces which suggest that the part of the narrative dealing with Muslim b. ʿAqīl in Kufa on the one hand and al-Ḥusayn's journey through the desert and the battle at Karbala on the other were originally transmitted as two separate stories. Investigation furthermore suggests that the Karbala story was not yet a fixed narrative at the time of al-Bāqir and Ibn ʿAbd al-Raḥmān. Although the basic structure is the same, details differ, and at times even conflict. By the time of Abū Mikhnaf, the story had attained much of its final shape, and had become an outline for authors and storytellers to follow. This, of course, has not hindered later narrators from further embellishing it, but the basic pattern is determined with Abū Mikhnaf.

At times my students have asked me whether the battle at Karbala actually happened, or if it is all fictional. My reply has always been that there is no reason to think that at least the core of the story is not historically correct, though many details are obviously added later – at least in the version of Abū Mikhnaf – and that it is difficult to know exactly which elements are later embroideries. I have never encountered any historian who has denied the historical veracity of the battle and what led up to it. While it has perhaps never been necessary to argue for the historicity of the core of the story, the present study further strengthens the impression that it recounts a historical event. The three early versions, independently of each other, give the same basic accounts of the affair, and several details in the story conflict with later Shiʿite tradition. Thus, both the criterion of multiple independent sources and the criterion of embarrassment argue for the historicity of the core story.[128]

In the account of Abū Mikhnaf, we see the first traces of the elevation of al-Ḥusayn to a figure of more than ordinary human capacities. Although

[128] As I will argue in Chapter 11, there is also some very early poetry which, although it does not narrate the story, testifies to the historicity of the event.

he does not have the miraculous powers or the semi-divine status given him (as well as the other imams) in the later Shiʿite tradition, he is described as very pious, totally trusting in God's mercy.[129] Thus, for example, he shows kindness to his enemies and gives them water when they are thirsty, and he refuses to initiate battle in spite of the martial advantages this would bring, and although he has dreams that predict what will happen he continues on the pre-ordained path. The inviolability of al-Ḥusayn owing to his relationship to the Prophet and his father ʿAlī is furthermore emphasised by Abū Mikhnaf. We also see in this version how the divine punishments of al-Ḥusayn's enemies are miraculously enacted immediately when he curses them, a sign of God's support for his cause. Likewise, much is made of the bravery of al-Ḥusayn and his followers, in contrast to the cowardliness and wickedness of their adversaries.[130] In other words, in the version of Abū Mikhnaf we see indications that the battle and al-Ḥusayn himself are removed from human history, as McCutcheon expresses it, and are lifted somewhat above 'the realm of human doings'. None of such hagiographical features is to be found in the earlier versions of al-Bāqir and Ibn ʿAbd al-Raḥmān. Furthermore, Abū Mikhnaf's rendering of the Karbala story is set in a theological context not found in the two earlier versions. While al-Bāqir and Ibn ʿAbd al-Raḥmān tell the story quite straightforwardly, Abū Mikhnaf gives the story and the death of al-Ḥusayn an ultimate significance by placing it in a covenantal structure. In the following chapter, we shall see how this is done.

[129] See Shoshan, *Poetics*, 245. However, I do not agree with Shoshan's interpretation that Abū Mikhnaf (or al-Ṭabarī) has parallel accounts 'which depict Ḥusayn as less determined' (Shoshan, *Poetics*). For a discussion about this, see Hylén, 'Ḥusayn, the Mediator', 186–8.

[130] For a more detailed discussion of these traits, see Hylén, 'Ḥusayn, the Mediator', 168–76.

4

Karbala and Covenant according to Abū Mikhnaf

Introduction

In previous chapters I have shown that modern scholars have varied in their attempts to assign a specific religious affiliation to Abū Mikhnaf. Some state that he did not identify as a Shiʿite, but was a historian primarily interested in writing the history of Iraq, his own family, and his tribe, al-Azd;[1] others see him as a 'soft' Shiʿite who thought that ʿAlī had been the rightful successor of the Prophet, but accepted the first caliphs as sinful, yet legitimate rulers.[2] Against this background, the analysis in this chapter will establish not only that Abū Mikhnaf's version of the Karbala story is thoroughly theological, but that it is the earliest theological framing that has survived intact right through until today. While, as we saw in Chapter 3, al-Bāqir and Ibn ʿAbd al-Raḥmān relate it in a quite straightforward manner, I will argue in this chapter that Abū Mikhnaf has a clear theological – if perhaps not necessarily Shiʿite – agenda in that he situates the tragedy at Karbala in the context of the divine covenant with humankind at large, and particularly with the Muslims.[3]

[1] Howard, 'Husayn the Martyr', 133; Bahramian et al., 'Abū Mikhnaf'; Athamina, 'Abū Mikhnaf'.
[2] van Ess, *Theologie*, vol. I, 311; Crone, *Political Thought*, 117–18.
[3] The present chapter is a development of my earlier study 'Hand of God', where I emphasised al-Ṭabarī as advocate of a covenant approach to the Karbala event. Here, I want to focus on Abū Mikhnaf, who was, as we have seen, al-Ṭabarī's main source. This by no means detracts from al-Ṭabarī's interest in the covenant ideology, as Mårtensson and others have argued (see e.g. Mårtensson, 'Discourse'; *Tabari*; Humphreys, 'Qur'ānic Myth', but cf. Shoshan, *Poetics*, 85–107). I am particularly grateful to Marianna Klar, editor of the issue of *Journal of Qur'anic Studies* in

Abū Mikhnaf's approach to this story apparently did not catch on among Shiʿites in the centuries to follow, however, even though the idea of the divine covenant was important in early Imami Shiʿite theology, as we will see. In the earliest purely Shiʿite biographies of al-Ḥusayn there is very little – if anything – of the covenant vocabulary and formulae that are so prevalent in Abū Mikhnaf. In spite of the enormous popularity and influence of his rendering,[4] Abū Mikhnaf's theological framing of the story has no early Shiʿite parallels. In a sense, it thus became a theological dead end. The analysis presented in this chapter, in other words, probably says more about Abū Mikhnaf and his view of the Karbala story (and perhaps of history at large) than about the reception of the story among Shiʿites.

In the following pages, I will argue that the notion of the divine covenant, which permeates the Qur'an, constitutes the framework through which Abū Mikhnaf views this event. The Qur'anic idea of the covenant will be traced in Abū Mikhnaf's account in structural/thematic continuity with the Hebrew Bible's account of the covenant between Yahweh and the Hebrew people – which has, in turn, been traced back in its basic form to Late Bronze Era treaties between rulers and their vassals.

I will focus on four speeches ascribed by Abū Mikhnaf to al-Ḥusayn when he encounters the vanguard of the Kufan army led by al-Ḥurr. I will analyse the use of Qur'anic covenant formulae and vocabulary in the four texts, and will also categorise them within the broader framework of the eight standard characteristics of Ancient West Asian (AWA)[5] and biblical covenants as presented by George Mendenhall and Gary Herion,[6] and further developed in a Qur'anic context by Rosalind Ward Gwynne.[7] I hope to show that Abū

which the article was originally published. Her pertinent remarks and numerous literature proposals greatly improved this study.

4 Bahramian et al., 'Abū Mikhnaf'; Dakake, *Charismatic Community*, 4.

5 The empires I discuss below span a huge time frame, from the late Bronze Age to the early Iron Age, and a vast geographical area including Anatolia and Mesopotamia (and at times also Egypt). Appellations like 'the Near East' or 'the Middle East' are colonial in origin. Thus, in the present context they are anachronistic (and of course filled with Eurocentric connotations). Although they might be convenient to use for modern times, I prefer the term 'West Asia' when talking about eras far back in history.

6 Mendenhall and Herion, 'Covenant'.

7 Gwynne, *Logic*. In her article 'Ancient Near East', Patricia Crone demonstrated that not only the notion of the covenant, but also other ideas and practices in Islam, have their roots in Ancient West Asia.

Mikhnaf's Karbala narrative presents the pact of loyalty (*bayʿa*) to al-Ḥusayn as an extension of the divine covenant.

The Covenant in the Qur'an …

Before focusing on the Karbala story, however, it is necessary to discuss the notion of the divine covenant in early Islam at large, and especially in the Qur'an. It is commonly accepted by scholars of Islam that the notion of the divine covenant with humankind is very important in the Qur'an.[8] Indeed, Andrew Marsham goes so far as to argue that 'as with the Bible, "covenant" is the "thematic centre" – *die Mitte* – of the Qur'ān'.[9] The two most common terms used in the Qur'an to denote the divine covenant are *mīthāq* (occurring 25 times; see for example Qur. 2:84; 3:187; 5:7; 57:8) and *ʿahd* (occurring 29 times, for example Qur. 3:77; 6:152; 13:25; 20:115).[10] The same words are also used at times to signify pacts and alliances between human individuals and groups (for *mīthāq* see Qur. 4:21, 90, 92 and 8:72, and for *ʿahd* see Qur. 23:8 and 70:32).[11] In the Qur'an, the two words appear to be used interchangeably. In spite of the importance of the theme, however, it is never dealt with at length in the Qur'an, nor in later exegesis or theology. Gwynne maintains that it is precisely because it is so fundamental to the Qur'an 'that the Covenant *as a discrete concept* does not have a clear profile in Islamic scholarship'.[12] One of the most important covenantal passages in the Qur'an is 7:172:

> (Remember) when your Lord took from the sons of Adam – from their loins – their descendants, and made them bear witness about themselves: 'Am I not your Lord?' They said, 'Yes indeed! We bear witness.' (We did

[8] To my knowledge the most comprehensive study (though by now a bit dated in many of its premises) of the Qur'anic notion of covenant is Darnell, 'Divine Covenant'. See also Böwering, 'Covenant', 1–24; Gwynne, *Logic*; Weiss, 'Covenant'. Recent discussions of the notion of the covenant in the Qur'an and its exegesis are Lumbard, 'Covenant'; 'Humanity in Covenant'; Jaffer, 'Covenant Theology'.

[9] Marsham, *Rituals*, 41. See also Weiss, 'Covenant', 54.

[10] The numbers of occurrences of these words mentioned here include only their forms as noun and verbal noun (*maṣdar*) respectively. In addition to these, both roots occur several times in verbal and other forms. For a good overview of the uses of these and other words with the meaning of 'covenant' in the Qur'an, see Böwering, 'Covenant'; Lumbard, 'Covenant', 2–4.

[11] Wansbrough, *Quranic Studies*, 9; Böwering, 'Covenant', 464b.

[12] Gwynne, *Logic*, 1–5. The quotation is from p. 4. Italics in original.

that) so that you would not say on the Day of Resurrection, 'Surely we were oblivious of this.'

Gwynne calls this 'the pivotal covenant-passage',[13] and Ebstein writes that it 'served as the focal point of later speculations on the primordial covenant between God and mankind'.[14] Though none of the words for 'covenant' occurs in this verse, it is often held by commentators of the Qur'an to relate the establishment of the primordial pact between God and humankind.[15] Other verses which describe covenants between God and the prophets, rather than with humankind as a whole, are Qur. 3:81 and 33:7.[16]

The emergence of Islam took place in an environment where Judaism and Christianity were already established and influential. Themes and concepts from these (as well as from other religious traditions such as Zoroastrianism and Manicheism) formed a pool of latent traditions from which the adherents of early Islam drew. They did not passively appropriate these ideas, however, but remoulded and adapted them in order to formulate a religious identity of their own.[17] It is also well-known that the Qur'an itself is replete with biblical motifs and notions. Thus, Reuven Firestone writes: 'in fact, [the Qur'ān] contains so many parallels with the Hebrew Bible and New Testament that it could not possibly exist without its scriptural predecessors as subtexts. The Qur'ān itself recognizes this in its extremely referential nature.'[18] One of the most important of these parallels is the idea of the divine covenant.[19]

[13] Gwynne, *Logic*, 2.

[14] Ebstein, 'Covenant'.

[15] For other, rationalist interpretations, see Ebstein, 'Covenant'; Jaffer, 'The Muʿtazila'.

[16] On all these verses and on the idea of 'covenantal pluralism' in the Qur'an, see Lumbard, 'Covenant'.

[17] Rippin, 'Literary Analysis', 157, referring to the ideas of Wansbrough, *Quranic Studies*. The literature on this subject is overwhelming. Besides all specialised studies, almost every introduction to Islam and its formative period begins with a section on the influence of Judaism, Christianity and other Late Antique religious traditions on the Arabian Peninsula. For a recent, very thorough overview, see Amir-Moezzi and Dye (eds), *Le Coran des historiens*, vol. I, Ch. 5–14.

[18] For an overview of some studies of such motifs, see Firestone, 'The Qur'ān and the Bible'; the quotation is from pp. 2–3. Indeed, the entire volume (Reeves (ed.), *Bible and Qur'ān*) of which Firestone's article is a contribution deals with this issue.

[19] For the adaptation and use of the biblical notion of the divine covenant in the Qur'an, see esp. Wansbrough, *Quranic Studies*, 1–12; Böwering, 'Covenant'; Gwynne, *Logic*, 1–24; Firestone, 'Divine Election'.

Just as the notion of the divine covenant in the Qur'an did not emerge in a vacuum, neither did that of the Bible. At least since the mid-twentieth century it has generally been recognised that the idea of the covenant of the Hebrew Bible, as well as its textual forms, were clearly influenced by suzerainty treaties from the Hittite empire (c. 1500–1200 BCE) and from the Mesopotamian and, especially, the Neo-Assyrian and Neo-Babylonian empires (tenth to sixth centuries BCE), even if the implications of the similarities have been much discussed.[20] The idea of a covenant between God and a chosen people continued, of course, into early Christianity.

Several scholars of the Qur'an have argued that there are close parallels between the biblical notion of the covenant and that found in the Qur'an. Thus, John Wansbrough writes, 'The source of the covenant imagery [in the Qur'an] was clearly Biblical, and predominantly Pentateuchal',[21] whereas Reuven Firestone holds that, although there are significant differences, 'the Qur'ānic references to covenant ... demonstrate both direct and indirect parallels with the Hebrew Bible and New Testament'.[22] While most scholars confine themselves to indicating similarities in the use of concepts and terms, Gwynne has taken a step further and attempts to find structural similarities as well, between the AWA and biblical notions of the covenant on the one hand and those in the Qur'an on the other. She finds that no single covenant-making event is related in the Qur'an which is 'equivalent to the Mosaic Covenant-event on Sinai'. 'On the contrary', she continues, '*the paradigmatic Covenant* is not set out in one place, even though its elements are integral to the Qur'ānic idiom.'[23] By 'the paradigmatic Covenant', Gwynne means a covenant-making occasion that includes several of the eight characteristics identified by Mendenhall and Herion in AWA covenants, as clearly manifest, for example, in the Sinai covenant (see below). Thus Gwynne maintains that,

[20] Mendenhall and Herion, 'Covenant'; Cross, 'Kinship', 17–19. For a good survey of studies on the biblical notion(s) of covenant, see Hahn, 'Covenant'. As Hahn and many of the scholars he surveys in his article show, there is not one single covenant related in the Hebrew Bible, but several (see esp. p. 286). Lumbard ('Covenant') argues that also in the Qur'an several covenants between God and humankind are mentioned.

[21] Wansbrough, *Quranic Studies*, 10.

[22] Firestone, 'Divine Election', 398. See also Böwering, 'Covenant'; Gwynne, *Logic*. Each of these gives further references.

[23] Gwynne, *Logic*, 6, emphasis mine.

although no such obvious event is described in the Qur'an, the many references and allusions to these features demonstrate a certain continuity between the Qur'anic understanding of covenant and the AWA covenants as mediated through the Hebrew Bible. When discussing the Sinai covenant in relation to older covenant formulae, Mendenhall and Herion make it clear that cultural forms are bound to be adjusted when transferred from one context to another and that, for that reason, the Sinai covenant had changed both in form and content to suit the new circumstances, despite keeping many of the traits of older covenants in the surrounding world.[24] The same should presumably be said about any adaptation of the concept to the context of late antique Arabia.

Here follows the list of the formal characteristics of covenantal texts as identified by Mendenhall and Herion. Some of the examples cited from the Qur'an are given by Gwynne, others are added by me.[25] At some points I also refer directly to Mendenhall and Herion's study and make comparisons with the ancient covenants, especially with the biblical texts relating the foundation of the Sinai covenant.[26]

1. THE COVENANT-GIVER IS IDENTIFIED
   Qur. 7:172 ('Am I not your Lord?'); 96:1 ('your Lord who created').

2. THE HISTORICAL RELATIONS ARE DESCRIBED RECIPROCALLY, SETTING OUT THE BENEFITS AND THE RESULTING OBLIGATIONS
   In the Qur'an there are many references to what God has done for humankind in the past. A short passage of this kind is Qur. 42:13:

   > He has instituted for you from the religion what He charged Noah with, and that which We have inspired you (with), and what We charged Abraham, and Moses, and Jesus with: 'Observe the religion, and do not become divided in it.'

[24] Mendenhall and Herion, 'Covenant', 1183b.

[25] The headings below are quoted verbatim from Gwynne, *Logic*, 7–20. Not all her references to the Qur'an are given.

[26] Mendenhall's and Herion's list is a model, that is, an abstraction of reality made from numerous covenantal documents from different historical contexts throughout the area and historical period that I have chosen to call Ancient West Asia. Thus, no single document or description of a covenant manifests all these characteristics, and the features can be given different relative weight in various documents (Mendenhall and Herion, 'Covenant', 1180b).

Mendenhall and Herion argue that in older covenants, traits (1) and (2) as listed above are often established separately and at length. At the giving of the covenant at Sinai, however, God identifies Himself through His acts in history much more succinctly: 'I am the Lord your God, who brought you out of the land of Egypt, out of the house of slavery.'[27]

3. THE STIPULATIONS OF BEHAVIOUR ARE GIVEN, OFTEN IN AN 'IF ... THEN' FORMAT
   In Arabic, conditional clauses can be formulated in many ways, and words like 'if' (*in*) or 'when' (*idhā*) in the first part of the clause express various nuances. One of many examples is Qur. 58:11:

   > You who believe! When (*idhā*) it is said to you 'Make room in the assemblies', make room! God will make room for you. And when (*idhā*) it is said 'Rise up', rise up! God will raise in rank those of you who have believed and those who have been given knowledge. God is aware of what you do.

4. PROVISION IS MADE FOR SAFEKEEPING OF THE DOCUMENT AND ITS PUBLIC READING
   Some examples are Qur. 2:78 ('Book'); 56:77–8 ('a hidden Book'); 85:21–2 ('a guarded Tablet'); 87:19 ('pages'); 96:1 ('Recite, in the name of your Lord!').

5. A LIST OF WITNESSES IS GIVEN
   Mendenhall and Herion speak of third-party witnesses. In the Qur'an, however, God is sufficient as witness: Qur. 2:84 ('And when We made a covenant with you ... then you agreed (to it) and bore witness'); 3:81 ('[God] said, "Bear witness, and I shall be with you among the witnesses"'); 4:166 ('But God bears witness to what He has sent down to you ... and the angels (also) bear witness. Yet God is sufficient as a witness'); 73:15 ('Surely We have sent to you a messenger as a witness over you').

[27] Ex. 20:2. I have used the translation of the New Revised Standard Version of the Bible.

6. Blessings and curses for obedience and disobedience are described

This feature is common in the Qur'an, in many different forms. A brief example is Qur. 5:1–11, which talks about God's blessing on those who believe and follow His precepts, and the punishment of unbelievers. An excerpt from this lengthy passage reads:

> Remember the blessing of God on you, and his covenant (*mīthāq*) with which He bound you, when you said, 'We hear and obey.'... God has promised those who believe and do righteous deeds (that there is) forgiveness for them and a great reward. But those who disbelieve and call Our signs a lie – those are the companions of the Furnace. You who believe! Remember the blessing of God on you.[28]

7. The covenant is ceremonially ratified, often by sacrifice of an animal

Several roots with the meaning of sacrifice occur in the Qur'an. The one which is used in explicit covenantal contexts, Gwynne argues, is *n-s-k*, 'the first meaning of which appears to be "worship", which includes the secondary meaning of sacrifice'.[29] It is in this sense, Gwynne maintains, that it is used, among other places, in Qur. 2:128 ('And show us our rituals [*manāsikanā*], and turn to us (in forgiveness)'), and in 6:162 ('Say: "Surely my prayer and my sacrifice [*nusukī*], and my living and my dying are for God, Lord of the Worlds"').

According to Mendenhall and Herion, in the AWA covenants, the killing of an animal symbolises the fate of the vassal if he were to break the covenant. They write that 'the sacrificed animal represented, and was identified with, the vassal who was being placed under oath; just as the animal was slaughtered, so would the vassal and his dependents be slaughtered if he violated his oath'.[30]

They show that this element is present in the sealing of the covenant at Sinai between Yahweh and the Hebrews, where a verbal statement

[28] Qur. 5:7–11.
[29] Gwynne, *Logic*, 14–15. For a longer discussion of this word, see Ådna, 'O Son', 308–10.
[30] Mendenhall and Herion, 'Covenant', 1182a.

('Everything that the Lord has spoken we will do') is combined with a blood sacrifice.[31] Gwynne, despite showing that various words for sacrifice are used in covenantal contexts in the Qur'an, fails to demonstrate that sacrifices in the Qur'an were used to ratify the covenant in the way Mendenhall and Herion indicate. The use of derivatives of *n-s-k*, as well as other words for sacrifice in the Qur'an, in my view seems to connote communion with God rather than a ratification of the covenant through blood.

Mendenhall and Herion furthermore argue that oaths seldom replace sacrifices in the ratification of covenants. Oaths in this context are what they describe as 'a conditional self-cursing: i.e. an appeal to the gods to bring certain penalties upon the oath taker if he violates the promise that he is swearing to keep. The sacrifice is thus the *enactment* of the oath.'[32] Although oaths are very prominent in the Qur'an, most conspicuously in the introductions to several suras,[33] they are uttered by God, and function not as self-cursings, but as 'solemn, unshakable undertakings by God that the relations between God and man, virtue and reward, sin and punishment, are the truth upon which all reasoning – indeed, all action – must be based'.[34] Thus, they are not ratifications of the covenant.

There are, however, passages in the Qur'an in which humankind verbally responds to God's invitation to seal a covenant. The verse about 'the primeval covenant' (Qur. 7:172) includes an oral ratification from the people when they answer God in the affirmative: '"Am I not your Lord?" They said: "Yes indeed! We bear witness."'

Similarly, when God makes a covenant with the prophets in Qur. 3:81, they respond:

> (Remember) when God made a covenant with the prophets: 'Whatever indeed I have given you of the Book and wisdom, when a messenger comes to you confirming what is with you, you are to believe in him and

[31] Ex. 19:8; 24:3. Mendenhall and Herion, 'Covenant', 1185a.
[32] Mendenhall and Herion, 'Covenant', 1182a, italics in the original.
[33] See the first verses of Qur. 51, 52, 77, 85, 92, 100, to give just a few examples.
[34] Gwynne, *Logic*, 21–2, quotation from 22.

> you are to help him.' He said, 'Do you agree and accept my burden on that (condition)?' They said, 'We agree.'

These affirmations of God's sovereignty and acceptance of His covenant, however, are not accompanied by sacrifices or oaths. Hence, it must be concluded that ratification ceremonies in the sense described in Mendenhall and Herion's list are not found in the Qur'an.

8. IF THE COVENANT IS ACTUALLY BROKEN, CURSES ARE IMPOSED AND PUNISHMENT FOLLOWS
Mendenhall and Herion argue that, although they are not found in the covenantal texts themselves, there must have been occasions on which the suzerain declared the covenant to be broken, and executed the punishments described in the text.[35] The Qur'an, according to Gwynne, is replete with actual cursings from God – not just threats of curses as in point (6) above. The first instance where the root *l-ʿ-n* ('curse') occurs is in Qur. 2:88 ('God has cursed them for their disbelief'), and Gwynne comments: 'Ṭabarī explains its meaning as "distancing" (*b-ʿ-d*) from God and His mercy, "expulsion" (*ṭ-r-d*), "humiliation" (*kh-z-y*), and "ruin" (*h-l-k*).'[36] Another case is Qur. 5:13 ('For their breaking of their covenant [*mīthāqahum*], We cursed them and made their hearts hard'). But in particular, there are the many so-called punishment narratives in the Quran, stories of peoples in history that have been punished for their disobedience.[37]

... and in Early Islamic Political Thought

Several passages in the Qur'an indicate a close relationship between believers' adherence to the divine covenant and their belief in the prophets sent by God (also, of course, Muḥammad) and their message (Qur. 2:40–1; 4:155; 5:12). This includes the expression of loyalty to Muḥammad as political authority (Qur. 33:15). He is described as a 'good example' (*uswa ḥasana*, Qur. 33:21); in several places believers are admonished to 'obey God and the messenger' (Qur. 3:32, 132; 4:59 and *passim*); and in Qur. 4:80 it is said that 'whoever

[35] Mendenhall and Herion, 'Covenant', 1182a–b.
[36] Gwynne, *Logic*, 16–17. See also al-Ṭabarī, *Jāmiʿ*, vol. I, 574.
[37] For discussions of these, see e.g. Marshall, 'Punishment Stories'; Wansbrough, *Quranic Studies*, 2–5.

obeys the messenger has obeyed God'. In Qur. 9:111; 48:10, 18 and 60:12 the making of a pledge of loyalty to Muḥammad is expressed through the verb *bāyaʿa*, a word which, together with the cognate noun *bayʿa*, had strong commercial connotations and often referred to the making of a contract between seller and buyer. The close relationship between the commercial and the spiritual senses of the word is particularly clear in Qur. 9:111:[38]

> Surely God has purchased [*ishtarā*] from the believers their lives and their wealth with (the price of) the Garden (in store) for them. They fight in the way of God, and they kill and are killed. (That is) a promise binding on Him in the Torah, the Gospel and the Qur'an. Who fulfils his covenant [*ʿahdihi*] better than God? So welcome the good news of the bargain [*bayʿ*] you have made with Him [*bāyaʿtum bihi*]. That is the great triumph!

The *bayʿa* was a reciprocal relationship in which both parties had obligations and rights towards one another; it was manifested through a public ritual in which the parties involved clasped hands. In the Qur'anic verses referred to above, the connection between the pledge of loyalty to Muḥammad and a similar pledge to God is made apparent. The pledge of loyalty to Muḥammad is therefore presented as a natural extension of the divine covenant.[39]

After the death of Muḥammad, this loyalty was directed towards the perceived ruler who was supposed to be following in the footsteps of the Prophet.[40] As the conflicts in the early history of Islam show, ideas about what this meant in practice differed. Thus, ideas about who was the legitimate ruler, the imam of the community, came to vary significantly.[41] This was a matter not only of politics as it is understood in the secular West today, but ultimately of salvation. It was crucial to belong to the right group – the true believers – in order to be able to do God's will, since divine guidance was to be found within that group. Patricia Crone suggested that the role of the imam was like that of the leader of a caravan in the desert. He had two fundamental tasks. He gave the

[38] For a discussion of the commercial and covenantal aspects of this verse, see Marsham, *Rituals*, 44–9.

[39] Tyan, 'Bayʿa'; Marsham, *Rituals*, 40–2; Landau-Tasseron, *Religious Foundations*, 5–6.

[40] Kister, 'Concepts of Authority'; Landau-Tasseron, *Religious Foundations*, 21–5.

[41] Here, the word *imām* does not specifically refer to the Shiʿite notion of the supreme leader. The concept was (and still is) used in a much wider sense for a leader by Sunni as well as Shiʿite Muslims. See e.g. Madelung, 'Imāma'. For the special case of Shiʿism, see below, Chapter 10.

community existence – without the leader, no caravan, only scattered travellers in the desert; and he guided it to its destination, because a true imam was, himself, guided by God:

> He knew better than anyone else because he was the best person of his time: it was his superior merit that made people follow him. His guidance was seen as primarily legal, or in other words he declared what was right and wrong, for it was by living in accordance with God's law that people travelled to salvation. The coercion he might use to prevent people from straying from his caravan, or sowing dissension in it, was part of his guidance too, for anyone who strayed from the right path was lost and everyone would perish if the caravan broke up ... Everyone who travelled with him would be saved, everyone else was lost.[42]

The earliest centuries of Islam, especially, were categorised by intense periods in which different groups vied with one another for political power in an attempt to make their specific forms of religion and polity the norm. As we have seen, it is around one of these contests about legitimate leadership that the Karbala event revolves.

The Speeches of al-Ḥusayn

I mentioned above that in early Islam, the relationship between the ruler and his subjects was seen in covenantal terms as an extension of the divine covenant. In the following, I will argue that the story of the death of al-Ḥusayn as a consequence of his efforts to gain religious and political power describes the battle at Karbala as a struggle to fulfil the covenant. This idea, often expressed through giving or refusing to give the *bayʿa*, but also through other covenantal language and symbols, is essential in the account. We have seen in previous chapters that the whole story begins with al-Ḥusayn's refusal to give his pledge of allegiance to the new Umayyad caliph Yazīd b. Muʿāwiya in 60/680.[43] As the loyalty of the people of Kufa vacillates, al-Ḥusayn attempts through his words and actions to gain their support. This becomes particularly clear in the passage describing al-Ḥusayn and his group's encounter with the vanguard of the Kufan army,

[42] Crone, *Political Thought*, 22.
[43] Al-Ṭabarī, *Taʾrīkh*, II, 217–23.

led by al-Ḥurr b. Yazīd al-Yarbūʿī. In that context, Abū Mikhnaf relates four speeches ascribed to al-Ḥusayn: the first three directed to the Kufans, and the fourth to his own followers. The first three speeches emphasise, each more emphatically than the previous one, the grave consequences to be faced in the hereafter of choosing not to pledge allegiance to al-Ḥusayn. The last speech portrays a gloomy vision of this world and al-Ḥusayn's longing for death and the meeting with God. My analysis of the four speeches below will demonstrate that they are filled with allusions and references to the divine covenant. I will not, however, discuss them in the order in which they appear in Abū Mikhnaf's account. Since the covenantal features are most clearly manifested in the third speech, I will begin with that before tracing the foreshadowing of its motifs in the second and then the first speech. Finally, I will say a few words about the fourth speech, which differs from the previous three in several respects. After each speech except the fourth, I will make a comparison with Mendenhall's and Herion's list of characteristics of AWA covenants related above.

The Third Speech

In the third speech ascribed to al-Ḥusayn, he is very outspoken against the Umayyads and the capricious Kufans:

> People, the Apostle of God said: 'Whoever sees an authority who is acting tyrannically, making permissible what God has forbidden, violating God's covenant [*ʿahd Allāh*], and opposing the Sunna of the Apostle of God by acting against the servants of God sinfully and with hostility, and does not correct[44] them by deed or by word, it is God's decree that that person will know the consequences [of his neglect] [*kāna ḥaqqan ʿalā Allāhi an yudkhilahu mudkhalahu*].'[45] Indeed, the present [authorities] [*hāʾulāʾi*]

[44] The text here and a few lines further down has the word *yuʿayyir*, and a couple of lines further down, *ʿayyara*, which means 'upbraid' or 'reproach' (al-Ṭabarī, *Taʾrīkh*, II, 300, lines 8 and 11). It is much weaker than *ghayyara* (lit. 'cause change', in contexts like these usually rendered 'put right'), which is normally used in similar contexts (Cook, *Commanding Right*, 34–5), and which is used by al-Balādhurī in the same place. Cook (*Commanding Right*, 231, n. 26) suggests that the word here should be read as *ghayyara*, and I have adopted this reading.

[45] I have not been able to find this hadith in any of the canonical collections. For the last two words (similar formulae are found in Qur. 4:31, 17:80, and 22:59), I have chosen this interpretation. The literal translation would be something like 'make him enter his entrance' (see Droge, *The Qurʾān*, on these passages).

> have cleaved to obedience to Satan and have abandoned obedience to the Merciful; they have made corruption visible; they have not administered the punishments laid down by God; they have appropriated the taxes exclusively to themselves; they have permitted what God has forbidden, and they have forbidden what He has permitted. I am more entitled than anyone else to put things right [*anā aḥaqqu man ghayyara*].[46]
>
> Your letters were brought to me, and your messengers came to me with your oath of allegiance [*bi-bayʿatikum*] that you would not hand me over or desert me. If you fulfil your pledge [*bayʿatikum*], you will attain your rectitude [*rushdakum*], for I am al-Ḥusayn, the son of ʿAlī, and the son of Fāṭima, daughter of the Apostle of God. My life is with your lives; my family is with your families. In me you have an example [*uswa*]. However, if you will not act, but you break your covenant [*ʿahdakum*] and lift off the pledge of allegiance to me [*bayʿatī*] from your necks, then, by my life, that is not a thing that is unknown of you. You have done that to my father, my brother, and my cousin Muslim. Anyone who was deceived by you would be gullible. Thus have you mistaken your fortune and lost your portion [in the hereafter].[47] For 'whoever breaks (his oath), only breaks it against himself' [Qur. 48:10]. God will enable me to do without you. Peace be with you, and the mercy and blessings of God.[48]

Here, the connection between the divine covenant and the pledge of loyalty to al-Ḥusayn is made obvious through their co-occurrence. In the speech, al-Ḥusayn benefits from his consanguineous relationship to the Prophet to legitimise his claims. First, the whole speech starts with a prophetical hadith, the implication of which is that al-Ḥusayn has the right to correct the present government; second, al-Ḥusayn calls attention to his position as the grandson

[46] See n. 36 above.

[47] That the words of this sentence, '*fa-ḥaẓẓakum akhṭaʾtum wa-naṣībakum ḍayyaʿtum*', refer to the hereafter is not entirely obvious. The word *ḥaẓẓ* can mean 'fortune', 'share' or 'lot'. Similarly, *naṣīb* means 'portion' or 'part of'. Both words are used in the Qurʾan regarding matters of this world as well as of the next. To me it seems evident, however, that in the present context these words refer to the hereafter. For Qurʾanic examples of this latter usage, see Qur. 3:176 for *ḥaẓẓ*; and Qur. 2:202, 7:37 and 42:20 for *naṣīb*.

[48] Al-Ṭabarī, *Taʾrīkh*, II, 300. In this and in the following quotations from al-Ṭabarī's *Taʾrīkh*, I have quoted, or relied heavily on, Howard's translation in *History*, vol. XIX. I have normally not provided page numbers for the translation, as the pagination of the Leiden edition is printed in the margins of the translation.

of Muḥammad – and thereby as the heir of the Prophet – who can provide guidance to rectitude (*rushd*) and be a model (*uswa*) just as the Prophet was (Qur. 33:21); and third, he refers to a passage from the Qur'an which, according to later exegesis, was originally directed to Muḥammad, and applies it to himself and his family:

> Surely, those who swear allegiance to you [*yubāyiʿūnaka*] swear allegiance to God [*yubāyiʿūna Allāh*] – the hand of God is over their hands. So whoever breaks [his oath], only breaks it against himself, but whoever fulfils what he has promised [*ʿāhada*] to God – He will give him a great reward.[49]

According to the mainstream of Islamic exegetical tradition, the context of the passage of which this verse forms a part is the treaty of Ḥudaybiyya, when Muḥammad was in a situation of distress and renewed the *bayʿa* with his followers by putting their hands together.[50] The argument in the verse quoted is that when Muḥammad and his followers clasped their hands, God held His hand over them and the pledge of loyalty was thus to God as well as to Muḥammad.[51] A few verses further on in the same sura, God's answer to this pledge is described:

> Certainly God was pleased [*raḍiya*] with the believers when they were swearing allegiance to you [*yubāyiʿūnaka*] under the tree, and He knew what was in their hearts. So, He sent down the Sakīna on them, and rewarded them with a near victory, and many spoils to take.[52]

The verb *raḍiya* (from the root *r-ḍ-y*), which is here translated 'was pleased', has given this event its name in Muslim tradition: *bayʿat al-riḍwān*, 'The pledge of [God's] pleasure'.[53] There is, then, a close connection between adhering to the covenant with God and being the object of His pleasure.[54]

[49] Qur. 48:10.

[50] For a discussion of this pledge and its relation to the divine covenant, as it is related in the Qur'an and the exegetical literature, see Darnell, 'Divine Covenant', 127–51.

[51] Ibn Hishām, *Sīra*, 749.

[52] Qur. 48:18–19.

[53] Darnell, 'Divine Covenant', 128.

[54] The root *r-ḍ-y* furthermore has connotations of divine election and can be regarded as a term included in the Islamic covenantal lexicon (Firestone, 'Divine Election', 402). For early Abbasid developments of the use of the term *riḍā* and its uses in connection to the *bayʿa* to the caliph and thereby to God, see Marsham, *Rituals*, 187–8, 295–9.

Another interesting word in this verse is *sakīna*, which is derived from the Hebrew word *shᵉkhinā* and has strong connotations of the presence of God. Qur'anic exegetes often gloss it as a kind of peace of mind (*ṭum'anīna*),[55] but as Darnell demonstrates, it has a wider meaning of 'an objective reality emanating from God', and is associated with God's presence and His assistance in gaining victory over the enemy.[56] Thus, the person to whom the pledge is given is Muḥammad, and in giving the oath of allegiance to Muḥammad, one is also giving the oath to God. The result is God's satisfaction, His sending down of His *sakīna*, and imminent victory over enemies. According to Marsham, at least from the 250s/860s, Qur. 48:10 became the *locus classicus* for the legitimacy of the Abbasid caliph and the *bayʿa* to him. But, he convincingly argues, the main idea of the verse was widespread long before that:

> The notion that the verse expresses – that blessings from God were the reward for loyalty to his representatives and violation of agreements with them led to material and spiritual destruction – was axiomatic in the late antique Near East and thus in early Islam.[57]

Thus, al-Ḥusayn tries to convince the people of Kufa that the divine covenant, which implies the acceptance of the authority of the Prophet, is extended to include the acceptance of *his own* authority. To submit to the religious and political authority of al-Ḥusayn is to submit to that of Muḥammad, which in turn means submitting to God.

In summary, the thrust of the argument in this speech is that it is the duty of all Muslims to correct a sinful ruler. Since al-Ḥusayn is the grandson of the Prophet and the son of ʿAlī, he has more right than anyone else to put bad conditions right. The people of Kufa have made a pact of allegiance with him (the two words *bayʿa* and *ʿahd* are used to denote this pact). By holding on to it and following his example, they will attain rectitude and, by implication,

[55] See e.g. al-Ṭabarī, *Jāmiʿ*, vol. XIII, 114.

[56] Darnell, 'Divine Covenant', 138–44; the quotation is from p. 139. See also Droge, *Qur'ān*, 26, n. 323; Mortensen, 'Sourate 20', 774; Firestone, 'Shekhinah', 590.

[57] Marsham, *Rituals*, 303.

God's pleasure and His presence.[58] Breaking the agreement means that they will be eternally lost, since a pact with al-Ḥusayn is equal to a pact with the Prophet, which, in turn, is a pact with God. Thus, it is of the utmost importance that the believer makes the correct decision, as it leads to a 'great reward' from God, whereas the wrong choice means eternal damnation.

Applying Mendenhall's and Herion's list of criteria to this speech, the following seem relevant:

1. and 2. Identification of the covenant-giver and historical prologue

Although al-Ḥusayn is not strictly the covenant-giver, he is the representative of God who instituted the covenant, and he is identified as such here: 'I am al-Ḥusayn, the son of ʿAlī and the son of Fāṭima, daughter of the Apostle of God.' Thus, al-Ḥusayn refers to his genealogy rather than directly to deeds that his family has performed in the past. As everyone knew the deeds of his ancestors, the Prophet and ʿAlī b. Abī Ṭālib, in the past, reference to genealogy must be regarded as equal to reference to deeds in history. Because of this, he can also say about himself: 'I am more entitled than anyone else to put things right.'

3. Stipulations

The people of Kufa have pledged through letters and messengers that they will not hand al-Ḥusayn over or desert him, and al-Ḥusayn in his turn promises, 'If you fulfil your pledge, you will attain your rectitude ... My life is with your lives; my family is with your families. In me you have an example.'

4. Deposits and public readings

I regard the letters sent by the Kufans to al-Ḥusayn with their pledges to support him as the text of the covenant here being referred to. I will have more to say about this below.

6. Blessings and curses

These are very clear in the speech: respectively, the attainment of rectitude and, by implication, God's pleasure, and punishment in the hereafter.

[58] For the connection between different forms of the root *r-sh-d* and guidance in the Qur'an, see Izutsu, *Ethico-Religious Concepts*, 194–5.

Items (5), (7) and (8) in Mendenhall's and Herion's list are not applicable to this speech.

The Second Speech

Al-Ḥusayn's second address to the Kufan army has a very tight structure. I have arranged the sentences so as to make the structure clear:

> O people,
> if you fear [God] [*in tataqqū*] and recognise the rights of those to whom they are due, this will be more satisfying to God [*arḍā li-Allāh*].
> We are the family of the house [*wa-naḥnu ahl al-bayt*],[59] more entitled to the authority of this government over you than [*min*] these who claim what does not belong to them, who bring tyranny and aggression among you.
> If you dislike us and are ignorant of our rights, and your view is different from what came to me in your letters and what your messengers brought to me, I will leave you.[60]

Excluding the vocative *Ayyuhā al-nās*, 'O people', the speech consists of three sentences. The first and the last are conditional (see Table 4.1), and commence with the Arabic conjunction *in*, 'if'; they deal with what will happen if the Kufans accept or reject al-Ḥusayn. Between these two is a statement in which al-Ḥusayn declares the merits of his own family, the *ahl al-bayt*, and the demerits of 'these who claim what does not belong to them', the present government, the Umayyads. The parallel structure of the speech is very clear. The Arabic preposition *min*, here translated 'than', in the middle of the sentence acts like a pivot for the whole speech. All the text before this word deals with the advantages of taking al-Ḥusayn as leader; everything after it gives the consequences of taking the Umayyads as leaders. Thus, the speech contrasts the *ahl al-bayt*, here represented by al-Ḥusayn, with the Umayyads. It furthermore states that the former are entitled to authority, whereas the latter are pretenders who bring tyranny and aggression. A closer look at the conditional sentences reveals an obvious antithetical parallelism, as can be seen in Table 4.1.

59 For discussions of the phrase *ahl al-bayt*, see Sharon, 'Ahl al-Bayt'.
60 Al-Ṭabarī, *Ta'rīkh*, II, 298.

Table 4.1 Parallelism of conditional sentences in al-Ḥusayn's second speech

If you fear [God]	and recognise the rights of those to whom they are due	this will be more satisfying to God
If you dislike us	and your view is different from what came to me in your letters and what your messengers brought to me	I will leave you

When they are tabulated in this way, it becomes clear that the sentences make up three important oppositions, arranged in columns in the table. In Column 1, the fear of God (*taqwā*) is opposed to the dislike of the *ahl al-bayt*. Column 2 opposes the acceptance of the authority of the *ahl al-bayt* to the breaking of the promises made to al-Ḥusayn. In Column 3, the outcomes of the choice facing the Kufans are opposed: God's satisfaction, against al-Ḥusayn leaving. Essential to al-Ḥusayn's message in this speech are the two words in the first conditional sentence: 'fear (of God)' and 'satisfying (to God)'. These words are so common in the Qur'an that it is easy to forget the covenantal implications they have. The former, from the root *w-q-y* (or possibly *t-q-w* or *t-q-y*),[61] is absolutely central in the Qur'an.[62] Derivatives of the root occur in several contexts dealing with the divine covenant. Thus, Qur. 5:7–8:

> Remember the blessing of God on you, and His covenant [*mīthāqahu*] with which He bound you [*wāthaqakum*], when you said, 'We hear and obey.' Fear God [*wa-ittaqū Allāh*]! Surely God knows what is in the hearts. You who believe! Be supervisors for God, witnesses in justice, and do not let hatred of a people provoke you to act unfairly. Act fairly! It is nearer to the fear of God [*taqwā*]. Fear God [*wa-ittaqū Allāh*]! Surely God is aware of what you do.[63]

In these verses, the fear of God is a precondition for the believer who wants to adhere to His covenant. Returning to al-Ḥusayn's speech, the word with

[61] For a short discussion of the alternatives, see Alexander, 'Fear', 194–5.

[62] For *w-q-y* and its derivatives in the Qur'an, see e.g. Alexander, 'Fear'; Izutsu, *Ethico-Religious Concepts*, 195–200 and *passim*; Ohlander, 'Fear of God'.

[63] I have departed from Droge's translation here. He translates the derivates of *w-q-y*: 'Guard (yourselves) against God'. Another place where the covenant (in this case the word *'ahd* is used) is used in conjunction with derivates of *w-q-y* is Qur. 3:76.

the meaning 'satisfying' (to God) is a derivative from the root *r-ḍ-y*, which I have discussed above with reference to its occurrence in Qur. 48:18 and its connection to the *bayʿa*. As we saw there, God promises His satisfaction as a reward for those who adhere to the covenant. In al-Ḥusayn's speech, no word for 'covenant' is used, but his mentioning of the fear of God together with God's satisfaction places it in a covenantal context, especially since Abū Mikhnaf has located the speech between two other speeches that make more overt reference to the covenant.

In summary, the message al-Ḥusayn is trying to convey is that the fear of God, a *sine qua non* for every Muslim, implies accepting the authority of al-Ḥusayn, the foremost living member of the *ahl al-bayt*, and his remaining in Kufa. That God should be satisfied is contingent on this acceptance.

A comparison of this speech with Mendenhall and Herion's list renders the following result:

1. AND 2. IDENTIFICATION OF THE COVENANT-GIVER AND HISTORICAL PROLOGUE
   Al-Ḥusayn explicitly states: 'We are the family of the house (of Muḥammad), more entitled to the authority of this government over you than these.'

3. STIPULATIONS
   The stipulation 'If you ... recognise the rights of those to whom they are due' is here embedded in the blessings and curses.

4. DEPOSITS AND PUBLIC READINGS
   Again, al-Ḥusayn is referring to the letters from the Kufans, with their invitations and their promises to support him.

6. BLESSINGS AND CURSES
   As demonstrated in Table 4.1 and the discussion pertaining to it, most of this speech is expressed in terms of the formal blessings and curses found in many AWA covenants, for example in the Sinai covenant, although in the latter case they are 'enormously elaborated'.[64]

[64] These words are used by Mendenhall and Herion, 'Covenant', 1184b, in referring to Deut. 28. See also the parallel text in Lev. 26.

The rest of the items in the list of covenantal characteristics are not found in this speech, at least not manifestly so.

The First Speech

Turning now to the first, short speech, al-Ḥusayn delivers this in front of the Kufan vanguard, at the time of the midday prayer:

> People, it is an excuse [for my coming here] [*innahā maʿdhira*], both to God the Mighty and Exalted and to you, that I did not come to you until your letters were brought to me, and your messengers came to me saying, 'Come to us, for we have no leader [*imām*]. God may unite us in guidance [*ʿalā al-hudā*] through you.' Since this was your view, I have come to you. Therefore, if you give me what you guaranteed in your pacts [*ʿuhūdikum*] and covenants [*mawāthīqikum*], I will come to your town. If you will not and are averse to my coming, I will leave you for the place from which I came to you.[65]

Al-Ḥusayn here explains that he has come because the people of Kufa have written to him and called on him to become their leader (imam). If the Kufans are prepared to give him what they guaranteed in their 'pacts and covenants' (*ʿuhūd*, *mawāthīq*, sg. *ʿahd*, *mīthāq*) he is willing to fulfil that mission; if not, he will return to Mecca. As I have mentioned above, there are many places in the Qur'an where the words *ʿahd* and *mīthāq* refer to alliances and pacts between humans. Similarly, in this context, the terms *ʿuhūd* and *mawāthīq* are clearly being used in a political sense to denote the promises and oaths of allegiance given by those who had summoned him. The references to God and His guidance through al-Ḥusayn, as well as the wider meaning of the words and the context, indicate, however, that there are also religious issues in play here.[66] It is interesting to note the parallel conditional sentences at the end

65 Al-Ṭabarī, *Ta'rīkh*, II, 297–8.
66 Here, I analyse only the words of al-Ḥusayn. Other aspects of this section of the text which add to the 'religious' context, such as his dress and the fact that he is allowed to lead all the people (his own group as well as the Kufan army) in prayer, are not dealt with. I have discussed these in 'Ḥusayn, the Mediator', 120–5.

of the speech. Although the receiving and renouncing of al-Ḥusayn are not explicitly followed here by divine sanctions, as in the second speech, they still augur the meaning of the conditional sentences of that address (see Table 4.1 and the discussion associated with it).

The following items from Mendenhall's and Herion's list are found in the speech:

3. Stipulations
   Ḥusayn refers to the 'pacts and covenants' from the Shiʿites of Kufa, where they guaranteed him support and help. In return, he was to give them divine guidance (*hudan*).

4. Deposits and public readings
   Here, al-Ḥusayn quotes verbatim from the letters from the Kufans and their invitation to him to come and give them guidance.

5. List of witnesses
   Ḥusayn invokes both 'God the Mighty and Exalted' and the people in front of him as witnesses that he has come because he was invited by the people of Kufa.

6. Blessings and curses
   The blessings and curses are here given in a weaker form than in the following speeches, as they refer only to his physical presence or absence, rather than to the spiritual consequences of this.

The other characteristics of the list are not applicable to this speech.

What is at stake in the three speeches analysed so far is the extension of the divine representation on earth to al-Ḥusayn himself. When he admonishes the Kufans to adhere to their promises to support him, the close connection between God's satisfaction and his own presence indicates that he presupposes and is building on the divine covenant with humankind, and that he regards loyalty to himself as an extension of the divine covenant. This is in no way unique in the early history of Islam; many pledges of loyalty to the caliphs, both Umayyads and, later, Abbasids, share the same premise. Indeed, it can be said that much of the discussion about the legitimate ruler in early Islam revolved around this question: who was to be accepted as the representative of God, and thus as the one worthy of the *bay'a*, the extension of the divine covenant?[67]

The Fourth Speech

In the fourth speech accounted for in Abū Mikhnaf's account, al-Ḥusayn turns to his followers rather than to the Kufan army:

> You have seen what this matter has come to. Truly, the world has changed and has become worse; its goodness has retreated and it has become very bitter. There remains only a small rest of it, like the dregs of a jar, a paltry life like an unhealthy pasturage. Can you not see that truth [*ḥaqq*] is no longer practised and falsehood [*bāṭil*] no longer desisted from, so that the believer rightly desires to meet God? I can only regard death as martyrdom [*shahāda*] and life with the oppressors as a tribulation.[68]

The words 'truth' (*ḥaqq*) and 'falsehood' (*bāṭil*) are very common in the Qur'an; the former is often used as a synonym for God's revelation and His guidance (see for example Qur. 2:119, 9:33, and 35:24), and is frequently opposed to the latter (for example Qur. 2:42; 34:49 and 47:1–3). Thus, al-Ḥusayn here regrets that the world has changed for the bad, and says that the believer rightly desires to meet God. Martyrdom is preferable to life 'with the oppressors'. In spite of the fact that the story of Karbala has become the main example of martyrdom in Shi'ite lore and theology, this is the only occurrence of the word *shahāda*, 'martyrdom', in the text. Although no word for 'sacrifice' is used in the text, the fact that al-Ḥusayn is prepared to die to keep his pact with God can be regarded as an allusion to self-sacrifice. When al-Ḥusayn has delivered his speech, one of his companions responds, speaking for all his men, and asserts their loyalty to him, even to death. In contrast to the lack of response from the people of Kufa after the previous speeches, here al-Ḥusayn's followers renew their pledge to support him.

In the speech itself, I find nothing except the reference to the sacrifice as ratification of the covenant (item 7) that can obviously be associated with the criteria in Mendenhall and Herion's list. The reactions of al-Ḥusayn's

67 Marsham, *Rituals*, 114–17, 168–80, 230–49 and *passim*.
68 Al-Ṭabarī, *Ta'rīkh*, II, 300–1.

followers are, however, important in this respect, and will be dealt with below.

Beyond al-Ḥusayn's Speeches

The speeches ascribed to al-Ḥusayn are saturated with formal allusions to and themes similar to those found in covenant formulae enacted in Ancient West Asia, particularly in the form these took in the Sinai covenant between Yahweh and the Hebrew people. It is to be noted that in later exegesis of Qur. 2:27, the covenant given to the People of the Book in the Torah is the same as that which Muḥammad preached. For al-Ṭabarī, for example, the divine covenant of the Bible includes acceptance of Muḥammad as a prophet.[69] What we have in the four speeches discussed here, however, are not covenantal formulae in themselves; they are, rather, attempts by al-Ḥusayn to re-enact the *bayʿa* that the inhabitants of Kufa have already made with him, and thus by extension with God, through their letters and envoys. Hence, the text refers to the divine covenant by allusions rather than accounting for it *in extenso*.[70]

Similar allusions to the covenant are found throughout the Karbala story. In what follows I will recapitulate the main arguments advanced in the analysis above by reviewing Mendenhall and Herion's list, at the same time giving further examples of passages from the story outside of the speeches whose themes fit into the characteristics of the covenant that they have suggested.

1. and 2. Identification of the covenant-giver and historical prologue

In the speeches analysed above, al-Ḥusayn refers to his genealogy rather than recounting a list of historical deeds. The same is true in speeches and addresses other than those analysed above in which he refers to his genealogy as an argument both for his inviolability and for the fact that those who invited him should adhere to their pacts. Thus, in a letter to the people of Basra written before he set out on the journey to Kufa, he declares:

> God gave preference to Muḥammad before all His creatures. He graced him with prophethood and chose him for His message. After he had

[69] Al-Ṭabarī, *Jāmiʿ*, vol. I, 263–5.

[70] As I have mentioned above, Gwynne argues that this is true also for the Qur'an.

> warned His servants and informed them of what he had been sent with, God took him to Himself. We are his family, those who possess his authority [*awliyāʾ*], those who have been made his trustees [*awṣiyāʾ*], and his inheritors; we are those who have more rights to his position among the people than anyone else.[71]

Similarly, al-Ḥusayn's genealogy is referred to in many places: by al-Ḥusayn himself, for example in a speech just before the battle,[72] by his son,[73] and by others, such as al-Ḥurr once he had joined al-Ḥusayn.[74] Hence, both al-Ḥusayn and his supporters argue that his authority derives from God, via his grandfather, the Prophet Muḥammad. The covenant-giver is ultimately God, not al-Ḥusayn, and his followers recognise this pattern of authority. One of his most ardent companions, Zuhayr b. al-Qayn, who initially disliked him but experienced an almost Pauline conversion on the road between Mecca and Kufa,[75] says to one of the Kufan opponents:

> By God! I did not ever write to him; I did not ever send messengers to him; I did not ever promise him my help. However, the road brought us together. When I saw him, I was reminded by him of the Apostle of God and of his position with regard to the Apostle of God. I knew his enemies and your party whom he was going toward. Then, I saw that it was right that I should help him, be in his party and put my life forward to protect his, because of the truth of God and the truth of His Apostle, which you have abandoned.[76]

[71] Al-Ṭabarī, *Taʾrīkh*, II, 240.
[72] Al-Ṭabarī, *Taʾrīkh*, II, 329–30.
[73] Al-Ṭabarī, *Taʾrīkh*, II, 356.
[74] Al-Ṭabarī, *Taʾrīkh*, II, 334–5. It is interesting to note that the function of the references to al-Ḥusayn's genealogy change slightly as the story moves. In the beginning it is used to argue for his political precedence; later, when he is surrounded by the army, it is used as an argument for his inviolability. (For a discussion of this, see Hylén, 'Ḥusayn, the Mediator', 168–76.) This use of one's genealogy is of course not unique to the family of the Prophet, as lineage in general was extremely important in pre-Islamic and early Islamic Arabia, and referring to one's ancestors was the main means for placing oneself on the status ladder among the Arabs. For many Shiʿites, though, ancestry was of paramount importance as the legitimacy of the whole movement depended on the descent of its leaders from the Prophet Muḥammad. See Chapter 10.
[75] Al-Ṭabarī, *Taʾrīkh*, II, 290–1.
[76] Al-Ṭabarī, *Taʾrīkh*, II, 319.

3. Stipulations

The mutual obligations stipulated in the *bayʿa* between al-Ḥusayn and the Kufans are referred to only in passing in the speeches analysed above. They are stated more directly, however, in the letters from the Kufans, where they promise to support him against the Umayyad authorities in the town. Thus, Sulaymān b. Ṣurad, al-Musayyab b. Najaba and Rifāʿa b. Shaddād – that is, some of the men who later became the leaders of the Tawwābūn (see Part II) – and others purportedly write to him:

> There is no imam over us. Therefore come, so God may unite us in truth through you. Al-Nuʿmān b. Bashīr is in the governor's palace; we do not gather with him for the Friday prayer. Nor do we accompany him out of the mosque for the Festival prayer. If we hear that you will agree to come to us, we will drive him away until we pursue him to Syria, if God wills.[77]

In another letter, some Kufan Shiʿites write: 'The region[78] has grown green; the fruit has ripened; the waters have overflowed. Therefore, if you want to, come to an army that has been gathered for you.'[79] It is furthermore stated that more than fifty letters with similar messages were sent to Al-Ḥusayn within a few days. Al-Ḥusayn's part of the obligations is described in his reply, a letter in which he states that if what they say is true, he will come and be an imam 'who acts according to the Book, one who upholds justice, one who professes the truth and one who dedicates himself to the essence of God'.[80]

4. Deposits and public readings

According to Abū Mikhnaf, al-Ḥusayn regarded the letters of invitation from the Kufans as binding treaties. He refers to them in the first three speeches, but also in a speech delivered just before the battle, in which he

[77] Al-Ṭabarī, *Ta'rīkh*, II, 234. On the refusal to pray with the governor as marker of political disunity, see van Ess, *Theologie*, vol. I, 17–19.
[78] Lit. *al-janāb*, 'region' or 'tract'; see Lane, *Arabic–English Lexicon*, vol. I, 467a. Howard has not translated this word.
[79] Al-Ṭabarī, *Ta'rīkh*, II, 235.
[80] Al-Ṭabarī, *Ta'rīkh*, II, 235.

quotes the last letter cited above.[81] We have also seen how his companion Zuhayr b. al-Qayn indirectly refers to the letters as documents of a binding treaty when he argues that he is supporting al-Ḥusayn despite having written no letters and made no promises. Implicit in Zuhayr's argument is that those who had written to al-Ḥusayn are even more obliged to stand by him.

An incident related after al-Ḥusayn's second speech emphasises the importance of the letters, and can be regarded as a case of 'public reading'. After the speech, al-Ḥurr b. Yazīd, the commander of the enemy, questions the existence of the letters:

> 'By God! We know nothing of these letters that you mention.' Al-Ḥusayn said: 'O, 'Uqba b. Sim'ān, bring out the two saddlebags in which their letters to me are kept.' He brought out two saddlebags that were full of documents and scattered them in front of them.[82]

Thus, the letters are kept by al-Ḥusayn and presented as a proof that he had actually received pledges of allegiance from the people of Kufa.

5. List of witnesses

No formal list of third-party witnesses is given in the text. Implied in the incident of the scattering of the letters is that al-Ḥurr becomes a witness to the pact between al-Ḥusayn and the people of Kufa. Furthermore, as we saw in the analysis of the first speech, God is called on as a witness. Indeed, God is the true covenant-giver, and in the Qur'an He is sufficient as a witness.

6. Blessings and curses

The blessings and curses are very obvious in the speeches; if the people keep their promises, al-Ḥusayn will come to them, God will be satisfied, they will attain rectitude and 'a great reward' from God, and so on. On the other hand, if they break the pact, al-Ḥusayn will leave them and they will lose their reward in the hereafter. Similar explicit formulae of blessings and curses do not occur elsewhere in the story.

[81] Al-Ṭabarī, *Ta'rīkh*, II, 330.
[82] Al-Ṭabarī, *Ta'rīkh*, II, 298–9.

7. Ratification

Al-Ḥusayn's speeches contain no trace of any ratification of the treaty they refer to. As I have shown above, the AWA treaties were frequently ratified through a blood sacrifice; less often, through an oath. In the Qur'an, neither oaths nor sacrifices are means used to confirm the covenant between God and humankind, though verbal assents to God and His covenant are mentioned on a few occasions. In Abū Mikhnaf's account of the Karbala story, al-Ḥusayn several times declares his loyalty to God, as in the following prayer just before the battle:

> O God! It is You in Whom I trust amid all grief. You are my hope in all my distress. You are my trust and provision in everything that happens to me, no matter how much the heart may seem to weaken, ingenuity to fail, the friend to desert and the enemy to rejoice. I have received it [the distress] through You and I complain to You out of my desire for You, You alone. May You dispel it for me and relieve me of it. You are the Master of all grace, the Possessor of all goodness and the Ultimate Resort of all desire.[83]

Furthermore, al-Ḥusayn's followers several times verbally assert their willingness to stand by his side. After the fourth speech analysed above, Zuhayr b. al-Qayn speaks for all of them, saying:

> We have heard God guide your words, son of the Apostle of God. By God! If, by helping and supporting you, we must abandon [this world], even if our world were eternal and we could be immortal within it, we would still prefer going with you to staying in it.[84]

Like al-Ḥusayn, his followers are prepared to die in order to uphold the covenant. Later, the night before the battle, al-Ḥusayn gives his followers permission to leave him. They re-assert their allegiance to him and promise that they will sacrifice their lives for him, saying:

> By God! We will not leave you. Rather, our lives will be a sacrifice [*al-fidāʾ*] for you; we will protect you with our necks [*bi-nuḥūrinā*],

[83] Al-Ṭabarī, *Ta'rīkh*, II, 327.
[84] Al-Ṭabarī, *Ta'rīkh*, II, 301.

> with our foreheads and with our hands. If we are killed, we have fulfilled and accomplished what we promised.[85]

The formula 'our lives will be a sacrifice for you' and similar expressions involving the word *fidan*[86] are very common in Arabic, denoting willingness to give one's life for another. In this passage, however, the sacrificial connotation is strengthened by the juxtaposition of the word *naḥr* (here in plural form: *nuḥūr*), which, besides signifying the upper part of the breast and the neck of the human body, also signifies the part of the camel's body where it is stabbed when sacrificed.[87] But it is not only through their words that the followers show that they are sticking to their pact with al-Ḥusayn. Almost all of them are in fact killed in the ensuing battle, and it can be argued that the deaths of al-Ḥusayn and his followers are described as a sacrifice, even if no word with that meaning is expressly used in the story. In this context it is noteworthy that each time blood is mentioned in the story, it is the blood of al-Ḥusayn, his family, and his supporters. Though many of his enemies are killed in the battle, nothing is said of their blood.[88]

Though Abū Mikhnaf describes the killings of al-Ḥusayn and his followers as sacrifices, they are, however, imbued with a different symbolic value from that of the ratification sacrifices as analysed by Mendenhall and Herion. Their deaths are not a warning of what will happen if they break the covenant with God, but the outcome of their keeping it, as we can see from the statement quoted above. Thus, while al-Ḥusayn and his followers ratify the covenant through verbal assent, neither oaths in the sense of 'self-cursings' nor enactments of such oaths through sacrifices are to be found in Abū Mikhnaf's account.

85 Al-Ṭabarī, *Ta'rīkh*, II, 323.

86 This word can also be translated 'ransom', but even so it has clear sacrificial connotations. See Ådna, 'O Son', 316–17. The word is also used in the same context by one of al-Ḥusayn's followers, when he says 'We will not [leave you]. Rather we will sacrifice (*tafdīka*) for your safety our lives, property and families' (al-Ṭabarī, *Ta'rīkh*, II, 322). Although the text seems to be corrupt here, the variants given in the Leiden edition use verbal derivatives of the root *f-d-y*.

87 Lane, *Arabic–English Lexicon*, vol. II, 2774b–c; see also Ådna, 'O Son', 340.

88 See e.g. al-Ṭabarī, *Ta'rīkh*, II, 351, 359, 360, 370. The only time the blood of al-Ḥusayn's adversaries is mentioned is when he says to the Kufans, just before his death: 'If you kill me, God will send misfortune among you and cause the shedding of your blood' (al-Ṭabarī, *Ta'rīkh*, II, 365).

8. The imposition of the curses, should the covenant be broken

This, again, is a feature absent from al-Ḥusayn's speeches. In the account of the battle that ensues, however, several situations are related where people are punished for their contempt and mockery of al-Ḥusayn – in other words, for their violation of the covenant. On one of these occasions, we are told that a certain ʿAbdallāh b. Ḥawza scorns al-Ḥusayn, who prays:

> 'My Lord! Drive him into the Fire!' Then [Ibn Ḥawza's] horse became troubled in a stream and made him fall. His leg was stuck in the stirrups and his head fell to the ground. The horse bolted and dragged him along, making his head strike every stone and clod of earth until he died.[89]

In this and similar situations, al-Ḥusayn does not personally have the power to punish those that have broken the covenant; instead, he curses them and lets God execute the punishment. This is yet another indication that it is in fact God, not al-Ḥusayn, who is the covenant-giver.

Karbala and Covenant in Abū Mikhnaf's Account

Abū Mikhnaf regards the Karbala event as a serious violation of the divine covenant with humankind. In his rendering of the affair, al-Ḥusayn, as the foremost representative of the family of the Prophet Muḥammad, is the person to whom God has given the authority to lead the community of believers.[90] To refuse to accept him as leader is to go against God's will and thus to break His covenant. On the contrary, holding fast to the *bayʿa* to al-Ḥusayn, whatever the cost, means adhering to the covenant. Abū Mikhnaf seems to regard the Karbala event as a kind of test which God put to the Muslim community. Thus, he makes Zuhayr b. al-Qayn, the zealous companion of al-Ḥusayn, say, in a speech just before the battle:

> People of al-Kufa, here is a warning to you of God's punishment, a warning insofar as it is the duty of a Muslim to advise his brother Muslim – and we are

[89] Al-Ṭabarī, *Taʾrīkh*, II, 337. Variant versions of the same event are given subsequently in the text. Other examples of al-Ḥusayn's curse leading to God's punishment of the cursed are found in al-Ṭabarī, *Taʾrīkh*, II, 312, 361–2.

[90] This may indicate that he actually identified as a 'soft' Shiʿite, as van Ess (*Theologie*, vol. I, 311) and Crone (*Political Thought*, 117–18) maintain.

> still brothers in one religion and one faith [*wa-naḥnu ḥattā al-āna ikhwatun wa-ʿalā dīnin wāḥidin wa-millatin wāḥidin*] as long as the sword does not strike between you and us. Therefore, you are still appropriate persons to receive advice from us. When the sword strikes, the protection will be cut asunder. We will be a community, and you will be a community. God has tested us and you [*inna Allāha qad ibtalānā wa-iyyākum*] through the offspring of His prophet Muḥammad so that He might see what we and you are doing. We summon you to help them and to desert the tyrant, ʿUbaydallāh b. Ziyād.[91]

The tragedy of the affair, according to Abū Mikhnaf, was that the majority of the Muslims did not pass the test; the community was split between those who adhered to the covenant and those who did not.

But even though the covenant vocabulary and structure are so prominent in his account of the Karbala drama, it is hard to say whether Abū Mikhnaf has intentionally adopted this language and style in his relation of the event. In other words, was this his usual way of describing the human–divine relationship, or has he endeavoured to structure this particular story within the covenant framework? Without more extensive studies of Abū Mikhnaf's writings, his vocabulary and his way of structuring his historiographical works, it is difficult to say. In the stories about the Tawwābūn and al-Mukhtār that will be discussed below, however, there are few of the overt references to the covenant that we find in his version of the Karbala story.

Al-Ṭabarī himself probably regarded the idea of the divine covenant as a major factor in history, and thus saw human history as a result of God's intervention.[92] If so, he would have been inclined to foreground, perhaps even amplify, Abū Mikhnaf's way of describing the Karbala event. In many other historiographies of early Islam that use Abū Mikhnaf's account of Karbala as a source, the covenant theology does not figure as ubiquitously as in al-Ṭabarī's version. Though most historians base their accounts on Abū Mikhnaf, many of them completely exclude the speeches: for example, Ibn Ṣaʿd, al-Yaʿqūbī and al-Iṣfahānī. Others include some of the speeches, but sometimes in

[91] Al-Ṭabarī, *Ta'rīkh*, II, 331.

[92] See the studies by Ulrika Mårtensson, for example her 'Discourse'; *Tabari*; 'Ibn Isḥāq', but cf. Shoshan, *Poetics*, 85–107.

abbreviated form. Thus, al-Balādhurī gives only a short version of the second speech,[93] while al-Mufīd has the two first speeches in full in his account.[94] Ibn Aʿtham al-Kūfī gives the three first speeches more or less complete, but he places them in contexts that differ from that given by Abū Mikhnaf. Thus, for example, he presents the third speech as a letter from al-Ḥusayn to the Shiʿite Sulaymān b. Ṣurad and his companions in Kufa, admonishing them to hold on to their promises.[95] The covenant setting that is so prominent in al-Ṭabarī's version of Abū Mikhnaf is thus played down in most of the accounts that are based on this one.

Abū Mikhnaf and Early Shiʿite Covenant Theology

Several scholars have argued that the idea of the divine covenant was a salient aspect of early Shiʿite theology, but in a way that is very different from how it was conceived in the Ancient West Asian tradition related above. The Shiʿite ideas about the covenant were, rather, placed in a late Antique esoteric framework influenced by Neoplatonism and Gnosticism. Most of these scholars base their research on collections of hadiths from the imams, collections that were compiled from the late third/ninth up to the end of the fourth/tenth centuries.[96] Mohammad Ali Amir-Moezzi, however, argues that, even though each separate hadith cannot with any certainty be said to derive from the imam to which it is ascribed, the ideas expressed are probably very old and originate in the time of the second/eighth-century imams like al-Bāqir and al-Ṣādiq.[97] Ideas on the covenant similar to those expressed in the hadiths examined by Amir-Moezzi are also found in the texts from Shiʿite 'extremists' (*ghulāt*) which are much earlier than the hadith collections, and which are examined by Mushegh Asatryan.[98] Here, I will only reiterate the most important points concerning the esoteric notion of the covenant expressed in these writings in order to enable a comparison with Abū Mikhnaf's Karbala account.[99]

[93] Al-Balādhurī, *Ansāb*, vol. III, 1,306.

[94] Al-Mufīd, *Al-Irshād*, 224–5.

[95] Ibn Aʿtham al-Kūfī, *Futūḥ*, vol. V, 143–5. The first and second speeches are found on pp. 135 and 137 respectively.

[96] The collections of Shiʿite hadiths will be further discussed in Chapter 10.

[97] Amir-Moezzi, 'On Spirituality'.

[98] Asatryan, *Controversies*.

[99] This section is based on Amir-Moezzi, *Divine Guide*, 33–7; 'Cosmogony'; Amir-Moezzi and Jambet, *Shiʿi Islam*, 11–18. See also Asatryan, *Controversies*, 67–8; Bar-Asher, *Scripture and*

The idea of the divine covenant in early Shiʿism is closely related to its cosmogony, as the covenant-founding events (in the plural, as we will see) occur before the creation of human beings in bodily form. As mentioned above, the Qurʾanic verse about the primordial covenant (Qur. 7:172) is central to the notion of the divine covenant in Islam. Imami Shiʿism, however, talks of a covenantal relationship between future Believers (*muʾminūn*) and God long before the occasion mentioned in that verse. According to early Shiʿite sources, God created humankind in several stages, in increasingly less subtle and more material forms. Very early on (if this expression can be used about a situation preceding historical time), He made a covenant with the true Believers while they were still in the form of 'particles' (Ar. *dharr*) or 'shadows' (Ar. *aẓilla*). This pact included not only a promise on the part of the Believers to worship and adore God, but also a vow of love and loyalty (*walāya*) towards the Prophet, towards the imams, and towards the Mahdi, the messianic saviour at the end of time.[100] Later, God created the descendants of Adam in the form of particles by mixing earth with water of different quality: this is the covenantal occasion between God and humankind referred to in Qur. 7:172. One hadith states:

> A man asked Abū Jaʿfar [al-Bāqir] about [the meaning of] God's word, '(Remember) when your Lord took from the sons of Adam – from their loins – their descendants, and made them bear witness about themselves: "Am I not your Lord?" They said, "Yes indeed!"' to the end of the verse [Qur. 7:172]. He replied, in the presence of his father [ʿAlī b. al-Ḥusayn, the fourth imam], 'My father reported to me that God took a fistful [*qabḍa*] of earth [*turāb*], the earth [*turba*] from which he created Adam. Then he poured fresh, sweet water on it and left it for forty days; then he poured salty, bitter water on it and left it for forty days. When the clay had fermented, He took it and kneaded it vigorously, and then [the descendants of Adam] came out like particles [*dharr*] from his right and from his left. He ordered

Exegesis, 132–6; Dakake, *Charismatic Community*, 145–55; Vilozny, *Constructing a World View*, 69–72, 125–6.

100 Amir-Moezzi, *Divine Guide*, 34; see also Amir-Moezzi, 'Cosmogony'. This first covenant God made not only with the believers (*muʾminūn*), but also with various spiritual beings such as angels, and with the prophets. Amir-Moezzi calls these entities 'the Pure Beings' (*Divine Guide*, 34).

> all of them to descend into the Fire, and so the People of the Right [*aṣḥāb al-yamīn*] entered, and it became cool and harmless for them, while the People of the Left [*aṣḥāb al-shimāl*] refused to enter.[101]

Here, the division of humankind between the true Believers who follow God's command (the People of the Right) and the unbelievers who disobey Him (the People of the Left) is made clear. Amir-Moezzi argues that according to the sources, the covenant mentioned in Qur. 7:172 includes all humankind, but that 'this oath covers only one point: the Unicity of the Creator'.[102] Thus, recognition of the unity of God (*islām*) is natural to all human beings. The true Believers, the People of the Right, are included in this covenant, but they have already taken the oath of *walāya* mentioned above, and will remain faithful to God, the Prophet and the imams. The People of the Left, on the other hand, have indeed declared their monotheism through the affirmation that God is their Lord – as expressed in the covenant verse – but since they have not promised *walāya* to the prophets and imams, they will inevitably fall into sin and will thus always be opposed to the true Believers.[103]

Amir-Moezzi further explains that the opposition between true Believers and non-believers is only a symptom of the conflict between cosmic good and evil powers that existed long before the creation of humankind. The first entities that were created, he writes, were the mutually opposed supreme intelligence (*ʿaql*) and ignorance (*jahl*), and their armies:[104]

> These, in turn, are symbols and archetypes of the Imam and his followers on the one side and of the Enemy of the Imam and his henchmen on the other. This primeval struggle has an echo in every age and in every historical cycle throughout all time.[105]

101 Al-Kulaynī, *Al-kāfī*, vol. II, 7, 'Kitāb al-īmān wa-l-kufr', Bāb 2, no 2. I have drawn on the translations of Dakake (*Charismatic Community*, 150) and Amir-Moezzi (*Divine Guide*, 36). Words in square brackets are added by me.

102 Amir-Moezzi, *Divine Guide*, 36. But cf. Dakake, *Charismatic Community*, 280, n. 32.

103 The notion of predestination inherent in this interpretation of the covenant was crucial in early Shiʿism, and is well-discussed by Dakake in *Charismatic Community*, 149–55. For similar Sunni views, see Jaffer, 'Covenant Theology', 107–11.

104 Amir-Moezzi, *Divine Guide*, 6–8, 36.

105 Amir-Moezzi and Jambet, *Shiʿi Islam*, 16.

Furthermore, Asatryan has demonstrated that already in the *ghulāt* texts from the second/eighth and third/ninth centuries, the battle at Karbala figures in connection with the esoteric cosmology reviewed above.[106]

I will return to the Imami Shiʿite idea of the cosmic struggle in Chapters 10 and 11. For now, it is enough to state that there are no indications that Abū Mikhnaf held the dualist ideas that are found in the Shiʿite sources referred to by Amir-Moezzi. This is not unexpected, of course, as he probably did not identify as a Shiʿite of the kind discussed by the latter – and maybe not as a Shiʿite at all. Perhaps more surprising is the total absence from the hadiths of references to the battle at Karbala which mention what Abū Mikhnaf describes as al-Ḥusayn's and his followers' adherence to the divine covenant and its violation by the enemy. One might have expected the importance of the cosmic battle and the notion of the divine covenant in early Shiʿism, in the context of the interpretation of the Karbala drama as 'the most tragic illustration of Shiʿism's dualistic vision',[107] to call for the use of Abū Mikhnaf's covenantal perspective on this event.

Again, we must remember that Abū Mikhnaf was probably not an Imami Shiʿite, and that it is unlikely that he shared the dualist world-view expressed in the early Imami sources. In his version of the Karbala story, the Muslim community is not pictured as divided in a cosmic conflict ordained throughout eternity. For him, the Muslims belonged together and should be united in faith and under one leader – although he probably thought that the Umayyad dynasty did not provide the leadership that was needed. An example of Abū Mikhnaf's wish to emphasise the unity of the Muslims is the common prayer on the occasion when al-Ḥusayn and his followers have just been intercepted by al-Ḥurr and his troop. The time for noon prayer is coming, and al-Ḥusayn prepares to pray. When he comes out of his tent, he delivers his first speech (see above), but receives no reaction from the Kufans. Abū Mikhnaf continues: 'al-Ḥusayn asked al-Ḥurr b. Yazīd whether he wanted to lead his followers in the prayer. He replied, "No, but you pray and we will pray with you leading the prayer."' After the common prayer, the two groups split up again and resume their former positions.[108]

[106] Asatryan, *Controversies*, 28–34.
[107] Amir-Moezzi and Jambet, *Shiʿi Islam*, 25.
[108] Al-Ṭabarī, *Taʾrīkh*, II, 298.

The tragedy of Karbala, according to Abū Mikhnaf, is that in this battle Muslims turned against Muslims, and, even more, that Muslims turned against the offspring of the Prophet Muḥammad and killed them. This is well-expressed in the words of al-Ḥusayn's companion Zuhayr b. al-Qayn in his address to the Kufans quoted above:

> we are still brothers in one religion and one faith as long as the sword does not strike between you and us ... When the sword strikes, the protection will be cut asunder. We will be a community, and you will be a community. God has tested us and you through the offspring of His prophet Muḥammad so that He might see what we and you are doing.[109]

A similar attitude can be seen in al-Ḥusayn's refusal to begin the battle – he prefers to wait for the enemy to open hostilities, even though it means less martial advantage for him and his companions.[110] In contrast to this, Abū Mikhnaf pictures the enemies as initiating the fight when he has the evil Shamir b. Dhī al-Jawshan incite the governor of Kufa and enemy army commander, ʿUmar b. Saʿd, to attack,[111] and makes ʿUmar shoot an arrow towards al-Ḥusayn's camp and say, 'Be witnesses that I was the first to shoot.'[112]

Passages such as these are far from the exclusivism found in Imami Shiʿite sources, and this might explain why later Shiʿite renderings of the Karbala story, while based on Abū Mikhnaf's version and making ample use of the details and imagery of his text, ignore his covenantal framework. Thus, if the early date of the esoteric Shiʿite ideas is accepted in accordance with the argument of the scholars mentioned above, we are able to compare two more or less contemporary views of the divine covenant with humanity that are nevertheless very different. This might also explain why al-Ṭabarī, whose interest in a more traditional view of the covenant Ulrika Mårtensson has forcefully argued,[113] has preserved Abū Mikhnaf's *Kitāb maqtal al-Ḥusayn* more or less unabridged, as far as we can tell.

109 Al-Ṭabarī, *Ta'rīkh*, II, 331.
110 Al-Ṭabarī, *Ta'rīkh*, II, 307–8.
111 Al-Ṭabarī, *Ta'rīkh*, II, 315–17.
112 Al-Ṭabarī, *Ta'rīkh*, II, 335.
113 Mårtensson, 'True New Testament'; *Tabari*; 'Ibn Isḥāq'.

According to Abū Mikhnaf, many people in Kufa felt that the killing of al-Ḥusayn at Karbala was very wrong, and regretted that they had not supported him at Karbala. It is to a group of these who wanted to do penitence for what they regarded as not only neglect of loyalty to the family of the Prophet, but also a sin against God, that we turn in Part II of the book.

PART II

REVENGE OR MARTYRDOM: THE STORY OF THE TAWWĀBŪN (THE 'PENITENTS')

5

Introducing the Story of the Tawwābūn

One of the earliest records of a reaction to the death of al-Ḥusayn at Karbala is the story of the Tawwābūn (the 'Penitents').[1] The story tells how some of the elders who had invited al-Ḥusayn to Kufa but failed to support him felt deep regret for their failure to come to the aid of the grandson of the Prophet. Soon after his death, they gathered, chose Sulaymān b. Ṣurad as their leader, and discussed how best to undertake penance (*tawba*) for this crime. In their deliberations over their sin, they likened what they had done to the Israelites' idolatrous worship of the Golden Calf. In that situation, Moses had commanded the children of Israel to execute all those among them who had taken part in the idolatry.[2] The Penitents therefore considered committing collective suicide, following this example. But since Muslims are not permitted to kill themselves, they decided against having recourse to this drastic measure and instead decided to take up arms and rise up against the Umayyad army, to kill those who had killed al-Ḥusayn or be killed themselves in the attempt to avenge him. The Penitents were well aware that this would probably lead to their own deaths, but they regarded their action as an act of martyrdom in the cause of loyalty to the Prophet and his offspring, hoping that it would cleanse them of their guilt. A few years later, in Rabīʿ II 65/November 684, they set out. Gathering at al-Nukhayla outside Kufa, they realised that the numbers of those joining their ranks were far below what they had expected. Furthermore, the Shiʿites from Basra and al-Madāʾin who had promised to

[1] The chapters in Part II draw heavily on two of my previously published studies (Hylén, 'Date'; 'Myth'). The analysis of the story that I make here is developed further, and as I have continued studying the text, I have reconsidered some of the conclusions from the previous analyses. Thus, some results presented in these chapters partly differ from those given in the articles.

[2] Qur. 2:54, cf. Ex. 32: 25–9. For a brief discussion of this verse from the Qurʾan, see Chapter 6.

support them had not shown up. In spite of this, they decided to set out. On their way to the battlefield, they stopped at al-Ḥusayn's tomb, dedicating themselves to prayer for his soul and remorseful weeping over their own sin. They continued on their way, eventually met the Umayyads in battle at ʿAyn al-Warda in northern Iraq, and were defeated. Some of the few survivors felt great shame that they had not been killed in the campaign.[3]

As far as I have been able to detect, the only independent account of the uprising of the Tawwābūn available to us is transmitted by Abū Mikhnaf; all other versions are dependent on his 'book', *Kitāb Sulaymān b. Ṣurad wa-ʿAyn al-Warda*.[4] Abū Mikhnaf's original text is lost to us but, as with the Karbala story, it seems to have been reproduced in its entirety by Hishām b. al-Kalbī (d. 204/819); Ibn al-Kalbī's version in its turn is transmitted by al-Ṭabarī (d. 310/923). Other Muslim historians, such as al-Balādhurī (d. 279/892), al-Masʿūdī (d. 345/956) and Ibn Aʿtham al-Kūfī (d. probably at the turn of the fourth/tenth century), have also given versions of the story.[5] Like that of al-Ṭabarī, their accounts are based on Abū Mikhnaf, but they show traces of heavy editing and are abbreviated. The only other source for the Tawwābūn movement that may be independent of Abū Mikhnaf's account is a long poem by the Kufan poet Aʿshā Hamdān (d. 82 or 83/701 or 702).[6] The poem is an elegy over the Tawwābūn, describing their longing to repent, their journey to ʿAyn al-Warda and their brave but futile stand against the Umayyads. If genuine, the poem certainly corroborates the narrative of Abū Mikhnaf. The problem is that it is only extant in al-Ṭabarī's rendering of the story, where it is appended to Abū Mikhnaf's account. It has been included in a couple of modern collections of Aʿshā's poems, and to my knowledge no one has

[3] The full text is given in al-Ṭabarī, *Taʾrīkh*, II, 497–513, 538–78. For more comprehensive summaries in translation, see Wellhausen, *Religio-Political Factions*, 121–4; Calmard, 'Culte', 66–9; Jafri, *Origins*, 222–34; Halm, *Shiʿa Islam*, 16–20; Denny, 'Tawwābūn'; Dakake, *Charismatic Community*, 90–5.

[4] Ibn al-Nadīm, *Fihrist*, vol. I, 93.

[5] Al-Balādhurī, *Ansāb*, vol. VI, 363–74; al-Masʿūdī, *Murūj*, vol. V, 213–21; Ibn Aʿtham al-Kūfī, *Futūḥ*, vol. VI, 47–53, 58–87. I accept Lindstedt's arguments for his approximate date of Ibn Aʿtham ('*Kitāb al-Dawla*', 118–23; 'Sources') against Conrad, who places it about a century earlier ('Ibn Aʿtham', 90–6). See now also McLaren, 'Dating', where Lindstedt's later dating is supported.

[6] Al-Ṭabarī, *Taʾrīkh*, II, 572–5. On Aʿshā Hamdān, see Seidensticker, 'Aʿshā Hamdān'.

doubted its authenticity,[7] but it is of course possible that it was created long after the death of Aʿshā on the basis of Abū Mikhnaf's account. I will return to this poem at the end of Chapter 8.

The present study uses al-Ṭabarī's rendering of Abū Mikhnaf's text as its main source, comparing it, when necessary, with the versions of al-Balādhurī and Ibn Aʿtham. The fact that ultimately there exists only one narrative source for the actions of the Tawwābūn is of course problematic for the historian. Of the three accounts of Kufan Shiʿite affairs studied in this book, the story of the Tawwābūn is the one with the least evidence for its historicity. The most probable reason it is not related by any other historian independently of Abū Mikhnaf is that in the turbulent years around the second *fitna* the movement was politically far too insignificant. It simply did not stir interest in the minds of most historians. That Abū Mikhnaf recorded this story is probably owing to the attention he devotes to his own family and tribe, al-Azd.[8] Sulaymān b. Ṣurad, the main leader of the Tawwābūn, came from the tribe of al-Khuzāʿa, which according to many traditions was a sub-tribe of al-Azd,[9] and one of the other initiators of the movement, ʿAbdallāh b. Saʿd b. Nufayl, was also an Azdī.[10] Another connection between Abū Mikhnaf and the Tawwābūn may be that, according to one account, his great-grandfather Mikhnaf b. Sulaymān al-Azdī, who had served under ʿAlī b. Abī Ṭālib at the battle of Ṣiffīn,[11] was one of the Tawwābūn killed at ʿAyn al-Warda.[12] As Borrut has demonstrated, however, there are several conflicting accounts of that death.[13] Be that as it may, Abū Mikhnaf's tribe, al-Azd, was amply represented among the Tawwābūn. But even if this was reason enough for Abū Mikhnaf to record the ventures of the group, we must be very careful about taking the story as an account of what 'really happened' – even more so than with the Karbala story itself, where several independent versions give a similar picture of the basic developments;

[7] Aʿshā Hamdān, *Dīwān*, 76–9 (poem no. 4); al-Aʿshā, *Gedichte*, 315–17. See also El-Achèche, *La poésie šiʿite*, 197–8, though I disagree with the opinion of this author that part of the poem is about al-Ḥusayn's death at Karbala.

[8] See the discussion about Abū Mikhnaf in Chapter 2.

[9] Kister, 'Khuzāʿa'; Webb, 'al-Azd'.

[10] Al-Ṭabarī, *Taʾrīkh*, II, 497.

[11] Al-Ṭabarī, *Taʾrīkh*, I, 3,303–4.

[12] Ibn Ḥajar al-ʿAsqalānī, *Tahdhīb*, vol. X, 78–9.

[13] Borrut, 'Remembering Karbalā'', 264, esp. n. 67.

the story of al-Mukhtār, as we shall see, is also attested by several independent sources. What we can glean from the story of the Tawwābūn is a glimpse of the trajectory of the early development of Shiʿism and of the role played by al-Ḥusayn's death in the emerging movement. This does not, of course, necessarily mean the story is entirely made up or false. My point is that, until the opposite is demonstrated, we do not know how much of this account is historical – when it comes to the details, at least.

It is the first half of the Tawwābūn story that is most interesting for the study of early Shiʿism. Ideological matters are to be found mainly in the speeches and letters of the first part and in the account of the visit to the grave, which is placed almost exactly in the middle of Abū Mikhnaf's 'book'. (The account of the dealings between Ibn al-Zubayr and the Kharijites, which breaks off the story of the Tawwābūn, must have been inserted by al-Ṭabarī in his annalistic work, as it deals with the year 64 AH; it was most likely not originally part of Abū Mikhnaf's work.[14]) Notably, even though al-Ḥusayn and his death at Karbala are almost omnipresent in the first half of the story, after the visit to the grave his name is never mentioned, not even once, and those few references made to him, to the supporters killed at Karbala and to the family of the Prophet are made only in passing.[15] Similarly, whereas words derived from the root *t-w-b* ('turning' or 'repentance') – one of the most important concepts of the story – occur at least twelve times in the first half of the text (a couple of times referring to God as the relenting one, the one who 'turns' from his anger), only four occurrences follow the visit to the grave.[16] In the first half of the text, the sin of treason against al-Ḥusayn is deliberated on and discussed; after the visit to the grave, the story becomes a common battle account, with many of the traditional topoi of such accounts.[17] Here, then, the ideological aspects of the Tawwābūn's mission are less frequent and are rendered in much more general terms.

[14] Al-Ṭabarī, *Ta'rīkh*, II, 513–37.
[15] Al-Ṭabarī, *Ta'rīkh*, II, 556, 558.
[16] Al-Ṭabarī, *Ta'rīkh*, II, 550, 555, 560, 567.
[17] For such topoi (e.g. how the armies are arranged and who are appointed as commanders of the different units, the succession of command, messages of victory sent to the caliph, etc.) see Noth and Conrad, *Early Arabic Historical Tradition*, 111–29.

Several scholars have claimed or presupposed, without really arguing for their position, that the story is much older than Abū Mikhnaf.[18] A problem when attempting to date the text is the dearth of independent versions to compare. Gerald Hawting does not explicitly state that the story is early in his article on the 'Āshūrā', but he seems to imply it when he writes that

> it could be maintained that it is only their preoccupation with the death of Ḥusayn, their identification of their 'great sin' with failure to support the grandson of the Prophet, which really places the Tawwābūn in a Muslim context. If one went through their speeches and letters and deleted the specific references to Ḥusayn and his family, what would be left would seem distinctly unusual in Islam.[19]

To me, this statement signals that Hawting believes the story of the Tawwābūn to be, indeed, very early. The reason he believes the story to be in many ways 'distinctly unusual in Islam', I infer, is that, at the early date when parts of it were composed, many tenets that were later considered as truly Islamic had not yet developed.[20]

In the following chapters, I will argue that a close analysis of the structure and content of parts of the text gives reason to believe that at least these parts go back to the end of the first/beginning of the seventh century, at the latest. Provided the story is indeed as early as I think, it gives a unique insight into some of the ideas and rituals of emerging Shi'ism. Two sections from the account of the Tawwābūn are particularly interesting in this regard for the ideational elements so evident within them: four 'programmatic' texts at the beginning of the story which I will discuss in Chapter 6, and the passage about the visit to al-Ḥusayn's grave in the middle of the story, to be analysed in Chapter 7. In Chapter 8, I will attempt to date the story and give some concluding reflections.

[18] Halm explicitly calls it an old text (*Shi'a Islam*, 18). See Hylén, 'Date', 176–84, for a more extended discussion of this matter.

[19] Hawting, 'Tawwābūn', 180.

[20] Hawting has confirmed this in a personal email to me, 19 January 2015. In support of Hawting's argument, see now Pregill, '"Turn in Repentance"', 142, n. 87.

6

Betrayal and Guilt in the Tawwābūn's Speeches and Letters

The Four Programmatic Texts

At the beginning of the story of the Tawwābūn, there are four texts – three speeches and one letter – which are programmatic in the sense that they lay out the emotions and thoughts of the group about their failure to support al-Ḥusayn and their ideas about what to do to atone for their sin. The first speech is ascribed to one of the leaders of the group, al-Musayyab b. Najaba, the second speech and the letter to its main leader, Sulaymān b. Ṣurad, and the final speech to the propagandist ʿUbaydallāh b. ʿAbdallāh al-Murrī.

Below, I reproduce what I regard as the most important parts of these four texts. The sections not quoted verbatim (mainly the introductions and/or the final parts) have been summarised.[1] To facilitate reference, each text has been assigned a roman number (I–IV), and the texts have been divided into sections. In order to distinguish the four programmatic texts from those about the visit to the grave (which will be analysed in the following chapter), I refer to them with a 'T'. Thus, for example, T.III.2 will refer to Text III, Section 2.

The Texts

The first two speeches, ascribed to al-Musayyab b. Najaba and Sulaymān b. Ṣurad respectively, are found in the same *khabar*. Its *isnād* is the following: Hishām b. Muḥammad [al-Kalbī] – Abū Mikhnaf – Yūsuf b. Yazīd – ʿAbdallāh

[1] I have followed Gerald Hawting's translation (al-Ṭabarī, *History*, vol. XX); when, in a few cases, I have made minor changes, I have noted this. Words within square brackets are added by me.

b. ʿAwf b. al-Aḥmar al-Azdī. Thus, there are two links in the chain of transmission between Abū Mikhnaf and the occasion described. All we know of Yūsuf b. Yazīd is that he was an authority frequently used by Abū Mikhnaf;[2] ʿAbdallāh b. ʿAwf was an accomplished poet.[3] The *khabar*, which is quite long,[4] relates how the group met in the house of Sulaymān b. Ṣurad, full of guilt and remorse over their failure to support al-Ḥusayn at Karbala. There, al-Musayyab and Sulaymān deliver their speeches.

Text I (Speech by al-Musayyab B. Najaba)

Al-Musayyab begins his talk by referring to the advanced age of all those assembled and the need to repent before life here on earth ends. He continues:

1. We were enamoured of self-justification and praising our party [*shīʿatinā*] until God put our best men to the test and found us sham on two of the battlefields of the son of our Prophet's daughter.[5]
2. Before that, we had received his letters and his messengers had come to us offering forgiveness, asking us to help him again in public and in private.
3. But we withheld ourselves from him until he was killed so near to us. We did not help him with our hands, argue on his behalf with our tongues, strengthen him with our wealth, or seek help for him from our clans.
4. What will be our excuse for our Lord and at the meeting with our Prophet when his descendant, his loved one, his offspring and his issue has been slain among us? No, by God, there is no excuse unless you kill his murderer and those who assisted him or unless you are killed while seeking that. Perhaps our Lord will be satisfied with us in that, for I have no security against His punishment after meeting Him.

Al-Musayyab finishes the speech by urging those assembled to elect a commander who can lead them in this act of vengeance.[6] The group chooses Sulaymān b. Ṣurad as their leader, and he delivers his speech.

[2] Sezgin, *Abū Miḫnaf*, 226.
[3] On him, see El-Achèche, *La poésie šiʿite*, 150–2.
[4] Al-Ṭabarī, *Taʾrīkh*, II, 497–501.
[5] One of the battlefields is, of course, Karbala. Which is meant by the other one is less certain. It could have been the insurrection of Ḥujr b. ʿAdī in 51/671, as Hawting suggests (al-Ṭabarī, *History*, vol. XX, 81, n. 374), or the raising of Muslim b. ʿAqīl, which is discussed in Chapter 3.
[6] Al-Ṭabarī, *Taʾrīkh*, II, 498–9.

Text II (Speech by Sulaymān b. Ṣurad)

Having praised God and confessed his faith in God and the Prophethood of Muḥammad, Sulaymān continues by lamenting that the times have sunk so low. Then he goes on:

1. What good is it for the most virtuous of this party [*hādihi al-shīʿa*] that we were yearning for the family of our Prophet [*āl nabiyyinā*] to come, offering them help and urging them to come,
2. but when they came we were weak and feeble and spineless, we delayed and waited to see what would happen, until the descendant of our Prophet, his offspring and his progeny, flesh of his flesh and blood of his blood, was killed in our very midst? He called for help but received none, he asked for justice but was not given any.
3. The impious ones made him a target for arrows and a butt for spears until they had broken him, assaulted him and stripped him.
4. Rise up indeed, for your Lord has been angered. Do not go back to your wives and children until God has been satisfied! By God, I do not think He will be satisfied unless you fight against those who killed him or perish. Do not fear death! By God, no man ever feared it without debasing himself.
5. Be like those Israelites when their prophet said to them, 'You have done evil to yourselves by your adoption of the Calf. Turn in repentance [*tūbū*] to your Creator and kill yourselves. That will be best for you with your Creator.'[7] And do what the people did. They fell on their knees and stretched out their necks and accepted the judgment, until they understood that nothing would save them from the magnitude of their offence except patient acceptance and slaughter.
6. How will it be with you, if you are summoned to something similar? Make sharp the swords, assemble the lances, 'and get ready against them what strength you can. Prepare for war'[8] so you can be assembled when you are summoned to fight.[9]

[7] Qur. 2:54.
[8] Qur. 8:60. Hawting has not indicated this passage as Qur'anic.
[9] Al-Ṭabarī, *Ta'rīkh*, II, 500–1.

Later, Sulaymān writes a letter to the Shiʿites of al-Madāʾin and Basra. The letter is recounted to Abū Mikhnaf by a certain al-Ḥuṣayn b. Yazīd b. ʿAbdallāh b. Saʿd b. Nufayl. Nothing is known of this man except that his grandfather, ʿAbdallāh b. Saʿd b. Nufayl, was purportedly one of the five leaders of the Tawwābūn and was killed at ʿAyn al-Warda as the deputy of Sulaymān b. Ṣurad.[10] Al-Ḥuṣayn b. Yazīd is the only authority in the *isnād* of the letter, and he states that he first read it at the time when Sulaymān (b. ʿAbd al-Azīz) was caliph, that is, 96–9/715–17.

Text III (Letter from Sulaymān b. Ṣurad)

After the traditional greetings, Sulaymān regrets the present state of the world, and states that 'the best servants of God' have decided to leave this world for the glories of the coming one. He continues:

1. The friends of God among your brethren and the party of your Prophet's family [*shīʿat āl nabiyyikum*] have reflected upon the way they were put to the test in the matter of the son of their Prophet's daughter.[11]
2. He responded when he was invited but received no answer when he called, wanted to go back but was detained, asked for safe conduct but was denied it.
3. He refrained from attacking the people although they did not refrain from him, but attacked and killed him, then plundered and stripped him wrongfully and in enmity, heedless and ignorant of God. What they did offended God and they will not return to Him. 'Those who commit evil will know the reversal which they will endure.'[12]
4. When your brethren considered and thought about the end to which they were coming, they saw they had sinned greatly in betraying the pure and good one, in delivering him up and refraining from aiding and helping him.
5. They saw there was no release for them and no repentance [*tawba*] apart from killing his murderers or killing themselves so that their spirits would be consumed in it. Your brethren have thought seriously, and you should too and prepare.

[10] Al-Ṭabarī, *Taʾrīkh*, II, 497, 556, 562. See also Sezgin, *Abū Miḫnaf*, 207–8.
[11] ... *ibn bint nabiyyihim*; Hawting has translated this 'their Prophet's grandson'.
[12] Qur. 26:227.

In the second half of the letter, Sulaymān sets a place and a time for the people of al-Madā'in and Basra to meet with the Kufans. He then exhorts the recipients to join them in the struggle and to be prepared to meet death in repenting of their sins.[13]

While it is of course impossible to determine whether even parts of this letter were actually written by Sulaymān, certain features in the second half of the rather long letter indicate that this part is a later addition to an earlier original. I will return to this question below.

Text IV (Speech by ʿUbaydallāh b. ʿAbdallāh al-Murrī)

The final speech is related by al-Ḥuṣayn b. Yazīd (that is, the same authority as for the previous text), on the authority of 'a man of Muzayna'. Of course, we cannot know who the latter was or what his credentials were as a source.[14] The speech is presented as a call to the Kufans to join the Tawwābūn, given by the propagandist (*al-dāʿī*) ʿUbaydallāh b. ʿAbdallāh al-Murrī, who is otherwise unknown to us.

ʿUbaydallāh begins his speech by recapitulating the position of the Prophet Muḥammad as God's elected, who has guided the community from destruction to God. He then continues:

1. Has God created among the first and the last anyone with a greater right to authority over this community than its Prophet? And have the descendants of any one of the prophets and messengers or anyone else a greater right to rule over this community than those of its Messenger? No, by God, there has not been and there will not be.
2. You belong to God. Have you not seen and have you not heard what evil was done to the son of your Prophet's daughter? Did you not regard how the people violated his sanctity [*ḥurma*], considered as weakness his solitariness, splattered him with blood, and pulled him down to the ground? In it they did not respect their Lord or al-Ḥusayn's kinship with the Prophet. They made him a target for arrows and left him a slaughter for the hyenas.
3. Blessed are the eyes of him who has seen the like of him, and blessed is Ḥusayn the son of ʿAlī. What a man was he they betrayed! He was true and patient,

[13] Al-Ṭabarī, *Taʾrīkh*, II, 502–4.
[14] Al-Ṭabarī, *Taʾrīkh*, II, 507.

trustworthy, helpful and resolute; he was the son of the first of the Muslims in Islam and the son of the daughter of the Messenger of the Lord of the Worlds.

4. His defenders were few while his foes flocked around him, and his enemy killed him while his friend betrayed him. Woe to the killer and shame on the traitor!
5. God will accept no plea from his killer and no excuse from his betrayer unless he sincerely turns to God in repentance [*tawba*], struggles against the murderers, and opposes the unrighteous. Perhaps on those conditions God will accept the repentance [*tawba*] and disregard the offence.
6. We call you to the Book of God, the Sunna of His Prophet, the seeking of vengeance for the blood of his family [*ahl baytihi*], and the struggle against the violators of God's law and renegades. If we are killed, that which God has prepared for us with Him is better for the God-fearing; if we are victorious, then we will restore this authority to the family of our Prophet [*ahl bayt nabiyyinā*]![15]

Formal Analysis

When these texts are placed side by side, it is evident that the first three texts, excepting the second half of Text III (the letter from Sulaymān, which will be discussed below), are similar in both structure and content. The following elements are included in all three texts, in roughly the same order:

a. The Tawwābūn begin by speaking of their advanced age and the prospect of departing this life. This leads to the considerations expressed in (f) and (g) below.
b. The speaker speaks of his group as the *shīʿa*, the 'party' (T.I.1; T.II.1; T.III.1).
c. Al-Ḥusayn is spoken of as the offspring or grandson of the Prophet (T.I.1, 4; T.II.2; T.III.1).
d. Al-Ḥusayn had been invited to Kufa by the Shiʿites and/or asked for their support (T.I.2; T.II.1; T.III.2).
e. But the Shiʿites did not help or support him, and he was killed (T.I.3; T.II.2, 3; T.III.2).

[15] Al-Ṭabarī, *Taʾrīkh*, II, 507–8.

f. God has been offended; the Shiʿites have committed a sin (T.I.4 [implied]; T.II.4; T.III.4).
g. The only way to show true repentance is to seek revenge for al-Ḥusayn's death, or to die in the attempt (T.I.4; T.II.4–6; T.III.5).

These similarities indicate that the first three speeches may go back to an earlier, probably oral tradition. Although we can hardly regard them as 'replays of tape recordings'[16] of what al-Musayyab and Sulaymān said and wrote, they could well be a rendering of an early tradition about the Tawwābūn relating the main ideas of the group. However, as indicated above, I doubt that the second half of Sulaymān's letter (Text III), which I have not rendered in full here, is part of the original text. There are three reasons for this.

To begin with, the first half of the letter is self-contained. After T.III.5, a date and a place for the mustering of the forces are set. (Whether these sentences belong to the original first half or the attached second part is unclear; see the discussion below.) What comes next is a general call to repentance through *jihād*. This is redundant, given the first half of the letter.

Furthermore, the content of the second half of the letter differs from that of the three documents quoted above. The motif of revenge for the death of al-Ḥusayn is totally absent; in fact, he is never mentioned, and the only time the family of the Prophet is brought up is in a general exhortation to fight against their enemies. Those addressed in the letter are several times exhorted to repent, but the nature of the sin is not discussed. This is indeed the section in the story of the Tawwābūn where derivatives of the root *t-w-b* ('turning' or 'repentance') are most frequent, with four of a total eighteen or so occurrences in the story occurring in these lines.[17] The writer of this part of the letter refers to those previously killed as martyrs and as exemplars of how one should behave when tested by God (a later narrator has added a gloss that this refers to Ḥujr b. ʿAdī and his followers). A similar pattern for imitation, alluding to the story of the Children of Israel and their acceptance of judgement after the incident of the Golden Calf, is already given in Sulaymān's

[16] This expression is taken from John P. Meier, who often uses it in a similar way in his books about the historical Jesus; see e.g. *A Marginal Jew*, vol. IV, 42, 521.

[17] I have not included the name of the group in this number.

speech in T.II.5. There, however, rather than martyrdom, the Israelites are described as humbly accepting God's punishment for the sin they committed. Furthermore, the interpretation offered of the Golden Calf incident in T.II.5 is very unusual, and also quite unorthodox,[18] as implied in the words ascribed to Khālid b. Saʿd that directly follow Text II, where he says that killing oneself 'is something which was ordered to a people who were before us while we have been prohibited from it'.[19] In my view, the insertion of such a strange interpretation of the Golden Calf incident at a later stage is unlikely, and I therefore agree with Gerald Hawting in regarding T.II.5 as very early. I am, however, inclined to think that someone has attached the second half of Text III to emphasise the motif of repentance. The editor has been following the pattern of T.II.5, but, unwilling to take such an unorthodox interpretation of the Qur'anic text, has taken a more acceptable example as a model for imitation.

Finally, the two halves of the letter use different words for 'family' in the expression 'the family of the Prophet'. Whereas in the first half of the letter (T.III.1) – and the second speech (T.II.1) – the word *āl* is used for 'family', in the second half of the letter the word used is *ahl*. Although the words are used more or less synonymously in classical Arabic, I find it difficult to believe that the same author should consistently have used one word in the first half of the text, then another in the second.[20]

Each of these arguments for the second half of the letter being a later appendage would hardly suffice in its own right, but the cumulative evidence indicates a process in which a later addition was attached to the original text. It is difficult to say exactly where to draw the line between the original and the addition. If, as I think most likely, the original document as we have it is not the words of Sulaymān himself but a rendering of the ideas of the Tawwābūn as they were remembered by those who came after

[18] See Hawting, 'Tawwābūn', 171. See Pregill, '"Turn in Repentance"', 138 n. 75, for another 'unique' instance of this interpretation. Pregill's article is an excellent study of early interpretations of Qur. 2:54.

[19] Al-Ṭabarī, *Ta'rīkh*, II, 501.

[20] For the meanings of these words, see Lane, *Arabic–English Lexicon*, vol. I, 121, 127. The Arab lexicographers do not agree on whether *āl* originates from *ahl* where the *h* is elided, or whether it was an original *a-w-l* with an elided *w* (Lane, *Arabic–English Lexicon*, vol. I, 127 b). See also Amir-Moezzi, *Spirituality*, 19 n. 37.

them, the place and time of the meeting could have been part of the original; by the time of writing, the place and time of the meeting and the group's departure would have been generally known. Still, such concrete details strike a discordant note with the other texts, and it is perhaps more probable that these were part of the subsequent appendage. Be that as it may, my main hypothesis, to which I adhere in what follows, is that the second half of the letter (with or without the time and place for meeting) is a later addition.

The final speech (Text IV) is also at variance with the first three texts. A couple of the elements listed from Texts I–III are missing. Thus, the introduction does not mention the impending encounter with God after death, and the term '*shīʿa*' is not used anywhere in the text to designate the group. Furthermore, several elements not found in the previous texts are present in Text IV. The introduction (T.IV.1) brings up the merits of the Prophet Muḥammad and his descendants' right to authority, rather than the brevity of this earthly life, and the text ends with a promise to restore authority to the family of the Prophet (T.IV.6). In addition, al-Ḥusayn is described not only as the grandson of the Prophet as in the texts examined above, but also as the son of ʿAlī, 'the first of the Muslims in Islam' (T.IV.2–3).[21] This is, moreover, the only time in these four texts that al-Ḥusayn's name is spelt out. Furthermore, the structural differences between Texts I–III on the one hand and Text IV on the other are striking. The content is arranged in a different manner, so that, while Texts I–III have more of a chronological outline of the material, Text IV revolves around al-Ḥusayn's position and character and the wickedness of his adversaries. Although this is not the place for a full structural analysis of Text IV, it is clear that that text is well-structured and that it features several literary and rhetorical devices. We have already seen that the theme of the authority of the descendants of the Prophet forms an *inclusio* which frames the speech. The text also contains other rhetorical tools, such as antithetical parallelisms and

[21] ... *ibn awwali al-muslimīna islāman*. Perhaps this phrase should rather be translated 'the son of the first of those who submitted among the submitters'. The question of how one should translate the words *muslim* and *islām* depends to a large extent on what position one takes regarding the question of when they began to be used as designations for a certain religious group and its adherents. For a date of this shift in use at the end of the first Muslim century (and also for the date I regard as the *terminus ante quem* for the origin of much of the story of the Tawwābūn), see Donner, *Muhammad and the Believers*.

chiastic structures.[22] The obvious conclusion of these arguments is that Text IV has an ultimate origin that differs from that of Texts I–III.

In summary, then, my analysis suggests that Texts I, II and the first half of Text III are based on early traditions about the Tawwābūn, but that the second half of Text III has a different origin and is probably a later addition. Text IV also has a source which differs from that/those of Texts I–III, though it is difficult to say whether or not this is later.

Content

The discussion above has touched on the content of the four programmatic texts. In what follows I will develop this subject a little more. Three themes are prominent in the texts: the image of al-Ḥusayn; the Karbala tragedy and the treachery of the Tawwābūn; and the dire consequences for the traitors and the need to repent.

The Image of al-Ḥusayn

All the texts emphasise that al-Ḥusayn is the progeny of the Prophet. He is 'the son of our/their Prophet's daughter' (T.I.1; T.III.1; T.IV.2, 3). In one passage he is described as 'the descendant of our Prophet, his offspring and his progeny, flesh of his flesh and blood of his blood [*walad nabiyyinā wa-sulālatuhu wa-ʿuṣāratuhu wa-baḍʿatun min laḥmihi wa-damihi*]' (T.II.2); similar terms occur in other texts as well (T.I.4; T.IV.2). Thus, all the texts trace his relationship with the Prophet through Fāṭima. In Text IV, however, al-Ḥusayn's kinship to ʿAlī is highlighted, along with his blood relation to the Prophet through Fāṭima (T.IV.3). Texts III and IV, furthermore, dwell on the character of al-Ḥusayn: thus in T.III.4 he is said to be 'the pure and good one [*al-zakiyyu al-ṭayyibu*]', and in T.IV.3 he is described as 'true and patient, trustworthy, helpful and resolute [*dhā ṣidq wa-ṣabr wa-dhā amāna wa-najda wa-ḥazm*]'.

The Karbala Tragedy and the Treachery of the Tawwābūn

There is nothing like a full description of the events before and during the battle of Karbala: these things are only alluded to. Everybody of course understands

[22] Although similar techniques are found in the previous texts as well (e.g. the parallelism in the last sentence of T.II.2), they are not at all as frequent and prominent as in Text IV.

what is referred to. The event is so well-known that it is unnecessary to relate it in these texts, and the emphasis is rather on the interpretation of what happened. Thus, the events themselves are outlined only very briefly in Texts I–III:

a. The first contacts between the Shiʿites of Kufa and al-Ḥusayn (the exchange of letters, the invitation to al-Ḥusayn).
b. The coming of al-Ḥusayn.
c. His plea for help and support from the Shiʿites and their failure to respond.
d. The attack on him and his killing by the evil-doers.

What is particularly interesting is that the sequence of the events is not only the same in all three texts, but corresponds to the accounts of the Karbala tragedy related in the three versions analysed in Chapter 3. As I will argue in Chapter 8, the story of the Tawwābūn (or at least the sections analysed in this and the following chapters) is probably earlier than those versions. In other words, a standardised account of the tragedy – probably in agreement with the historical order of events – began to emerge soon after its occurrence.

In Text IV, only the treachery (c) and the killing (d) are mentioned.

The Dire Consequences for the Traitors, the Need to Repent and the Manner of Repentance

This is perhaps the most conspicuous theme in these texts. It distinguishes the ideology of the Tawwābūn from that of other Shiʿites, and it is found in all four texts (T.I.4, T.II.4–6; T.III.4–5; T.IV.4–6). The Tawwābūn regard their betrayal of al-Ḥusayn as a mortal sin against God. It must be atoned for by avenging his death or by dying in the attempt. If – as I will argue in Chapter 8 – the parts of the story that I analyse here originate in the late first/early eighth century, then the call for repentance or penitence, *tawba*, is indeed one of the earliest instances of this theme preserved for us in Islamic literature outside of the Qur'an. In early Sufism it occurs frequently, but the literature that preserves the deliberations over what is to be done is several decades later.[23]

[23] For this concept in the Qur'an, see Denny, 'Qur'ānic Vocabulary of Repentance', and, more recently, Reynolds and Moghadam, 'Repentance', 382–5. For its use in early Sufism, see Böwering, 'Early Sufism'.

The root *t-w-b* and its derivatives can literally be translated 'to turn'. In the Qur'an, this verb is used both with human actors and with God as subjects: the two are interdependent.[24] Thus Qur. 5:39 says, 'Whoever turns [in repentance] [*man tāba*] after his evildoing and sets [things] right – surely God will turn to him [*fa-inna allāhu yatūbu 'alayhi*]', and Qur. 9:118, 'He [God] turned to them [in forgiveness] so that they might [also] turn [in repentance] [*tāba 'alayhim li-yatūbū*]'. In the story of the Tawwābūn, both these uses of the root *t-w-b* appear, but with a heavy preponderance on the side of human repentance and turning to God; of the eighteen occurrences of the root that I have found, only two refer to God's turning or relenting towards humankind.[25] So the emphasis in the story is clearly on the need for the Shiʿites to repent of their sin in betraying al-Ḥusayn. As the texts quoted above demonstrate, the Tawwābūn believe that the only way for them to show sincere repentance for this offence is to be prepared to die to atone for their sin.[26] An important example of this idea is the unusual interpretation in T.II.5 of Qur. 2:54. The full verse goes:

> And when Moses said to his people, 'My people! Surely you have done yourselves evil by taking the calf. So turn [*tūbū*] to your Creator (in repentance), and kill yourselves.[27] That will be better for you in the sight of the Creator.' He turned to you (in forgiveness) [*tāba*]. Surely He – He is the One who turns (in forgiveness) [*al-tawwāb*], the compassionate.

Sulaymān quotes only the first part of the verse. Hawting argues that in the Tawwābūn's interpretation of this verse we find the link between the Jewish celebration of the Day of Atonement and the Shiʿite 'Āshūrā' festival. The common denominator, according to Hawting, is the yearning for atonement,

[24] Denny, 'Qur'ānic Vocabulary of Repentance', 655; Reynolds and Moghadam, 'Repentance', 382–5.

[25] Both these occurrences are found in Qur. 2:128, which is quoted in the account of the visit to the grave. See Chapter 7.

[26] On the discussion about the need for an outward expression of an inner repentance, see van Ess, *Theologie*, vol. IV, 579–90, esp. 586. Although van Ess mentions the Tawwābūn on p. 586, most of his discussion relates to later developments in Islamic theology.

[27] Droge has translated the words *uqtulū anfusakum* 'kill one another'. This is probably more in line with the original intention of the text in the Qur'an. Here I have followed Hawting's more literal translation (al-Ṭabarī, *History*, vol. XX, 83; Hawting, 'Tawwābūn') as this seems to be how these words were understood by the Tawwābūn. See also n. 67 in Droge's translation of this verse.

something which the Tawwābūn thought could only be reached by sacrificing their own lives in the attempt to exact revenge for the killing of al-Ḥusayn. However, there is nothing in the story that indicates a commemorative ritual foreshadowing the ʿĀshūrāʾ, as we will see in the following chapters.

It was the hope of the Tawwābūn that if they turned to God in repentance, sacrificing their own lives, God would likewise turn to them in forgiveness. Although this second meaning of the root *t-w-b* is unusual in the story, this reciprocity is clearly implied throughout. The Tawwābūn hoped and prayed that God would forgive and 'turn' to them if they sincerely repented. This is also understood by the citation from Qur. 2:54. As we have seen above, God's 'turning' to his human subjects in forgiveness comes in the second part of the verse (which Sulaymān does not quote) as a corollary to human repentance. Although God's *tawba* towards the human being is only implied in Sulaymān's speech, in the narrative of the story, that hope is expressed explicitly many times.

After the battle against the Umayyad army at ʿAyn al-Warda, where most of the Tawwābūn were killed, ʿAbdallāh b. Ghaziyya, one of the survivors, reportedly says of those who had died in the battle: 'May God have mercy on you! You have been true and borne your suffering patiently. We have been false and fled.'[28] Thus it seems that the survivors believed they had failed to secure God's forgiveness.

Summary

In this chapter I have examined four texts which, I argue, are capable of revealing deeply significant ideas and motives of the Tawwābūn. The analysis has demonstrated that the similarities in structure and content of Texts I and II and the first half of Text III strongly suggest that these have a common origin, while the second half of Text III is probably a later addition, and Text IV has a different origin of undetermined date. Three themes figure prominently in these texts. First, the lineage of al-Ḥusayn is highlighted. All four texts describe him as the grandson of the Prophet Muḥammad through the latter's daughter Fāṭima; in Text IV, his father ʿAlī is also mentioned. Furthermore, Texts III and IV draw attention to his blameless character. The second theme is the

[28] Al-Ṭabarī, *Taʾrīkh*, II, 570.

tragedy at Karbala. Although these texts give no full account of what occurred there, the order of events mentioned in Texts I–III is the same as in the complete versions, which are probably later. Finally, the Tawwābūn express their deep sense of guilt for failing to support al-Ḥusayn at Karbala. In betraying the grandson of the Prophet, they have committed a major sin; they will be punished by God unless they can atone for it by avenging al-Ḥusayn or be killed in the attempt.

In the next two chapters I will analyse the account of the visit to the grave of al-Ḥusayn, arguing for an early date for the traditions that form the basis for that section. In Chapter 8, I will also compare the analysis with that given in the present chapter, and will argue that Texts I–III discussed above have a similar date of origin.

7

The Visit to al-Ḥusayn's Grave

The previous chapter argued that the profound sense of guilt felt by the Tawwābūn, as expressed in the four programmatic texts that introduce their story, caused them to take up armed resistance against the Umayyads with the aim of avenging the death of al-Ḥusayn or dying as martyrs in the attempt. They longed, in other words, to make their sincere repentance manifest, and they were prepared to sacrifice their lives to do so. The story tells how, on the way to the battlefield, the Tawwābūn stopped at al-Ḥusayn's grave, and the description of this visit at the grave, the subject of the analysis in this chapter, displays features that foreshadow aspects of the later trajectory of Shiʿism. The visit to the grave therefore merits deeper analysis in its own right. This is made possible by the fact that this passage, alone in the entire Tawwābūn story, is presented in more than one version. The visit to the grave is related through three *khabar*s whose slight differences aid comparative analysis. A close examination of these three texts reveals features of the redactional history that are important because through them it is possible to distinguish layers of the text that have originated at different times.

In this chapter, I will argue that the three *khabar*s derive from two earlier reports which have been adapted and supplemented with extra material. Within the *khabar*s, various alterations and additions are often separated by the word '*qāla*', 'he said'.[1] This word is problematic as a delimiter, however, since it is used in several ways in early Islamic historiography in general and in this account in particular. Sometimes 'he' (the pronoun is implied in the verb) refers to the earliest authority in the previous *isnād*, and thus the word simply functions as an introduction to a new section of the text; at other times, it

[1] Hawting has not indicated these *qāla* instances in his translation.

indicates that Abū Mikhnaf or Hishām b. al-Kalbī have summarised the text that follows.[2] In the present context it is quite clear that '*qāla*' is mostly used to indicate a seam between two earlier reports that have been juxtaposed in the *khabar*. As we do not know who placed the traditions side by side, or at what stage in the redactional history this was done (though it probably preceded Abū Mikhnaf's compilation), it is impossible to know to whom the pronoun 'he' refers. Furthermore, as we will see, in at least one instance, a '*qāla*' is missing where one might have been expected. This suggests that the editors were applying it quite arbitrarily, and that it must therefore be used with care as a tool in the analysis of the text.

The Text

In the following, the account of the visit to the grave is given in full, the three *khabars* being given with their chains of authorities. To facilitate reference, each *khabar* has been assigned a roman number (I–III) and has been divided into sections with Arabic numbers. Each section except the first begins where there is a *qāla* in the text. To distinguish these texts about the visit to the grave from the programmatic texts discussed in Chapter 5, I will refer to them with a '*K*'. Thus, for example, *K*.III.2 refers to *Khabar* III, Section 2.[3] Bold text signifies the oldest layer, as will be clear from the analysis below.

Khabar I

'Abd al-Jabbār b. 'Abbās al-Hamdānī[4] – 'Awn b. Abī Juḥayfa al-Suwā'ī:[5]

1. Next morning they came [*ṣabbaḥū*] to the tomb of al-Ḥusayn. **There they remained for a night and a day praying over him and asking God's pardon for him.**

[2] Sezgin, *Abū Miḫnaf*, 91–2; see also Fishbein's note in al-Ṭabarī, *History*, vol. XXI, 6, n. 31.

[3] As in the previous chapter, I have used Hawting's translation throughout (al-Ṭabarī, *History*, vol. XX), though I have at times slightly amended it. At times I compare it with Fishbein's translation ('Life of al-Mukhtār', 153–7), which is close to Hawting's, but differs on certain important points. I have normally not included transcriptions of Arabic terms that Hawting has inserted within square brackets in his translation. On the other hand, I have added transcriptions of words and phrases within brackets where this is important for the analysis that follows.

[4] Died probably between 140/757 and 150/767, according to Sezgin, *Abū Miḫnaf*, 190, but she gives no source for this, and I have not been able to confirm this information.

[5] Died 116/734, according to Ibn Ḥajar al-'Asqalānī, *Tahdhīb*, vol. VIII, 170.

2. *Qāla*: **When the people reached the tomb of al-Ḥusayn, they shouted with one voice and wept.** Never was a day seen when there was more weeping.

Khabar II

ʿAbd al-Raḥmān b. Jundab[6] – ʿAbd al-Raḥmān b. Ghaziyya:[7]

1. *Qāla*: **When we reached the tomb of al-Ḥusayn (Peace be upon him) the people wept together, and I heard most of the people expressing the wish that they had fallen with him.** Sulaymān said: 'Oh God, have mercy on al-Ḥusayn, the martyr [*al-shahīd*] son of the martyr, the right-guided one [*al-mahdī*] son of the right-guided one, the righteous one [*al-ṣiddīq*] son of the righteous one. Oh God, we call you to witness[8] that we follow their religion and their path, and we are enemies [*aʿdāʾ*] of those who killed them, and friends [*awliyāʾ*] of those who love them.' Then he went away, and he and his companions encamped.

Khabar III

Al-Aʿmash (Sulaymān b. Mihrān al-Asadī)[9] – Salama b. Kuhayl[10] – Abū Ṣādiq:[11]

1. *Qāla*: **When Sulaymān b. Ṣurad and his companions reached the tomb of al-Ḥusayn, they cried in unison, 'Oh Lord, we have betrayed the son of our Prophet's daughter! Pardon us for what we did in the past "and**

[6] He is only referred to as *rāwī* by Abū Mikhnaf (al-Ṭabarī, *History*, vol. XIX, 22, n. 98). The date of his death seems to be unknown. On him, see Sezgin, *Abū Miḫnaf*, 195–6.

[7] This might be the same person as ʿAbdallāh b. Ghaziyya, who is reported as taking part in the movement and surviving the battle, and who transmits reports later in the story (al-Ṭabarī, *History*, vol. XX, 141, n. 515; see also Sezgin, *Abū Miḫnaf*, 200).

[8] The word here is *nushhiduka*; Hawting translates this '… we testify to you …' (al-Ṭabarī, *History*, vol. XX, 132). However, the fourth form of the verb *sh-h-d* is causative, and rather means 'to make someone a witness' (see Lane, *Arabic–English Lexicon*, vol. II, 1610a; see also Fishbein, 'Life of al-Mukhtār', 153). I have made a similar change in the following *khabar*.

[9] A famous traditionist who died between 145/762 and 151/768. See e.g. al-Mizzī, *Tahdhīb*, vol. XII, 90. On him, see also Kohlberg, 'Aʿmaš'; Haider, *Origins*, 221–7; and van Ess, *Theologie*, vol. I, 237–9.

[10] Died between 121/739 and 123/741 according to al-Mizzī, *Tahdhīb*, vol. XI, 317. See also Sezgin, *Abū Miḫnaf*, 218; van Ess, *Theologie*, vol. I, 244.

[11] Of al-Azd. A well-known Kūfan traditionist, whose date of death seems to be unknown. On him, see Ibn Saʿd, *Ṭabaqāt*, vol. VI, 206–7; Sezgin, *Abū Miḫnaf*, 206.

relent [*tub*] toward us, for you are the relenting one [*al-tawwāb*] and the compassionate one".[12] Have mercy on al-Ḥusayn and his companions, the martyrs [*al-shuhadā'*] and the righteous ones [*al-ṣiddīqīn*]. We call you to witness, O Lord, that we are doing the same as they were when they were killed. "If you do not pardon us our sin and have mercy on us, then we are among the losers.'"[13]

2. *Qāla*: **They remained there a day and a night praying over him, weeping and abasing themselves. And from that time onwards the people did not cease to plead for mercy on him and his companions until they made the early morning prayer by his tomb on the following day, and that increased their fury. Then they mounted up and Sulaymān ordered the people to proceed. And no man would pass on until he had come to the tomb of al-Ḥusayn, stood in prayer[14] over it, and asked for mercy on him and pardon for him.**
3. *Qāla*: And by God, I saw them thronging more thickly than the people throng around the Black Stone.
4. *Qāla*: Sulaymān stood by his [al-Ḥusayn's][15] tomb, and whenever a group prayed for him and asked for mercy on him, al-Musayyab b. Najaba and Sulaymān b. Ṣurad said to them, 'Join your brethren, may God have mercy on you!' He continued in this manner until about thirty of his companions were left, and then Sulaymān and his companions made a circle around the tomb and Sulaymān said, 'Praise be to God who, if He had wished, would have honoured us with martyrdom with al-Ḥusayn. Oh my God, since you forbade us it together with him, do not forbid us it on his account after him.' And 'Abdallāh b. Wāl said, 'Verily, by God, I consider al-Ḥusayn and his father and brother as the best of Muḥammad's community [who will be] imploring God's favour [on behalf of the Muslims] on the Day of

[12] Qur. 2:128. Hawting has not indicated this passage as Qur'ānic.

[13] Qur. 7: 23. Hawting has not indicated this passage as Qur'ānic. Similar expressions are found in Qur. 7:149 and 11: 47.

[14] The words 'in prayer' are not found in the Arabic text. Obviously Hawting regards them as implied, and I agree on this, as similar formulae are found in other places of the text. Fishbein ('Life of al-Mukhtār', 155) translates this sentence: 'but before leaving, each man came to the grave of al-Husayn, stood by it, and asked God to have mercy upon him and forgive him'.

[15] The name of al-Ḥusayn is not mentioned here in the Arabic text, although it is clear that it is his tomb that is meant. Both Hawting (al-Ṭabarī, *History*, vol. XX, 133) and Fishbein ('Life of al-Mukhtār', 155) have inserted it.

Resurrection. Are you not amazed at the test to which this community has been subjected by its enemies? They killed two and brought the third to the brink of death.'[16]

5. *Qāla*: Al-Musayyab b. Najaba said, 'I am one of those who will kill them. I dissociate myself from whoever shares their views. Them I will treat as an enemy and fight.'[17]
6. *Qāla*: All of the leaders spoke most eloquently. Al-Muthannā b. Mukharriba was a companion of one of the leaders and notables, and it pained me when I did not hear him making a speech with the people in a manner similar to their speeches.
7. *Qāla*: Before long, however, he delivered a speech which was not inferior to any of the others. He said, 'God made these men, whose status you have mentioned relative to their Prophet, superior to anyone except their Prophet. A mob to whom we are enemies and with whom we recognise no ties killed them. We have left our homes, our people and our properties seeking the extirpation of those who killed them. By God, even if the fight against them is where the sun goes down or the earth ends, it is incumbent upon us to seek it until we attain it. That is our booty and it is martyrdom, the reward for which is heaven.' We said to him, 'You have spoken the truth, you have achieved your end, and you have been granted success.'
8. *Qāla*: Then Sulaymān b. Ṣurad travelled on from the tomb of al-Ḥusayn and we went with him. We took the road by al-Ḥaṣṣāṣa, then al-Anbār, then al-Ṣadūd, then al-Qayyāra.[18]

Formal Analysis

Sections K.*I.1–2*

Khabar I is actually quite long, extending over almost two pages in the Leiden edition of al-Ṭabarī's *Ta'rīkh*.[19] Most of it relates the departure of the

[16] Here, perhaps, Fishbein's translation is to be preferred: 'They killed two of them, and then satisfied their thirst for killing with the third' ('Life of al-Mukhtār', 155).

[17] The words here translated 'dissociate myself' and 'treat as an enemy' come from the Arabic roots *b-r-'* and *ʿ-d-w* respectively.

[18] Al-Ṭabarī, *Ta'rīkh*, II, 546–8.

[19] Al-Ṭabarī, *Ta'rīkh*, II, 544–6. The following formal analysis is quite technical. The reader who does not need to follow the detailed argument may jump to the analysis of the content below.

Tawwābūn from their camp at al-Nukhayla outside Kufa. Only the last few lines, *K*.I.1 and 2 as reproduced above, deal briefly with the visit to the grave. These two sections probably originate from two earlier reports which have been joined, with the fissure indicated by the word *qāla*, 'he said'. '*Qāla*' is used several times in the *khabar*, but it seems mostly to refer back to the last-named authority in the *isnād* and is thus used mainly to indicate a new section in the narrative. At this point between *K*.1.1 and 2, however, it is quite clear that '*qāla*' signals a break between two earlier reports. There are both internal and external grounds for this conclusion. Internally, *K*.I.2 repeats the arrival of the Tawwābūn at the grave, which has already been stated in *K*.I.1. This repetition is hardly necessary either to give information or for narrative purposes, and it signals that two previously independent reports have been brought together at this point, but have not been sufficiently edited so as to create a smooth narrative. The external grounds for hypothesising two antecedent reports here will emerge from the subsequent analysis of the two following *khabars*, as well as from comparison with the accounts of Ibn A'tham and al-Balādhurī, where the same or very similar sentences are used to introduce longer reports.

Apart from repeating the arrival at the grave, the two reports give different information. *K*.I.1 tells us about the duration of the stay at the grave – a night and a day – and also says that the Tawwābūn prayed over al-Ḥusayn and asked God's pardon for him. *K*.I.2, on the other hand, dwells on the shouting and weeping at the grave. Both these features recur in the two *khabars* that follow.

Section K.*II.1*

Khabar II is relatively short, and is entirely devoted to the visit to the grave. This *khabar* at first sight seems to constitute a single redactional unit. Although we are presented with three scenarios – the arrival at the grave and the people's weeping in unison, Sulaymān's prayer, and the departure and encampment – the narrative runs relatively smoothly, and each scene adds new information. However, I will argue later in this chapter that the wording of Sulaymān's prayer original to the tradition has been altered. In this *khabar*, it has received a more 'Shi'ite' mark than it had from the beginning.

The introductory sentence of the *khabar* is close in wording to the first sentence of *K*.I.2, though with some variations. The main difference is that the narrator here speaks as an eyewitness in the first person plural. Also, different words are used for the collective outpouring of grief. Furthermore, in *K*.II.1 the sentence is not placed at the end of a longer passage, as in *K*.I.2, but introduces a separate tradition. I will have more to say about this shortly.

Four important features of this *khabar* which are not found in *Khabar* I but are extant in *K*.III.1 should be noted:

a. The Tawwābūn wish they had fallen with al-Ḥusayn at Karbala. In this way they declare that they have betrayed al-Ḥusayn and that they repent of their sin. Here, though, their repentance is expressed less explicitly than in the following *khabar*.
b. In Sulaymān's prayer, three epithets (two of which recur in *K*.III.1) are used to describe al-Ḥusayn and his father ʿAlī: they are called 'martyrs', 'right-guided', and 'righteous'.
c. Sulaymān prays for God's mercy on al-Ḥusayn.
d. Sulaymān declares that he and his companions are following the religion (*dīn*) and path of al-Ḥusayn and ʿAlī. He furthermore uses the words 'enemy' (*ʿadūw*, pl. *aʿdāʾ*) and 'friend' or 'associate' (*wālī*, pl. *awliyāʾ*), a pair of concepts that have always been immensely important for distinguishing between Shiʿites and non-Shiʿites.[20]

Section K.*III.1–2*

Khabar III is quite long, but, like *Khabar* II, it deals solely with the Tawwābūn's visit to the grave.[21] *K*.III.1 and 2 are introduced by sentences very close to *K*.I.1 and 2, but with key elements presented in reverse order.

The opening words of *K*.III.1 are almost exactly the same as those of *K*.I.2, and very close to the introductory sentence of *K*.II.1 (see the synopsis in Table 7.1). As in *K*.II.1, the sentence introduces a longer report. *K*.II.1 and

[20] See e.g. Amir-Moezzi, *Spirituality*, 262–70; Dakake, *Charismatic Community*, 65–7; Haider, *Shīʿī Islam*, 32–5.

[21] This is the only occasion in the entire story of the Tawwābūn when three authorities are given in the *isnād*.

K.III.1 have several further elements in common. Although the wording partly differs, it is striking that in *K*.III.1 the following elements recur in the same order as in *K*.II.1: (a) The Tawwābūn confess their betrayal of al-Ḥusayn; (b) they ask for mercy on him and his companions (not, however, his father as in *K*.II.1); (c) they use the epithets 'martyrs' and 'righteous' for them; and (d) they declare that they 'do the same' as al-Ḥusayn and his companions did when they were killed. Furthermore, a fifth element is introduced here, not found in *K*.II.1: (e) a quotation from the Qurʾān saying that if God does not forgive them, they will be 'among the losers'. The similarities to *K*.I.2 and *K*.II.1 are thus striking, and would be very difficult to explain other than by the hypothesis that behind them lies an older report which has been transmitted through different chains of authorities and has been modified by the transmitters on the way.

Then there follows (*K*.III.2) a '*qāla*', which introduces a sentence very similar to *K*.I.1. The main difference, apart from the reversed order of the words 'night and day', is the last clause of the sentence. In *K*.I.1, the Tawwābūn ask for forgiveness for *al-Ḥusayn* (*yastaghfirūna lahu*), whereas in *K*.III.2, they weep and abase *themselves* (*yabkūna wa-yataḍarraʿūna*).[22]

Moreover, in *K*.III.2 the introductory sentence is placed not at the end of a longer passage, as in *K*.I.1, but introducing a separate tradition. The obvious conclusion, and one that I have already indicated above, is that the sentences in *K*.I.1 and 2 have been extracted from the beginning of two longer reports and juxtaposed at the end of *Khabar* I. This raises the question of why the opening sentence of *K*.I.1 is not preceded by a '*qāla*'. Had it been part of an independent tradition, one would have expected the compiler to indicate this. Still, the close correspondence between the first sentences of *K*.I.1 and *K*.III.2 convinces me that both these sections are dependent on a single original report. This hypothesis, as I will demonstrate below, is corroborated by a comparison with Ibn Aʿtham's version of the story. The absence of a '*qāla*' to introduce the sentence in *Khabar* I just shows how unreliable this word is as a tool for tradition criticism. In order for us to discern the break between two

22 The expression *yastaghfirūna lahu* is found later in the tradition. It is a common phrase, however, and this isolated occurrence in a different position in the text as compared with *Khabar* I can at the most be considered an indirect indication for its being part of a fixed tradition.

reports that have been merged in a text, the '*qāla*' must be supplemented with other criteria, such as the interior coherence of a text unit, comparisons with other texts, and so on.

These similarities lead me to believe that the text from *K*.I.1 to *K*.III.2 is based on two older reports: Report A, traces of which are found in *K*.I.2, *K*.II.1, and *K*.III.1, and Report B, which has been used as the basis for *K*.I.1 and *K*.III.2. This older layer is in bold type in the text of the *khabar*s reproduced above and in Table 7.1. (See also Figure 8.1 in the following chapter.)

My hypothesis – that the three *khabar*s in Abū Mikhnaf's account of the visit to the grave are based on two older reports – is corroborated by a comparison with the same passage as presented by Ibn Aʿtham and al-Balādhurī. Ibn Aʿtham's version is clearly an abbreviation of *Khabar* III, with a long interpolation between Reports A and B.[23] Although Ibn Aʿtham has in certain respects edited the *khabar*, it is in the latter part (*K*.III.4–7, to be discussed below) that the main changes have been made. In his text, the two anonymous reports A and B as formulated here are kept relatively intact in comparison with Abū Mikhnaf's version, and the interpolation of the long passage containing a speech and a poem by a certain Wahb b. Zamʿa al-Juʿfī is placed between the two traditions.[24] This indicates that Ibn Aʿtham regarded Reports A and B as original units.

Al-Balādhurī's account is very short, and based on Report A with some modifications. It goes:

> When Sulaymān and his companions reached the tomb of al-Ḥusayn [*lammā intahā Sulaymān wa-asḥābihi ilā qabr al-Ḥusayn*] they cried out in unison and wept [*ṣarakhū ṣarkhatan wāhidatan wa-bakaw*]. Sulaymān said: 'Oh God [*Allāhumma*], have mercy on al-Ḥusayn, the martyr son of the martyr!' They called out: 'Oh, avengers of al-Ḥusayn!' and they expressed their repentance [*tawba*] for neglecting to help him.[25]

[23] Ibn Aʿtham al-Kūfī, *Futūḥ*, vol. VI, 67.

[24] For Ibn Aʿtham's 'interpolations', see Conrad, 'Ibn Aʿtham', 99–101. In this context, however, the interpolation is less overt than those Conrad discusses. The speech and poem ascribed to Wahb in fact have very little to do with the sentiment and the mission of the Tawwābūn, as it is expressed in the rest of the story.

[25] Al-Balādhurī, *Ansāb*, vol. VI, 369–70.

That Ibn A'tham's and al-Balādhurī's versions are similar to that of Abū Mikhnaf is of course no surprise, as they based their accounts of the Tawwābūn on his account. What is significant here, however, is that, although they have made amendments to Abū Mikhnaf's text, they have kept the two anonymous reports A and B basically intact. In all cases (Ibn A'tham's versions of Reports A and B, and al-Balādhurī's version of Report A), the introductory words are essentially the same as in those reports in Abū Mikhnaf's version. In every case, moreover, the introductions are followed by expressions that are entirely consistent with each of the respective traditions. Thus, an introduction from Report A is never combined with elements from Report B, or vice versa. Finally, although elements from each of the traditions may be cut out in the various versions, when they do occur, they always do so in the same order.

Before going on, I will focus on the differences between the two versions of Report A as given in *K*.II.1 and *K*.III.1. If, as I argue above, these two sections have their origin in an older, anonymous report, why are they different? Is it possible to determine which of the two versions is nearer to the original? There is in fact a grammatical anomaly in *K*.II.1 which may be of some help in tracing the tradition history of the two versions. A close reading reveals that the pronominal suffixes at the end of the section, which refer to al-Ḥusayn and his father 'Alī, are in the plural form, even though the dual form would have been grammatically correct. Thus, the text first refers to them as 'the martyr son of the martyr, the right-guided one son of the right-guided one, the righteous one son of the righteous one'. This is followed by an invocation to God to act as a witness that the Tawwābūn follow '*their* [al-Ḥusayn's and 'Alī's] religion and *their* path and are enemies of those who killed *them* and friends of those who love *them*'.[26] Had the text been grammatically correct, each of the pronouns italicised above would have been dual (*-humā* or *-himā*), as they refer to the two persons, al-Ḥusayn and 'Alī; but instead, they are plural (*-hum* or *-him*). It is true that such grammatical anomalies are not unusual, even in Arabic texts of high literary quality.[27] The corresponding sentence in *K*.III.1 is grammatically correct: 'We call You to witness, O Lord, that we are doing the

[26] Al-Ṭabarī, *Ta'rīkh*, II, 546.
[27] I am grateful to Meir Bar-Asher for pointing this out to me.

same as [what *they* were] when *they* were killed'.[28] Here, the italicised pronouns (which are implied in the passive verb *qutalū*), which refer to Ḥusayn and his companions who fought at Karbala, are, correctly, in the plural.

To conclude this argument. In my view, the wording of *K*.III.1 is probably closer to, if not *the*, original rendering. The text was then later 'Shiʿitised' in *K*.II.1 by substituting ʿAlī for the fighters at Karbala, by emphasising the filial relationship of al-Ḥusayn to ʿAlī, and by adding the epithet *mahdī* (rightly guided) to those of *shahīd* (martyr) and *ṣiddīq* (righteous).[29] The suffixed pronouns from the original version in the new rendering were, however, not changed, resulting in the slightly inaccurate grammar of *K*.II.1. A further, perhaps even more probative indication that the rendering of *K*.III.1 is older is that the reverse process is not likely. In other words, it is difficult to imagine ʿAlī being replaced by al-Ḥusayn's companions at Karbala in a later version.

Sections K.*III.3–8*

In what follows, I analyse the approximately four-fifths of *Khabar* III that has not yet been discussed. The question I now address is the extent of anonymous Report B. Its beginning is quite clear, but where does it end? Does it extend to the end of *Khabar* III, or is much of that *khabar* composed of material that was added later? Unlike the first sentence of the tradition, and unlike Report A, there are no independent parallels that can be compared with the latter part of the *khabar*. In Ibn Aʿtham's account there is a shorter version of the *khabar*, but this is clearly based on Abū Mikhnaf and thus cannot be used for comparison.[30] Thus in this part of the study we must rely mainly on internal criteria, such as content and the flow of the narrative.

When it comes to *K*.III.6 and 7, however, there are quite clear indications that these sections were added later, even if they are written as part of *Khabar* III. These sections relate a speech by a certain al-Muthannā

[28] Al-Ṭabarī, *Taʾrīkh*, II, 546; *History*, vol. XX, 132. The passage is difficult to translate literally, which is why the words which I have placed within square brackets are inserted by the translator. In fact, in the Arabic text, only one pronoun is implied.

[29] For early instances of the formula '*mahdī ibn al-mahdī*', see the poetry by the Kaysānī poet Kutayyir ʿAzza, e.g. *Dīwān*, 496.

[30] In a previous study, I more or less took for granted that Report A was roughly equal to *K*.III.2–5 ('Date', 200). As will be seen, I have changed my view on this matter.

Table 7.1 Synopsis of the khabars *about the Tawwābūn's visit to al-Ḥusayn's grave*

***Khabar* I**	***Khabar* II**	***Khabar* III**
	Report A	
K.I.2. **When the people reached al-Ḥusayn's tomb, they shouted out in unison and wept;**	*K*.II.1. **When we reached the tomb of al-Ḥusayn (P) the people wept together;**	*K*.III.1. **When Sulaymān b. Ṣurad and his companions reached the tomb of al-Ḥusayn, they cried in unison;**
Lammā intahā al-nās ilā qabr al-Ḥusayn ṣāḥū ṣayḥatan wāḥidatan wa-bakū.	*Lammā intahaynā ilā qabr al-Ḥusayn* (ع) *bakā al-nās bi-ajmaʿihim.*	*Lammā intahā Sulaymān b. Ṣurad wa-aṣḥābihi ilā qabr al-Ḥusayn nadaw ṣayḥatan wāḥidatan.*
	Oh God, have mercy on al-Ḥusayn, the martyr son of the martyr, the right-guided one son of the right-guided one, the righteous one son of the righteous one.	**Oh Lord ... have mercy on al-Ḥusayn and his companions, the martyrs and the righteous ones.**
	Allāhumma, irḥam Ḥusaynan, al-shahīd ibn al-shahīd, al-mahdī ibn al-mahdī, al-ṣiddīq ibn al-ṣiddīq.	*Yā Rabb... irḥam Ḥusaynan wa-aṣḥābahu, al-shuhadāʾ wa-l-ṣiddīqīn.*
	Oh God, we call you to witness that we follow their religion and their path, and we are enemies of those who killed them, friends of those who love them.	**We call you to witness, Oh Lord, that we are doing the same as what they were when they were killed.**
	Allāhumma, inna nushhiduka annā ʿalā dīnihim wa-sabīlihim, wa-aʿdāʾa qātilayhim wa-awliyāʾa muḥibbayhim.	*Wa-innā nushhiduka, yā Rabb, annā ʿalā mithlimā qutalū ʿalayhi.*
	Report B	
K.I.1. **They remained there a night and a day praying over him and asking God's pardon for him;**		*K*.III.2. **They remained there a day and a night praying over him, weeping and abasing themselves;**
Aqāmū bihi laylatan wa-yawman yuṣallūna ʿalayhi wa-yastaghfirūna lahu.		*Aqāmū ʿindahu yawman wa-laylatan yuṣallūna ʿalayhi wa-yabkūna wa-yataḍarraʿūna.*

b. Mukharriba, a leader of the Basra Shiʿites.[31] They make up a narrative unit, and the '*qāla*' separating them probably does not, therefore, indicate a fissure between two traditions. Several features in the incident related here, as well as its position in the story at large, indicate that these two sections were not part of the original account.

To begin with, the incident is not consistent with other parts of the story of the Tawwābūn where al-Muthannā is mentioned. The first time he shows up in the story, it is as recipient of Sulaymān b. Ṣurad's letter to the Shiʿites of al-Madāʾin and Basra, asking them to join the Tawwābūn in their mission (analysed in Chapter 6). As leader of the Shiʿites of Basra, al-Muthannā responds positively to the call and promises to come when summoned.[32] When the Tawwābūn are about to set out from their camp at al-Nukhayla, they realise that the people of Basra and al-Madāʾin have not come; they decide to go anyway, and let these groups catch up later.[33] During the battle at ʿAyn al-Warda, three messengers from al-Madāʾin arrive at the battlefield to encourage the Tawwābūn and tell them that the Madāʾinīs and the Basrans (the latter under the leadership of al-Muthannā) are on their way.[34] Help does not arrive in time, however, and the next time we hear of al-Muthannā is when he and his men (as well as the people from al-Madāʾin) meet the remnants of the Tawwābūn, who are on their way back to Kufa.[35] Thus, the structure of the story at large speaks against al-Muthannā's presence at the grave of al-Ḥusayn.

Nevertheless, there are traditions which support the version that al-Muthannā was indeed present at the grave, or at least took part in the battle at ʿAyn al-Warda. Thus, al-Madāʾinī begins his account of al-Muthannā's support for al-Mukhtār in Basra some time later with the words: 'Al-Muthannā b. Mukharriba al-ʿAbdī was among those who had witnessed [the battle of] ʿAyn al-Warda with Sulaymān b. Ṣurad.'[36] Al-Balādhurī has no record

[31] According to Hawting, he was from ʿAbd al-Qays of Rabīʿa (al-Ṭabarī, *History*, vol. XX, 89, n. 388 and 133, n. 499). The name is differently given in the sources, e.g. Muthannā b. Makhrama (see al-Masʿūdī, *Murūj*, vol. V, 217; Ibn Aʿtham al-Kūfī, *Futūḥ*, vol. VI, 52, n. 4). Like Hawting, I have followed the version given in the *Addenda et emenanda* in the Leiden version of al-Ṭabarī's *Taʾrīkh*.

[32] Al-Ṭabarī, *Taʾrīkh*, II, 505.

[33] Al-Ṭabarī, *Taʾrīkh*, II, 544–5.

[34] Al-Ṭabarī, *Taʾrīkh*, II, 561–2.

[35] Al-Ṭabarī, *Taʾrīkh*, II, 568.

[36] Al-Ṭabarī, *Taʾrīkh*, II, 680.

of al-Muthannā at the grave, but when he relates the meeting between the defeated Tawwābūn and the delayed support from al-Madā'in and Basra, he adds a note: 'Some people allege that ... Ibn Mukharriba showed up at the grave of al-Ḥusayn (peace be upon him) at the beginning of the expedition and were present at their battle. God knows best.'[37] This little note further indicates that there were traditions in circulation which gave al-Muthannā a role at the grave (as well as in the battle, perhaps), but that al-Balādhurī regarded them with suspicion.

There are, moreover, internal traces that suggest that this part of the text is not original. Although the scene described is basically the same, it differs from the preceding sections in several respects. Thus, in *K*.III.4 and 5, short speeches by Sulaymān and by two of the other leaders of the Tawwābūn, ʿAbdallāh b. Wāl and al-Musayyab b. Najaba, are recounted, but none by any other participant at the grave. Furthermore, the leaders' speeches are not praised by the other participants. In *K*.III.6 and 7, however, the account suddenly changes into the first person, and we read that the narrator is sad that al-Muthannā at first does not give a speech like the other leaders, but that after he has spoken, the others commend him for what he said. Thus, both the structure and the content of the passage about al-Muthannā's speech differ from those of the speeches preceding it, factors which differentiate his speech from the rest of the *khabar* and signal that it is added later. Finally, *K*.III.6 and 7 add nothing to the story at large (except for the alleged presence of al-Muthannā at the grave, of course), and the narrative would have run smoothly without it.

Ibn Aʿtham gives an abbreviated version of this segment of the story, in which parts of al-Muthannā's speech are related, merged with other phrases, but his name is not mentioned. Instead, this speech is presented as a collective outcry of the Tawwābūn gathered around the grave.[38]

Thus, both structure and content argue that the passage about al-Muthannā b. Mukharriba here is a later insertion. The motive for the creation of such a tradition is probably the wish to give al-Muthannā, who was later active in support of al-Mukhtār in Basra,[39] a more significant role – for

[37] Al-Balādhurī, *Ansāb*, vol. VI, 372.
[38] Ibn Aʿtham al-Kūfī, *Futūḥ*, vol. VI, 69.
[39] Al-Ṭabarī, *Taʾrīkh*, II, 680–3.

himself and for Basra – in the Shiʿite movement at large. His embarrassing belatedness in the affair of the Tawwābūn perhaps did not contribute to his image as a champion for the Shiʿite cause, and it might be that the traditions under discussion here, as well as other traditions which are now lost, were attempting to remedy this. It is difficult to know when this addition was made. I find it hard to believe that Abū Mikhnaf himself made such a flagrant break with the narrative structure of his own work. Whatever the background, in the following discussion of the traditions of the Tawwābūn's visit to the grave of al-Ḥusayn, I regard *K*.III.6 and 7 as an insertion, probably not included by Abū Mikhnaf in his *Kitāb Sulaymān b. Ṣurad* but added later to enhance al-Muthannā's reputation. It must, however, have been part of the text by the time of Hishām b. al-Kalbī at the latest (that is the turn of the third/beginning of the ninth century), as all the sources mentioned above use that edition of Abū Mikhnaf's account.

K.III.8 is merely a description of the course that the journey took after the visit to the grave of al-Ḥusayn. The accounts given by al-Ṭabarī and al-Balādhurī are very similar; they may give a correct picture of the journey, although this is impossible to establish with any certainty. Ibn Aʿtham's description ('[they] stuck to the main road'[40]) is probably his own condensed rendering of the journey. It is plausible that a description of the journey of the Tawwābūn was included in the earliest versions of the story.

What remains is a discussion of the remainder of the *khabar*, from the latter part of *K*.III.2 to *K*.III.5. I noted above that only the first sentence of *K*.III.2 has a parallel which can be used for comparative purposes, namely *K*.I.1 (see Table 7.1). However, the content of the entire section *K*.III.2 is well in line with that of the original rendering of Reports A and B, to the extent that these have been identified. The two anonymous reports relate how the Tawwābūn weep, abase themselves, and ask God for mercy and forgiveness for themselves and al-Ḥusayn. This is very much also the message of *K*.III.2. Furthermore, *K*.III.2 is self-contained, in that it gives a brief but complete account of the visit to the grave from the arrival of the Tawwābūn, their sojourn overnight and their departure. Hence, it is plausible that *K*.III.2 more or less corresponds to the original rendering of Report B.

40 Ibn Aʿtham al-Kūfī, *Futūḥ*, vol. VI, 70.

K.III.3, however, clearly breaks the narrative flow. There, the story switches to the first person, with the narrator relating how he saw the people crowding around al-Ḥusayn's tomb 'more thickly than the people throng around the Black Stone [of the Kaʿba]'.[41] This is an example of the rhetorical device of *mimesis* (i.e. creating the illusion of having directly witnessed what actually happened), a frequent device in early Arabic historiography.[42] By speaking in the first person, the narrator tries to convey a 'photographic' image of the scene and thus 'to inscribe history "as it really was"'.[43] After this section, which consists of only one sentence, the narrative reverts to an account in the third person. To my mind, *K*.III.3 is likely a later addition, the purpose of which is to demonstrate the high status of al-Ḥusayn, to make the story livelier, and to inspire confidence in the narrator and the story.

K.III.4 and 5 relate in further detail what happened when the group prepared to leave the grave. The first part repeats the departure scene, but adds a description of how the Tawwābūn are blessed by their leaders as they leave. This is followed by short speeches given by the same leaders, but here the tenor of their words differs from the renditions in *K*.III.1 and 2. Rather than crying out to God for forgiveness and mercy, here the Tawwābūn laud the family of al-Ḥusayn, accuse their enemies, and assert their wish to fight against the latter. As I will show below, the content of these contributions contains elements that probably did not develop within Shiʿism until later. This is also the only time in the story of the Tawwābūn when al-Ḥusayn's brother al-Ḥasan is mentioned, even if not by name. Taken together, the redundant description of the departure and the short speeches that convey a partly different message suggest that *K*.III. 4 and 5 belong to neither of the two anonymous reports, but are later additions.

Content

The foregoing, rather detailed analysis of the account of the Tawwābūn's visit to the grave of al-Ḥusayn suggests that the text is based on two anonymous reports, which I have called A and B. Of the texts, *K*.III.1 and *K*.III.2 are

[41] Al-Ṭabarī, *Taʾrīkh*, II, 547.

[42] For a discussion of the use of *mimesis* in al-Ṭabarī's *Taʾrīkh*, see Shoshan, *Poetics*, 3–60; the employment of eyewitnesses in this respect is particularly discussed on pp. 25–41.

[43] Shoshan, *Poetics*, 25

probably the closest to the original Reports A and B respectively. *K*.I.1 consists of the first sentence of Report B, and *K*.I.2 is taken from the introduction to Report B. *K*.II.1 is a modified version of Report A. It is not improbable that *K*.III.8, the onward journey from the site of the grave, is also very early. The rest of *Khabar* III (*K*.III.3–7), however, is, I think, made up of later additions (see Figure 8.1).

It should now be possible also to recognise which aspects of the content of the account are early, and perhaps to detect traces of the development of some of the ideas expressed within early Shiʿism. In the oldest sections of the text, *K*.III.1 and 2, two of the themes that we found in the four programmatic texts examined in Chapter 5 figure prominently in the account of the visit to the grave: the role and the image presented of al-Ḥusayn, and the repentance of the Tawwābūn. The theme of the Karbala tragedy and the treachery of the Kufans, so important in the texts analysed in the previous chapter, is much less conspicuous here, though clearly implied.

The Image of al-Ḥusayn

As I have mentioned above, the two anonymous reports relate how the Tawwābūn asked for God's mercy on and forgiveness for al-Ḥusayn. Thus, in Report A (*K*.III.1 in the outline above), they pray, 'Have mercy on al-Ḥusayn and his companions', and in Report B (*K*.III.2) we read that on departure, every one of them stopped at the grave and 'stood in prayer over it and asked for mercy on him and pardon for him'. In the light of later Shiʿism – in which al-Ḥusayn is one of the fourteen *maʿṣūmūn*, those members of the family of the Prophet who are 'impeccable' or immune from error and sin – this is unexpected.[44] Though the earliest attestations of the concept of *ʿiṣma* or 'impeccability' being applied to the Shiʿite imams, dating from the third quarter of the second/late eighth century,[45] seem to use it to refer to the infallible transmission

[44] For the concept of *ʿiṣma*, 'inerrancy' or 'impeccability', see e.g. Madelung, "Iṣma', and Algar, 'Čahārdah Maʿṣūm'. There are, however, traditions in which the Prophet asked for forgiveness for *himself*, though he was sinless (see Crow, 'Death', 82–9; the tradition is quoted on p. 84). This is a different matter, though, and probably a later idea.

[45] Both Madelung ("Iṣma') and Algar ('Čahārdah Maʿṣūm') maintain that the notion of the inerrancy of the Imāms was held at least from the first half of the second/eighth century. It is unfortunate, however, that neither of them substantiates their statements with examples or references, but having claimed this, both scholars move on to discuss the concept of *ʿiṣma* in the writings of

of the Prophetic message, it soon came to mean the complete impeccability of the Prophet Muḥammad, his daughter Fāṭima and the imams.[46] Furthermore, both the anonymous reports mention al-Ḥusayn and his followers side by side, almost as equals; all of them are called martyrs and righteous, and the Tawwābūn's prayers for mercy are extended to all those killed at Karbala. The only difference here between the companions and al-Ḥusayn is the latter's blood relation to his grandfather, the Prophet Muḥammad. Again, as in the programmatic texts examined in Chapter 5, the connection to the Prophet goes through Fāṭima. In other words, both Reports A and B portray al-Ḥusayn as an ordinary human being, standing in the same position towards God as all other humans, except for his close relation to the Prophet.

In the amendments of and additions to the two original reports, however, another image of al-Ḥusayn begins to emerge. Earlier in the chapter I have already discussed the association between al-Ḥusayn and his father ʿAlī in *K*.II.1, where both are called martyrs and righteous, epithets that in Report A were originally given to his companions at Karbala. In *Khabar* II, al-Ḥusayn and ʿAlī are moreover described as rightly guided, *mahdī*. This term was originally probably a kind of honorific title given to those leaders and prophets who were thought to be guided by God; it did not originally have the meaning of eschatological redeemer that it later acquired. In the latter sense, the *mahdī* is never portrayed as being or having a son, so here the more general meaning of the title is certainly meant.

In *K*.III.4, however, al-Ḥusayn, his father and his brother are said to be 'the best of Muḥammad's community [*umma*] [who will be] imploring God's favour on the Day of Resurrection [*wasīlatan ʿinda Allāh yawma al-qiyāma*]'. According to Jean Calmard, this is the first time al-Ḥusayn is invoked as an intermediary (*wasīla*) between God and humanity, even if the word here does not have the meaning it received in later Shiʿism.[47] Calmard,

Hishām b. al-Ḥakam, who was active at the *end* of the same century. On Hishām and his opinion on *ʿiṣma*, see also Bayhom-Daou, 'Hishām b. al-Ḥakam', 78–9. See also the discussion relating to this issue by Crow, 'Death', 82–9. Crow seems to take the authenticity of the sources for granted; if that is correct, the concept of *ʿiṣma* at least began to be discussed as early as Madelung and Algar suggest. For an extended discussion of *ʿiṣma* in early Shiʿism, see also Bar-Asher, *Scripture and Exegesis*, 159–79.

46 Madelung, "Iṣma'.

47 Calmard, 'Culte', 68–9.

however, seems to accept that the text gives a more or less correct description of the actual event, while I regard this (as argued above) as a later addition. Thus, I think Calmard's bold assertion that this is the earliest instance of this idea exceeds the bounds of the evidence.

Finally, the association made between the grave of al-Ḥusayn and the Black Stone of the Kaʿba in *K*.III.3 is interesting.[48] I agree with Dakake when she writes, 'To connect this stone with the tomb of al-Ḥusayn is a statement of immense symbolic significance for understanding the concept of the sanctity of Ḥusayn as the bearer of Prophetic blood.'[49] As we have seen, the notion of the sanctity and inviolability of al-Ḥusayn and the family of the Prophet is very prominent in the Karbala story,[50] and the idea is certainly present even if the word *ḥurma* ('inviolability') is mentioned only once in the account of the Tawwābūn with regard to al-Ḥusayn.[51] Again, this section is probably a later addition to Report B, and it is uncertain when it was appended.

There are, therefore, obvious indications in the account of the visit to the grave that the image of al-Ḥusayn developed over time. In the earliest sections, those that probably quite faithfully recount the two anonymous reports A and B, he is described as an ordinary man, more or less on a par with his companions at Karbala except for the fact that he is the grandson of the Prophet. By contrast, in the parts amended or added later, he is clearly depicted as standing above his followers and the Tawwābūn. He is partly removed from human history, to use the words of McCutcheon.

The Karbala Tragedy and the Treachery of the Tawwābūn

The oldest parts of the account contain no description of what happened at Karbala; the event is only alluded to in Report A (*K*.III.1) as the Tawwābūn

48 Al-Ṭabarī, *Taʾrīkh*, ser. II, 547; *History*, vol. XX, 133.

49 Dakake, *Charismatic Community*, 94. Dakake indicates a similar statement of one of the Tawwābūn after the battle proper, where he calls the enemy 'destroyers of the sacred sanctuary' (*yā mukhribī al-bayt al-ḥarām*) (al-Ṭabarī, *Taʾrīkh*, II, 571; *History*, vol. XX, 156). However, I find Dakake's conclusion that 'the sacred sanctuary' here refers to the *ahl al-bayt* less probable. The reference might very well be literal, referring to the bombardment of the Kaʿba by the troops of the caliph Yazīd in 64/683 (see al-Ṭabarī, *Taʾrīkh*, II, 424–7). The later connection and contrast between the grave of al-Ḥusayn at Karbala and the Kaʿba will be further discussed with regard to the merits of pilgrimage to the grave in Chapter 11.

50 See Chapter 4.

51 See above, Chapter 6 on Sections T.II.2.

ask for forgiveness for their sin of failing to support al-Ḥusayn and his companions. In Reports A and B, the tragedy is thus implied when the Tawwābūn cry out over their betrayal. The treachery, on the other hand, is conspicuous in both the older reports. Thus, Report A begins with the outcry, 'Oh Lord, we have betrayed the son of our Prophet's daughter!' In Report B, the confession of betrayal is less explicit, but the weeping and self-abasement of the Tawwābūn clearly signify their consciousness of the sin they have committed.

As will be seen in the next section, in the later amendments and additions to the three *khabar*s, this sense of guilt is played down.

The Dire Consequences for the Traitors, the Need to Repent and the Manner of Repentance

Report A (*K*.III.1) ends with a quote from Qur. 7:23: 'If you do not pardon us our sin and have mercy on us, then we are among the losers.' In the Qur'ān, this is actually Adam and Eve's plea for God's forgiveness when they have sinned against His command not to eat of the tree in the Garden (of Eden). In quoting this verse, the report thus signals that the treachery of the Tawwābūn against al-Ḥusayn is a sin of the gravest order, an offence that will bring perdition on those who committed it if they are not forgiven. Thus, in another quotation from the Qur'ān in the same section, the Tawwābūn plead to God, 'relent [*tub*] toward us, for you are the relenting one [*al-tawwāb*] and the compassionate one' (Qur. 2:128). This verse contains the only two occurrences in the entire story of the root *t-w-b* where it is God who is the 'turning' or relenting subject. In the Qur'ān, God's 'turning' towards the human is normally conditioned by human repentance. Referring to the passage of the Golden Calf discussed above, Reynolds and Moghadam write, 'As a rule, human *tawba* precedes, and is a condition of, divine *tawba* (Q 2:160; 5:39). In Q 2:54 the Israelites, after the sin of the (golden) calf, are told to return (*tūbū*) to God that he might turn to them (*tāba 'alaykum*).'[52] Report A, like other parts of the story, therefore clearly demonstrates the Tawwābūn's awareness that God's forgiveness can only follow their own *tawba* and that they consider it necessary to manifest their repentance publicly to show their sincerity. Their plea to God for forgiveness is therefore closely associated with their declaration that they are now

[52] Reynolds and Moghadam, 'Repentance', 383.

doing what al-Ḥusayn and his companions did at Karbala when they were killed. Turning their backs on their previous cowardly negligence, they are now prepared to follow the example of his companions on the battlefield. The weeping and self-abasement related in Report B signify the same kind of plea for forgiveness, even if that report foregrounds the prayer for al-Ḥusayn's soul.

The amendments and additions to the original reports give a slightly different picture of the feelings of the Tawwābūn. The profound sense of guilt and the plea for God's forgiveness are toned down, and what is accentuated in their place is their bold declarations of loyalty and love towards al-Ḥusayn and his family, as well as enmity and the desire to fight against their enemies. It is in these parts of the account that we find various forms of the concepts *walāya* ('love' or 'loyalty') towards the family of the Prophet, and *ʿadāwa* ('enmity') towards and *barāʾa* ('dissociation') from its enemies (*K*.II.1; *K*.III.5).[53] The more recent layers of the account, in other words, contain markers of a Shiʿite group identity that are not found in the earliest reports.

Ritual Aspects

The section dealing with the visit of the Tawwābūn to al-Ḥusayn's grave is, furthermore, one of the earliest accounts of a Shiʿite ritual that was later to emerge.[54] Although what is described here is not a *ziyāra*, a pilgrimage ritual, as it developed later, the way Randal Collins talks of interaction rituals – as encounters between people where they mutually focus their attention on something – is applicable here.[55]

To set the visit to the grave in a more general context, I will briefly, before analysing the text, summarise the relevant parts of Leor Halevi's book on death rites in the emerging Islamic community.[56] Halevi argues that rituals regarding death and the dead body are crucial in the establishment and preservation of the identity, what I call 'social formation', of a religious community.[57] He contends that the early pre-Islamic rituals of washing the corpse, visiting

[53] On these concepts and their significance for the early Shiʿite community, see Dakake, *Charismatic Community*, 49–57. On *walāya*, see Amir-Moezzi, *Spirituality*, 231–75.

[54] Dakake, *Charismatic Community*, 94. See below, Chapter 11.

[55] See Chapter 2.

[56] Halevi, *Muhammad's Grave*. For the importance of visits to graves in later Shiʿism, see also Schöller, *The Living and the Dead*, vol. II, 29–33.

[57] Halevi, *Muhammad's Grave*, 1–5, 234–40.

the graves of the dead and praying for God's mercy and forgiveness for the deceased, together with other customs associated with death and burial, gradually became 'Islamicised' during the second and early third/eighth and early ninth centuries in order to distinguish the Muslims from other communities and strengthen the unity within the Islamic *umma*.[58] One such marker, he argues, where the process of Islamisation is clearly visible is that of epitaphs.

On a tombstone bearing one of the earliest inscriptions known from a Muslim context, we read:

> In the name of God, the Merciful the Compassionate, this grave belongs to 'Abd al-Raḥmān ibn Khayr al-Ḥajrī.
> Forgive him, O God, and make him enter [Paradise] by your mercy, and let us go with him.
> Seek forgiveness for him whenever this inscription is read, and say 'Amen!'
> This inscription was written in Jumādā II of the year 31 [January or February of the year 652 CE].[59]

Halevi asks to what extent this inscription can be called 'Islamic', as the only unambiguous indication that the deceased belonged to the movement that later came to be known under the label 'Islam' is the reference to the *hijrī* calendar. Although there is no reason to doubt that this 'Abd al-Raḥmān identified himself as 'Muslim', or perhaps as a 'Believer' (*mu'min*) or 'Emigrant' (*muhājir*), the inscription itself can hardly be said to be 'Islamic'. Halevi demonstrates that over the first centuries of Islam, epitaphs increasingly came to include particular characteristics such as references to the Prophet Muḥammad, quotations from the Qur'ān and formulaic confessions of faith. Similarly, burial customs such as the washing of the dead body, the procession and communal prayer at the burial, and the physical appearance of the grave

[58] Halevi, *Muhammad's Grave*, 14–32. The term 'pre-Islamic religious traditions' here does not necessarily mean the *jāhilī* tradition that was supplanted by Islam, but includes traditions which existed before the emergence of Islam and continued to exist beside it (in, for example, Judaism, Christianity and Zoroastrianism) and which to a certain extent were also taken over and integrated into Islam.

[59] The translation is from Halevi, *Muhammad's Grave*, 14, and the discussion of the lack of Islamic characteristics on the following pages of this book. For a slightly different translation of the same text, see Donner, *Narratives*, 85. The Arabic text is available in El-Hawary, 'Most Ancient Islamic Monument', 322.

were given specific 'Islamic' characteristics. Consequently, a tombstone at a woman's grave about four decades later has more 'Islamic' characteristics, such as the reference to the Muslims as a family (the *ahl al-islām*), the lament over the Prophet's death, and the *shahāda* (although in slightly different form from the classical one). Still, though, there is no quotation from the Qur'ān. These only emerge towards the middle of the second/eighth century.[60]

My point here is that many supposedly Islamic traditions associated with death and burial already existed within other religious traditions in the area – among Christians, Jews and Zoroastrians, for example. To a certain extent, the Muslims maintained these customs and rituals but placed them in a new context, adapted them and, in certain cases, gave them new content. In the same process, some earlier traditions were completely prohibited, while others were added. (This is true not only of rituals surrounding death and burial, of course, but also other rituals such as prayer, pilgrimage and fasting.)

The account of the visit of the Tawwābūn to Ḥusayn's grave is a further example of the process of 'Islamisation' – or perhaps, rather, a 'Shiʿitisation' of pre-Islamic rituals. In the oldest layers of the story, that is, in Reports A and B (*K*.III. 1 and 2), part of what is described – the visit to the grave and the pleas to God for forgiveness and mercy for al-Ḥusayn – constitutes a ritual that was familiar in this context. By later Shiʿite standards, however, asking God to forgive al-Ḥusayn's sins was absurd, as we have seen. Yet, already in these old strata there are some elements that are less usual in this setting: the Tawwābūn's repentance and their prayers for forgiveness for *themselves* rather than just for al-Ḥusayn. In these reports we probably come closer to a description of the actual event than in the later additions and emendations; in the later parts of the text, we find activities and words that have more of a Shiʿite tinge.

Another aspect of interest is the role of the Kufan tribal burial grounds, the *jabbānāt*, as spaces where rebellions were often instigated and prepared. When the men of the tribe gathered at their *jabbāna* to get ready for battle, the women customarily wailed and spurred the fighters on to avenge the dead

[60] Halevi, *Muhammad's Grave*, 20–2. For the establishment of the Qur'an as a text common to all Muslims at the turn of the second/eighth century, see Shoemaker, *Creating the Qur'an*.

of the tribe.[61] As Parker Selby has indicated, several features in the description of the Tawwābūn's visit to al-Ḥusayn's grave correspond to this practice. He writes: 'this is not to deny the soteriological notions of atonement motivating the participants in the revolt, but to suggest that the Tawwābūn's revolt also be understood as a prototypical social institution of Arab tribal politics'.[62] I agree with Selby's conclusion. Thus in *K*.III.2, for example, we read that 'the people did not cease to plead for mercy on [al-Ḥusayn] and his companions until they made the early morning prayer by his tomb on the following day, *and that increased their fury*'. The last clause, italicised here, clearly points in this direction. The scenes described in the early layers of this story thus amply express the intense emotions of the Tawwābūn – in Durkheimian language, their collective effervescence – which intensified their determination to avenge the death of al-Ḥusayn or to die in the attempt. Still, *wailing* in the sense of expressing sorrow for the death of al-Ḥusayn is conspicuous by its absence from the account. The grief that the Tawwābūn manifest is not so much at having lost al-Ḥusayn as of having sinned gravely against God and the family of the Prophet.[63] Furthermore, while their visit to the grave foreshadows the developed Shiʿite ritual of the *ziyāra*, we see nothing of the miraculous qualities of the grave that are found in later traditions and pilgrimage manuals.[64]

Summary

The account of the Tawwābūn's visit to the grave of al-Ḥusayn is interesting in several respects. The composition of the text reveals some of the history of its tradition and shows that it consists of at least two layers. The earlier one is made up of two anonymous traditions about the visit to the grave, where ideas are expressed which disagree with, or are less common in, later Shiʿism, such as the tenet of the infallibility of the imam and the sense of deep guilt of the Tawwābūn for neglecting al-Ḥusayn. In this layer, furthermore, ʿAlī is absent, and the genealogy of al-Ḥusayn is traced through his mother Fāṭima to the

61 Halevi, *Muhammad's Grave*, 132–3.
62 Selby, 'Ḥusayn's Dirt', 23–4.
63 This in agreement with Halm (*Shiʿa Islam*, 19), but contrary to what Dakake assumes in her analysis of the story (*Charismatic Community*, 90–5).
64 See Chapter 11.

Prophet. The later layer is merged with and appended to these two early traditions and displays more 'markers' of Shiʿism as it developed later. Here, then, we see clear traces of the imam (whether ʿAlī, al-Ḥasan or al-Ḥusayn) being elevated to a figure above ordinary humanity. Thus, within this story, most of which was composed before the end of the second/eighth century, we can already see a certain development of Shiʿite doctrine. In the following chapter, I will discuss the dating of the text in more detail.

8

The Story of the Tawwābūn: Date and Concluding Remarks

In the two previous chapters, I have argued that, of the four programmatic texts, the first two, as well as the first half of the third, have a similar structure and content, while the fourth is sufficiently divergent from the first three for it to be necessary to hypothesise a different origin. The second half of the third text is almost certainly a later addition. I have furthermore maintained that the account of the visit to the grave is based on two old reports, which have subsequently been amended and extended. So, the question of the date of these passages must now be dealt with. This is difficult, and any such attempt must be taken with a generous pinch of salt. The discussion of the date will begin with the grave section, and then proceed to the programmatic texts.

Is it Possible to Date the Story of the Tawwābūn?

A starting point for any attempt to date the story is of course Abū Mikhnaf's presumed date of death some time before 170/786–7, which must be regarded as a *terminus ante quem* for his *Kitāb Sulaymān b. Ṣurad wa ʿAyn al-Warda*; but we have already seen that the question of a latest date for the story is not straightforward. Layers of text from various dates have been compiled, and the analysis above has already demonstrated that those sections in the account of the visit to the grave that recount the speech of al-Muthannā were probably added after Abū Mikhnaf.[1] Nevertheless, although changes have certainly

[1] There is reason to believe that another alteration is the date given for the battle at ʿAyn al-Warda, which is probably wrong, as the text first says it occurred in Jumādā I 65/January 685, while a few lines further on it is placed in the reign of ʿAbd al-Malik, who became caliph in April 685 (al-Ṭabarī, *Taʾrīkh*, II, 558; see also Rotter, *Bürgerkrieg*, 187–92). This has caused some confusion

been made in various parts of the story of the Tawwābūn, I see no reason to believe that the account of the visit to the grave has been substantially modified since Abū Mikhnaf. It cannot, of course, be established beyond doubt that such alterations did not take place, however, and further studies may come to a different conclusion.

To summarise the foregoing analysis of the grave text in this context. The structure of the text indicates that there are two major reports, which I have called Reports A and B, underlying Abū Mikhnaf's account. These reports may very well have been transmitted orally in the earliest stages; subsequently, however, they were moulded by the transmitters according to their respective contexts and were used in three separate *khabar*s which were then compiled by Abū Mikhnaf into the story analysed here.[2] We do not know when he wrote his book about the Tawwābūn, but to be safe, let us postulate some time towards the end of his life, in the third quarter of the second/eighth century.[3] Given the different wordings and structures of the three *khabar*s, it is most unlikely that Abū Mikhnaf could have made these up himself. It would have been extremely hard to forge traditions like these, and it is difficult to see any motive for him to do so in this case. Thus, the probability is that the three *khabar*s he used to create this account were extant when he wrote it. If this is correct, traditionists from the generation before Abū Mikhnaf would have compiled the longer *khabar*s that make up the account (that is *Khabar* I, II, and III), and in this process they would have used the two anonymous reports from a previous generation of narrators, amended them, and added material to fit their needs. As with the preceding generation of transmitters, one single person could hardly have forged the two reports that are at the basis of the *khabar*s. My argument, then, is that Reports A and B have their origin two

among later historians. Al-Yaʿqūbī, for example, first writes that it was the caliph Marwān who sent his army against the Tawwābūn, and then adds a disclaimer, 'It is also said that Sulaymān was not killed in the days of Marwān, but in the time of ʿAbd al-Malik' (*Taʾrīkh*, vol. II, 306), and both al-Balādhurī and al-Masʿūdī place the battle in the reign of ʿAbd al-Malik (al-Balādhurī, *Ansāb*, vol. VI, 370–1; al-Masʿūdī, *Murūj*, vol. V, 221). Personally, I would not give too much attention to the date for the battle purportedly given by Abū Mikhnaf. He was an experienced historian who would scarcely have made a mistake of this kind. This date might well have been inserted by a later copyist or editor. If so, we have yet another indication that the text has been altered after him.

2 For a discussion of such processes, see e.g. Schoeler, *The Oral and the Written*, 28–44.

3 For a discussion about the chronology of Abū Mikhnaf's works, see Bahramian et al., 'Abū Mikhnaf'.

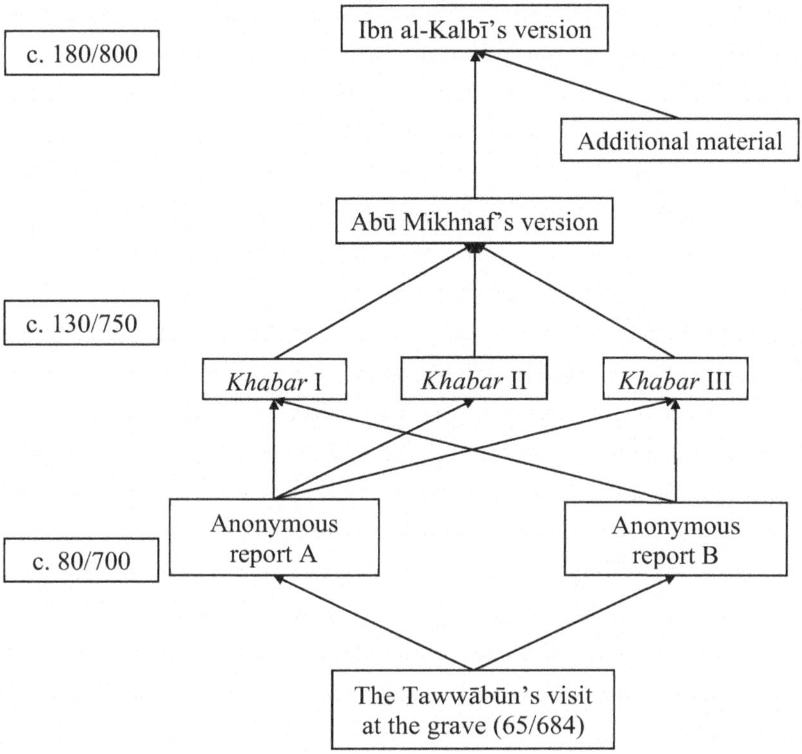

Figure 8.1 Tradition history of the account of the Tawwābūn's visit to al-Ḥusayn's grave. The leftmost column indicates years.

generations before Abū Mikhnaf, that is, at least as early as the end of the first/ the beginning of the eighth century (see Figure 8.1). They might, of course, have originated before that and might even go back to eyewitnesses of the event; but there is no way we can know this for sure.

Unlike the section on the visit to the grave, each of the four programmatic texts is extant in only one version. This makes it much more difficult to date them accurately. However, there are a few indications which in my view point towards a date as early as the visit to the grave, at least for the first three texts.

First, there is the curious interpretation of the Qur'anic verse relating the incident of the Hebrews and the Golden Calf (Qur. 2:54), already discussed in Chapter 6. There, I mentioned Hawting's opinion that the Tawwābūn's application of this verse to their situation is unusual in Islam and indicates an early date for the text. This argument, however, sets only a relative date in relation to the emerging movement of Islam: namely, 'early'.

Second, I mentioned above that Text III – the letter purportedly written by Sulaymān b. Ṣurad to the Shiʿites of al-Madā'in and Basra – was transmitted to Abū Mikhnaf by al-Ḥuṣayn b. Yazīd, grandson of 'Abdallāh b. Sa'd b. Nufayl, one of the five leading figures of the Tawwābūn. Al-Ḥuṣayn b. Yazīd says that he he had access to it during the caliphate of Sulaymān b. 'Abd al-Azīz (96–9/715–17). If correct, this date would give us a *terminus ante quem* for the origin of the letter. In my opinion, statements like this cannot be taken at face value unless supported by other evidence; the date could have been made up by the narrator to make his story seem more truthful, or he could have been mistaken. But in the present case the date provided is backed up (though, of course, not absolutely verified) by the dating of the section dealing with al-Ḥusayn's grave to the end of the first century AH/beginning of the eighth century CE. If Text III originates at this time, so too, probably, do Texts I and II. As outlined above, the similarities in structure and content between Texts I, II and the first half of III argue for a similar origin for these texts. (It will be remembered that I think that the second half of Text III as well as Text IV have different origins.)

Third, the similarities between the ideas expressed in the first three programmatic texts on the one hand and Report A and B in the grave section on the other also argue for a similar date of origin. Unique to both sets of text is the profound sense of guilt and the need to express true repentance by seeking vengeance for al-Ḥusayn. These features are not present in the texts that, partly on other grounds, I have judged to be later additions to the story. Supposing these sections to have been inserted at a later date, the omission of the theme of guilt could be accounted for either by later editors not sharing this feeling or by a conscious de-emphasis of it, whether for religious or other reasons. The expression of guilt is furthermore completely absent from the story of al-Mukhtār b. Abī 'Ubayd, the leader of a Shiʿite rebellion in Kufa just after the affair of the Tawwābūn. In Chapter 9, I will argue that important elements of that story, including al-Mukhtār's successful vengeance for the killing of al-Ḥusayn, are probably historical.[4] Whatever his motives for

[4] See also Hylén, 'Mukhtār and the *Mahdī*'; 'Emerging Patterns'.

avenging al-Ḥusayn, there are no traces of a sense of guilt in the various versions of the story about al-Mukhtār. This feature, then, seems to have been quite unique to the Tawwābūn. The fact that it is important both in the four programmatic texts and in the section dealing with the visit to the grave argues, in my view, for these two sets of text being based on traditions with a similar date of origin.

Taken by itself, none of the above three arguments is probative. Nevertheless, in my opinion the cumulative weight of the argument makes a case for the origin of the programmatic texts in their present form at about the same time as the text about the visit to the grave – that is, in the late first/early eighth century for Texts I, II and the first half of Text III, at least. Text IV, as demonstrated above, is considerably at variance with the first three, and probably has a different origin. Given its more developed argument, it may be that it is later, but this is impossible to conclude with safety. Yet, while my view is that Texts I, II and the first half of Text III originated at least at the turn of the second/eighth century, there is no reason to assume that the second half of Text III and Text IV were not part of Abū Mikhnaf's original text.

A final argument for an early date for the traditions that form the basis of Abū Mikhnaf's account is the poem by the famous Kufan poet Aʿshā Hamdān (d. 82/701 or 83/702), quoted by al-Ṭabarī as an appendix to Abū Mikhnaf's story.[5] If this poem is genuine (and I really see no reason to suspect otherwise), it constitutes very early support for the historicity of the Tawwābūn movement and for the ideas and sentiments expressed in Abū Mikhnaf's narrative. A few verses of this long poem will suffice to illustrate this:

11. He[6] made entreaties to God truthfully
    and fear of God achieves the best of rewards.
12. And he abstained from this world and did not get involved in it
    but turned in repentance to God, the Lofty, the Most High.

[...]

[5] Al-Ṭabarī, *Taʾrīkh*, II, 572–5. On Aʿshā Hamdān, see El-Achèche, *La poésie šiʿite*, 197–9 (note that El-Acheche mistakenly says that his poem is about the Karbala event); Seidensticker, 'Aʿshā Hamdān'

[6] The subject here is Sulaymān b. Ṣurad.

15. It caused him to set out on the signposted roads
    against Ibn Ziyād[7] leading troops who put all to flight.
16. With a throng who were people of divine fear and understanding,
    one who was active in courage and noble of lineage.
17. They passed on, leaving Ibn Ṭalḥa[8] to his own thoughts
    and answering not the governor who addressed them.[9]
18. They journeyed on together with the seeker after piety
    and another one repenting what he had done in the past.
19. At ʿAyn al-Warda, they met the army which was setting out
    against them, and they slaughtered them with cutting swords.[10]

These verses bring up several of the key concepts and events related by Abū Mikhnaf. Repentance, leaving this world behind, seeking piety, paying no heed to the admonitions of the Kufan governor and his officials, turning against the Umayyads and battling them at ʿAyn al-Warda – all these elements are found in the narrative. Given that the poem was composed at least fifty years before Abū Mikhnaf's *Kitāb Sulaymān b. Ṣurad*, the presence of these themes makes the end of the first/seventh century all the more likely as a time of origin for the traditions that form the basis of this story.

In summary, my analysis of the four programmatic texts and of the account of the visit to the grave suggest that the earliest parts of the story – that is, the programmatic Texts I and II and the first half of Text III, as well as Reports A and B (*K*.III.1–2) of the visit to the grave – stem from the late first/seventh or the early second/eighth century.

[7] As we saw in Chapter 3, he was the Umayyad governor of Kufa, responsible for al-Ḥusayn's death. In the time of the Tawwābūn, he was active in Damascus, working in close proximity to the caliph, and was in charge of the troops against the Tawwābūn at ʿAyn al-Warda.

[8] Ibrāhīm b. Muḥammad b. Ṭalḥa, who was at this time the Kufan official in charge of collecting the taxes.

[9] This probably refers to a letter that the present Zubayrid governor of Kufa, ʿAbdallāh b. Yazīd al-Anṣarī, sent to the Tawwābūn after they had set off, trying to make them return. The Penitents refused, however. (See Al-Ṭabarī, *Taʾrīkh*, II, 548–51.)

[10] Al-Ṭabarī, *Taʾrīkh*, II, 573–4.

Concluding Remarks

The early date of the oldest strata of the story of the Tawwābūn suggests that they probably go back further in time than the versions of the full Karbala story that are related by al-Bāqir and Ibn ʿAbd al-Raḥmān. Yet, with the exception of the story of Muslim b. ʿAqīl's mission and death, the main elements of the story of al-Ḥusayn's death are also to be found in these early traditions: the invitation to al-Ḥusayn by the Kufan Shiʿites; their failure to support him when he was attacked by the evil-doers; his death at the hands of his enemies. This shared pattern indicates that, even if the full story was not fixed at this time, its skeleton at least is very old.

In the oldest layer of the story of the Tawwābūn, the most salient feature is the profound sense of guilt expressed by the group for their betrayal of al-Ḥusayn. They view this treachery not only as an act of the utmost disloyalty to the family of the Prophet, but also as a grave sin against God that will be punished in the hereafter. The only way to be relieved of the guilt and to find peace with God is to repent, and to express this repentance through seeking revenge for the killing of al-Ḥusayn, or dying in the attempt. In these early texts, beyond the fact that he is the grandson of the Prophet Muḥammad through Fāṭima, al-Ḥusayn is pictured as an ordinary man, on a par with his companions. Thus, it is necessary to pray for God's mercy on him and his followers at Karbala. Such ideas are unusual in Shiʿism, and indeed in Islam at large, and are in themselves an indication of the early origin of these traditions.

In the sections with a different origin, whether these are likely to be later additions and amendments (the latter part of *K*.II.1, and *K*.III.3–7) or whether their date is just difficult to ascertain (T.IV), the guilt feelings of the Tawwābūn are much less prominent. In these sections, rather than the sense of guilt, what is foregrounded is exhortations to reinstate and uphold the authority of the family of the Prophet, love for the family of the Prophet, and dissociation from the family's enemies. In other words, we see more Shiʿite 'markers' in these sections. Here, al-Ḥusayn is associated with the family of the Prophet not only through his mother Fāṭima, but also, and to an even greater extent, through his father ʿAlī. Furthermore, al-Ḥusayn is described as a person who is above other human beings. He is inviolable, he is rightly guided, and he is the link between God and humanity on the Day of Judgement. In Chapter 3, we saw that the image of al-Ḥusayn developed in the interval between the two shorter versions of al-Bāqir and Ibn ʿAbd al-Raḥmān on the one hand, and the long version of Abū Mikhnaf on the other. Here, then, a similar development, a removal of al-Ḥusayn and the battle at Karbala from human history, can be discerned within the story of the Tawwābūn as we have it now. This process of mythmaking continued after Abū Mikhnaf's compilation of his books, and in Chapter 11 we will see how it flourished in the following centuries as an element of the elaboration of the notion of the Imam in Twelver Shiʿism. Before that, however, it is necessary to take a brief look at the story of the rebellion of al-Mukhtār in Kufa.

PART III

FROM SKIRMISH TO COSMIC BATTLE

9

Al-Mukhtār and the Mahdi

The revolt of the Shiʿite leader al-Mukhtār b. Abī ʿUbayd al-Thaqafī (d. 67/687) marks a kind of completion of the Karbala drama, with he and his followers exacting vengeance on those responsible for the death of al-Ḥusayn.[1] A tradition in one of the earliest collections of hadiths about the twelve imams, *Ithbāt al-waṣiyya li-l-imām ʿAlī b. Abī Ṭālib*, ascribed to al-Masʿūdī (d. 345/956),[2] describes how the skies were blood-red after the killing of al-Ḥusayn. Then follows a tradition which says, 'It is narrated that the blood did not calm down until al-Mukhtār b. Abī ʿUbayda rose in rebellion and killed seventy thousand in it.' Later tradition thus regards al-Mukhtār's revenge as a kind of settlement (though the tradition also makes him state that the killing of seventy thousand was in no way sufficient to make up for the death of al-Ḥusayn).[3] In later popular Shiʿite literature from the Turco-Persian cultural sphere, the Karbala drama, the story of the Tawwābūn and the story of al-Mukhtār and his revenge have at times been fused to make a kind of literary cycle.[4]

But beyond the vengeance for al-Ḥusayn, the Karbala affair is conspicuous by its absence in the earliest accounts of al-Mukhtār, given the fact that he was active in Kufa during and after the actions of the Tawwābūn and that some of the survivors from the battle of ʿAyn al-Warda joined his insurrection on their return. Al-Mukhtār's movement was politically important, challenging the

[1] This section draws to a certain extent on two of my previous publications, 'Mukhtār and the *Mahdī*' and 'Emerging Patterns'.
[2] On him and the discussion about the authorship of the *Ithbāt*, see Pierce, *Twelve Infallible Men*, 21–3.
[3] Al-Masʿūdī, *Ithbāt*, 164.
[4] Calmard, 'Culte', 220–59; 'Popular Literature', 318–23.

two main contenders for power at the time: the Umayyad caliphate, based in Damascus, and the caliphate of ʿAbdallāh b. al-Zubayr, centred in Mecca. His revolt and the Kaysāniyya movement that emerged after him are furthermore significant for the study of the development of the Shiʿite ideology, as several of the concepts and ideas promoted in these two movements were later developed and are still visible even in Shiʿism today. The political and religious impact of al-Mukhtār's revolt and the Kaysāniyya is an important reason why his movement is one of the most fully recorded groups in the first century of Islam, as well as one of the early movements most thoroughly investigated by modern scholars.[5] In this short chapter, I will summarise the story of al-Mukhtār as it is related by al-Ṭabarī, and then briefly discuss the development of the Kaysāniyya with special regard to issues that are important for later Shiʿism.[6] The chapter does not contain the kind of close textual analyses as found in Parts I and II, but is more of a survey based on previous research, my own and that of other scholars.

The Insurrection of al-Mukhtār

In Chapter 1, I mentioned that the religio-political situation in the region in the second quarter of the first/last quarter of the seventh century was turbulent. Two caliphates, one headed by Ibn al-Zubayr in Mecca and the other by the Umayyads in Damascus, were competing for power. At the same time,

[5] Some important studies of al-Mukhtār and his movement from different perspectives are Dixon, *Umayyad Caliphate*, 25–81; al-Qadi, *Al-kaysānīya*, 71–137; Wellhausen, *Religio-Political Factions*, 125–45; Halm, *Die islamische Gnosis*, 43–83; Fishbein, 'Life of al-Mukhtār'; Hawting, 'Al-Mukhtār'; Tucker, *Mahdis*, 19–33; Anthony, *The Caliph*, 256–90; 'Kaysāniya'. These studies are of shifting quality. Some (notably Anthony, *The Caliph*) are truly critical in the sense that they investigate and problematise the sources according to criteria normally used in modern academic scholarship; others (particularly Dixon and Wellhausen) are mainly compilations and attempts to harmonise the sources. Halm's study differs from the others in that it is based on translations of early heresiographical accounts about al-Mukhtār and his movement. An excellent study on al-Mukhtār from various perspectives in Islamic historiography is Haider, *Rebel*, 26–114, much abbreviated in Haider, 'al-Mukhtār'.

[6] The revolt of al-Mukhtār and his rule in Kufa is related by several sources, e.g. al-Ṭabarī, *Taʾrīkh*, II, 599–746 (English translations in al-Ṭabarī, *History*, vols XX and XXI by Hawting and Fishbein respectively); Ibn Saʿd, *Ṭabaqāt*, vol. VII, 99–107; al-Dīnawarī, *Akhbār*, vol. I, 296–316; as well as the Syriac chronicle *Rīš Mellē* by the contemporary Christian writer John bar Penkāyē (Brock, 'North Mesopotamia', 64–7). For more detailed discussions of the sources, see Hylén, 'Emerging Patterns', 11–12; 'Mukhtār and the *Mahdī*', 145–8. See also the important discussion of sources and their various perspectives in Haider, *Rebel*, 26–114.

apocalyptic ideas were in the air, inspiring several anti-authoritarian political movements, including that of al-Mukhtār. After the defeat of the Tawwābūn, he rose to power as the most prominent political leader of the Shiʿites in Kufa. The early sources often regard him with great suspicion, describing him as a political opportunist more interested in power than in adhering to political or religious conviction.[7] Al-Mukhtār claimed to have been sent by a living son of ʿAlī, Muḥammad b. al-Ḥanafiyya. Ibn al-Ḥanafiyya was ʿAlī's son, not (like al-Ḥasan and al-Ḥusayn) with Fāṭima the daughter of the Prophet, but with a slave woman from the tribe of Ḥanīfa; hence his appellation Ibn al-Ḥanafiyya, 'the son of the Ḥanafī woman' (see Figure 'Genealogy of the imams'). He seems, however, to have been hesitant, if not outright negative, about being associated with al-Mukhtār, who called Ibn al-Ḥanafiyya *al-mahdī*, 'the rightly guided [by God]'. It should be clarified at this point that in the first decades of the movement of believers, the term *al-mahdī* probably had no eschatological connotations but was simply used to describe a person, normally some kind of leader, as divinely guided. Several studies about al-Mukhtār have asserted – without really advancing any arguments – that he was the first figure to use this concept with the meaning 'messianic redeemer'. I have demonstrated elsewhere, however, that, while his use of the title *al-mahdī* for Ibn al-Ḥanafiyya can be historically maintained with some probability, it is much less certain that he used it in an eschatological sense.[8]

Al-Mukhtār gathered around him large numbers of Shiʿites, and several sources indicate that his followers called themselves *shurṭat Allāh*, 'the troops of God'.[9] They seem to a large extent to have consisted of two categories; *mawlā*s, non-Arab clients to an Arab tribe; and members of South Arabian tribes who had settled in Kufa. Most of the sources attest the significant proportion of *mawlā*s among the supporters of al-Mukhtār.[10] The *mawlā*s were the non-Arabs who formed part of the Arab society of believers, converts and freed slaves. In pre-Islamic Arab society, which was based on a system

[7] This view of al-Mukhtār has also been forwarded by some modern scholars. So, for example, Howard in al-Ṭabarī, *History*, vol. XIX, 28, n. 131; Shaban, *Islamic History*, 94. For various opinions about him from Western scholars, see Dixon, *Umayyad Caliphate*, 26–7.

[8] Hylén, 'Mukhtār and the *Mahdī*'.

[9] For references, see Anthony, *The Caliph*, 282–5.

[10] See e.g. Crone, *Political Thought*, 85; Fishbein, 'Life of al-Mukhtār', 15–42; Urban, 'Early Islamic *Mawālī*', 98–104.

of genealogically defined tribes, membership of a tribe was necessary in order to be part of society.[11] Those not born into a tribe could become a member of society only by becoming affiliated to a tribe in a kind of contractual relationship; becoming a *mawlā*, a client, to an Arab who was a member of a tribe allowed a person to become connected to that tribe.[12] Thus, in the first/seventh century, to join the movement of believers was to join Arab society. During the Arab conquests of the surrounding, non-Arab societies, some individuals and groups among the conquered peoples converted to the new faith and joined the ranks of the Arabs. Of those who did not convert immediately, many were taken as slaves, some of whom were later manumitted on conversion. Both these categories – immediate converts and freed slaves – became *mawlā*s and thus became incorporated into Arab society.[13] But despite their shared faith, the *mawlā*s were regarded as second-class citizens by the Arabs under the Umayyad rulers. Patricia Crone argued that their situation was much like that of indigenous peoples in the European colonies in the nineteenth and twentieth centuries. One way for the *mawlā*s to assert their identity in the new society, she held, was for them to separate themselves from the chauvinist Umayyad Arab ideology. The main alternative open to them was to align with the Shiʿites and adopt their reverence for the family of the Prophet, which 'formed a sacred lineage so greatly elevated above Arabs and non-Arabs alike that the differences between the two were drained of importance'.[14] At the same time, the *mawlā*s could identify with the sufferings of the *ahl al-bayt*, as both groups had been treated badly by the Umayyads and those affiliated with them. Thus to seek vengeance for al-Ḥusayn – the grandson of the Prophet, killed by the Umayyads – was a very concrete way of breaking ties

[11] The following discussion about the *mawālī* is based on Crone, '*Mawālī*'; *Political Thought*, 84–6; Hoyland, *In God's Path*, 157–69; Urban, 'Early Islamic *Mawālī*'. For a discussion problematising the concepts of Arabs and Arabic tribes in pre-Islamic times, see Webb, *Imagining the Arabs*.

[12] The correct Arabic plural is *mawālī*.

[13] Hoyland, *In God's Path*, 157–69; but cf. Webb, *Imagining the Arabs*, 17, n. 18, 242–4, and esp. 280, n. 18.

[14] Crone, '*Mawālī*', 186. Although Urban ('Early Islamic *Mawālī*', 86–98) expresses problems with Crone's and others' 'ethnification' of the concept of *mawlā*, she accepts the view that the *mawlā*s tried to create new and inclusive forms of nobility, based on Islamic virtue rather than birth and lineage. In her thesis, Urban views the phenomenon of the *mawlā*s from an interesting perspective that is quite different from that of many earlier historians. A problem, however, is her often uncritical use of single sources and isolated traditions as bases for her arguments.

with Arab society in its then-current form in an attempt to shape something new.[15] Within the ranks of al-Mukhtār's movement, the *mawlā*s were regarded by many as a threat to the Arabs rather than as a part of society.

To make a sharp distinction between Arabs and non-Arabs, however, is to oversimplify. Plenty of *mawlā*s were loyal to their tribes in early Umayyad times, just as many Arabs loathed and fought against the Umayyads and joined the Shiʿite movement. As already mentioned, several sources indicate that the second major group constituting al-Mukhtār's following were Arabs belonging to South Arabian tribes. The Southern Arabs seem to have been politically and religiously divided, with rifts between the followers and opponents of al-Mukhtār extending even within the tribes. The sources do not reveal the reasons why certain Southern groups or individuals joined his movement while others did not. Hichem Djaït points to social stratification as one possible factor; many of the southerners who joined al-Mukhtār seem, according to Djaït, to have belonged to the lower classes, while few of the Southern tribal leaders took part in the movement.[16] If this is true, then a substantial proportion of al-Mukhtār's followers (both the *mawlā*s and a large number of southerners) were socially deprived in one way or another. Crone argues that it was poverty that made many of them carry wooden clubs as arms rather than real weapons of iron; hence this group of poor foot soldiers of the *shurṭat Allāh* were often pejoratively called *Khashabiyya*, 'bearers of wooden clubs'.[17]

In the present context, the vengeance for al-Ḥusayn is of particular interest as it brings one phase in the trajectory of the Karbala drama to a close. The various sources normally express this as vengeance 'for the blood of al-Ḥusayn' or 'for the blood of the Prophet's family' or something similar. Al-Mukhtār was able to win over the nobleman Ibrāhīm b. al-Ashtar (of the Southern Arabian tribe of Madhḥij) by producing a letter that he alleged to have been written by the Mahdi, Ibn al-Ḥanafiyya; Ibn al-Ashtar subsequently became one of al-Mukhtār's most successful commanders, and the movement

[15] Crone, '*Mawālī*', 184–6; *Political Thought*, 84–5.

[16] Djaït, 'Les Yamanites', 168–70; see also Rotter, *Bürgerkrieg*, 99–101; Crone, 'Wooden Weapons'. Watt's hypothesis ('Shiʿism', 161–2) that South Arabian ideas about a charismatic leader were behind their promotion of ʿAlī and his descendants has not been supported by later studies, to my knowledge.

[17] Crone, 'Wooden Weapons', 174–80; Anthony, *The Caliph*, 280–4.

then managed to oust Ibn al-Zubayr's governor in Kufa. The chronology of the events that followed is unclear, as the sources differ, but all agree that al-Mukhtār and his movement took a harsh revenge on the Kufans who had taken part in the battle against al-Ḥusayn. We are told that al-Mukhtār and his companions sought out and killed the men who were involved in the battle of Karbala on the Umayyad side, including Shamir b. Dhī al-Jawshan, ʿUmar b. Saʿd and other leaders of the Karbala campaign living in Kufa. In 67/686, al-Mukhtār sent an army led by Ibn al-Ashtar against a great Umayyad force; he managed to defeat it, and killed ʿUbaydallāh b. Ziyād at the River Khāzir, close to Mosul in Northern Iraq. (Ibn Ziyād, as described in Chapter 3 and 4, had been governor in Kufa when al-Ḥusayn approached the town, and was ultimately responsible for his killing.) The victorious battle against Ibn Ziyād is mentioned also by the Christian, John bar Penkāyē. Although the latter does not mention vengeance for al-Ḥusayn as the motive for the Kufan troops (he singles out political and economic motives for the rebellion), he confirms the battle at Khāzir and its outcome.[18] Finally, a few months later, al-Mukhtār's movement was crushed by an army led by the governor of Basra, Musʿab b. al-Zubayr, brother to ʿAbdallāh b. al-Zubayr. Kufa was retaken, and al-Mukhtār was besieged in the palace of the town for some weeks before he was killed.

The account that the sources give of the Tawwābūn clearly shows the centrality of the deep longing of the Shiʿites in Kufa to avenge al-Ḥusayn's killing (see Part II above). Although, as we have seen, the main elements of this story cannot be established before the beginning of the second/eighth century, it would be very difficult to explain the Tawwābūn movement without taking account of a real sense of guilt among its members, and also among many of the Kufan Shiʿites, even those who had not joined the Tawwābūn on their march. Given this, it is not surprising that al-Mukhtār succeeded in raising support for himself as leader with a purported mission from al-Ḥusayn's half-brother to exact the vengeance that the Tawwābūn had failed to complete for the hideous crime committed at Karbala.

Apart from the vengeance for al-Ḥusayn, however, the Karbala story, its protagonists and the events it recounts are alluded to only here and there in the story of al-Mukhtār. Al-Ḥusayn himself is almost invisible, except as the

[18] Brock, 'North Mesopotamia', 65–6.

cause to be avenged. As al-Mukhtār and his companions are described, it is not so much the family of the Prophet that is in focus as ʿAlī and his sons. In this story, we see how many of the followers of al-Mukhtār enthusiastically embraced 'the religion of ʿAlī' (*dīn ʿAlī*).[19] His adoption of Ibn al-Ḥanafiyya – son to ʿAlī, rather than to al-Ḥasan or al-Ḥusayn – as *al-mahdī*, 'the rightly guided', is a clear indication of this. Since ʿAlī was the legatee (*waṣī*) of the Prophet, it was his descendants that were now carrying on this heritage, irrespective of whether they were descended from the Prophet (as were al-Ḥasan and al-Ḥusayn through Fāṭima) or not. In associating himself with Ibn al-Ḥanafiyya, al-Mukhtār was using his position to defer to ʿAlī himself, and thereby as a way of promoting his own authority.

Furthermore, the movement of al-Mukhtār has clear eschatological overtones. As Sean Anthony argues, this may have been a further factor in the great number of followers attracted. Many of al-Mukhtār's more enthusiastic acolytes belonged to the Sabaʾiyya movement, mentioned in Chapter 1.[20] The idea that ʿAlī was not dead but would soon return was widespread; at his return (*rajʿa*), he would cause a major reversal (*dawla*) and set everything right. The apocalyptic character of the movement is apparent in the curious affair of ʿAlī's chair. Several sources relate that, before embarking on the campaign against the Syrians, al-Mukhtār presented a chair (*kursī*) to his followers, which he claimed had belonged to ʿAlī.[21] This chair aroused great enthusiasm among some of his followers. The sources relate that it immediately became a kind of cultic object to some of them, who regarded it as being on a par with the Israelite Ark of the Covenant. It was covered with silk and brocade, and the people raised their hands, circled around it, and shouted. Attendants were appointed to it, and it was placed on a grey mule and brought out into the battle at the banks of the Khāzir River against the Umayyad army as a kind of talisman – a battle that, as we have seen, was very successful.

The allusion to the Ark of the Covenant is consistent with al-Mukhtār's attempt to portray himself as the representative of Ibn al-Ḥanafiyya. Although it is nowhere reported that al-Mukhtār stated that the chair of ʿAlī *was* the

19 On this, see Chapter 1 above.

20 Anthony, *The Caliph*, 256–90.

21 On this issue, see the comprehensive analysis that Anthony (*The Caliph*, 261–90) has made of the accounts of the chair and its significance, and Hylén, 'Emerging Patterns', 19–22.

Ark of the Covenant, one source relates him as saying: 'Among the children of Israel there was the Ark, in which there was a remnant of what the family of Moses and the family of Aaron left behind. Among us, this is like the Ark.'[22]

The Ark of the Covenant is important in Islamic tradition.[23] It is mentioned only once in the Qur'an, in an account where the people of Israel have asked their prophet Samuel to give them a king (Qur. 2:246–8). The prophet replies that God has chosen Ṭālūt (Saul) as their king, but they do not want him. He then says:

> Surely the sign of his kingship is that the ark will come to you. In it is Sakīna from your Lord, and a remnant of what the house of Moses and the house of Aaron left behind. The angels (will) carry it. Surely in that is a sign for you, if you are believers.[24]

Thus, in the Qur'an the Ark has the function of legitimising authority.[25] Al-Mukhtār's association of the chair of ʿAlī with the Ark of the Covenant further strengthened his authority by creating the kind of link between himself and Ibn al-Ḥanafiyya that, according to tradition, had first existed between Moses and Aaron.[26] Anthony furthermore points to the pervasiveness of the idea about the return of the Ark at the end of time. It had mysteriously disappeared during the Babylonian destruction of the Jerusalem Temple in 587 BCE, and according to Jewish and Christian apocalyptic beliefs God would bring it back as a sign of the end times.[27] Indeed, the words 'a remnant of what the house of Moses and the house of Aaron left behind' in the verse quoted probably also refer to the staff of Moses, which was closely associated with the Ark. As we saw in Chapter 1, this staff was a messianic insignia, to be carried by ʿAlī in the final battle against the evil powers of the world.

22 Al-Ṭabarī, *Ta'rīkh*, II, 703. See also the poem by Aʿshā Hamdān in the version given by al-Ṭabarī (*Ta'rīkh*, II, 704–5). The verse where the Ark is mentioned differs in al-Jāhiz's version of the poem (Anthony, *The Caliph*, 278, n. 122).

23 Rubin, 'Traditions'.

24 In the biblical version of this story (1 Sam. 8–10), the Ark is not mentioned.

25 Rubin, 'Traditions', 200.

26 This relationship was mirrored in the relation between the Prophet Muḥammad and ʿAlī. (Rubin, 'Traditions', 209–10; Anthony, *The Caliph*, 267–8; Hylén, 'Emerging Patterns', 13–14).

27 Anthony, *The Caliph*, 273–5.

The quoted verse from the Qur'an, moreover, reveals the connection between the Ark and the concept of *sakīna*. In the discussion in Chapter 4 we saw that in the Qur'an this concept is connected with the presence of God. Reuven Firestone summarises its Qur'anic significance by writing that it always 'denotes divine aid and proof of the authenticity of God's agent in the face of disbelief and adversity, and this aid or proof (or divine presence) comes in the form of divine victory in battle or its potentiality'.[28] Though the word is used by only one source in connection with the chair of ʿAlī in the story of al-Mukhtār,[29] its close connection with the Ark and its connotation of the presence of God make it likely that the chair was seen as a vessel of God's *sakīna* by his followers.

Finally, it seems that the chair of ʿAlī was regarded as some kind of medium for divine revelation in that it inspired prophecy (*waḥy*). According to Abū Mikhnaf, one man said of the chair, 'Today there has been established for us a [source of] inspiration (*waḥy*) the like of which men have never heard of. In it there is news of what will come to be.'[30] It seems that at times al-Mukhtār attempted to predict future events, and was criticised as a liar when he was mistaken. This caused him to develop the idea that God could change His mind, a doctrine known as *badāʾ* ('emergence [of new circumstances]'), which later became an important theological concept in Shiʿism.[31]

Many of al-Mukhtār's followers were thus filled with enthusiasm over the 'discovery' of the chair. At the same time, there were those who warned against the danger of falling into disbelief and committing polytheism. As far as we can tell, the chair was rather short-lived; after the battle of the Khāzir River, nothing more is heard of it. The sources relate that both the chair and the enthusiasm it had evoked were severely criticised, and al-Ṭabarī reproduces two poems by Aʿshā Hamdān and al-Mutawakkil expressing outright hostility towards it.[32] The fact that the whole affair was passed over in silence by most later authors, notably by a Shiʿite like Ibn Aʿtham who certainly had recourse

[28] Firestone, 'Shekhinah', 590.

[29] The source is a highly polemical poem by Aʿsha Hamdān related by al-Ṭabarī (*Taʾrīkh*, II, 704).

[30] Al-Ṭabarī, *Taʾrīkh*, II, 706. See also *Taʾrīkh*, II, 705 for direct and indirect references of *waḥy* in connection with the chair.

[31] See Madelung, 'Badā''. For al-Mukhtār's prophesy, see further the discussion in Anthony, *The Caliph*, 287–90. See also below, Chapter 10.

[32] Al-Ṭabarī, *Taʾrīkh*, II, 702–6.

to Abū Mikhnaf's account, indicates that it was viewed by them as an embarrassment. Together with the fact that it is mentioned by several sources, this embarrassment, in my opinion, is a strong argument in favour of its historicity, as it is hardly likely to have been invented by later generations.

The Kaysāniyya

From the foregoing discussion, it should be clear that al-Mukhtār and many of his followers emphasised ʿAlī and his legacy rather than the family of the Prophet Muḥammad and their descendants. While some groups among the Shiʿites stuck to the Prophetic bloodline in their search for a leader – groups that later developed into the Ismaili and the Imami branches, which are still very much alive (see Chapter 10) – a group, or rather a cluster of groups which later heresiographers have called 'the Kaysāniyya', arose out of the movement of al-Mukhtār. Though it only survived for a couple of centuries, many of the Kaysāniyya's central ideas, as we will see, survived and were adopted in various forms by later Shiʿism, in particular notions regarding the eschatological features of the imam.[33]

There is no record that the group named itself Kaysāniyya, and the name was probably a label given by people who did not belong to the movement. One attempt to explain the origin of the name derives it from a commander of al-Mukhtār's *shurṭat Allāh*, Abū ʿAmra Kaysān; another explanation is that Kaysān was a nickname given to al-Mukhtār himself, perhaps for his shrewdness and cleverness (*kays*).[34] Many of the followers of al-Mukhtār survived the death of their leader and were able to set up a base for their activities in the northern Iraqi town of Nisibis for a few years. They held on to the imamate of Ibn al-Ḥanafiyya and continued to view him as the Mahdi. For that reason, the movement experienced two major crises related to him: the first when he declared his loyalty (*bayʿa*) to ʿAbd al-Malik, the caliph of the hated Umayyads, after the victory of the latter over Ibn al-Zubayr in 73/692, and the second on the occasion of the imam's death in 81/700. The movement subsequently split into a number of sects offering various explanations that could accommodate

33 The following section is based on Anthony, 'Kaysāniya', unless stated. For more comprehensive overviews of the Kaysāniyya, see the references in n. 5.
34 Al-Qadi, *Al-kaysānīya*, 58–9.

the seeming impossibility of these events. Most of them declared that Ibn al-Ḥanafiyya was not dead but living in concealment (*ghayba*) from the world, and here we find the notion of the imam's occultation in Shiʿism for the first time. Some of them were of the opinion that God had concealed him from the world as a punishment for his *bayʿa* to the caliph, that he was living in the mountains and would return in due time and set everything right, while meanwhile the imamate was temporarily upheld by his son Abū Hāshim.[35] Others held that it was to protect Ibn al-Ḥanafiyya from evil that God had hidden him until his time would come, and that while he bided his time, he was living on Mount Raḍwa in the vicinity of Medina. Thus, in a poem ascribed to the Kaysānī poet Kuthayyir ʿAzza (d. c. 105/723), we read of ʿAlī and his three sons, al-Ḥasan, al-Ḥusayn and Muḥammad b. al-Ḥanafiyya:

> Verily, the imams are of [the tribe of] Quraysh,
> the rightful masters, four alike,
> ʿAlī and three of his sons
> they are the grandchildren [of the Prophet] and the successors.
> One is a grandson of faith and gentleness,
> and one is a grandson whom Karbala took away (*ghayyabat*).
> and one grandson who will not taste death until
> he will lead the horses [of war] with the banner in front,
> hidden (*taghayyaba*), invisible to them for a time
> at Raḍwa, where there is honey and water.[36]

This belief, Leonardo Capezzone writes,

> marks the first time a Shīʿī sect took on the features of a religious confession marked by a chiliastic tension focused on the eschatologic [*sic*] role of redeemer assigned to its leader, thus developing concepts that, later on, even

[35] On him, see Bayhom-Daou, 'Abū Hāshim'.

[36] I have only translated the five verses given by al-Qummī, *Maqālāt*, 29, though I have followed the reading of al-Kuthayyir's *Dīwān*, 521, vv. 3, 4, 7, 10 and 11. See also Halm, *Die islamische Gnosis*, 51 for a German translation based on al-Qummī. Kuthayyir's authorship of this poem is contested, see *Dīwān*, 522. For a more comprehensive discussion of the poetry of Kuthayyir, see al-Qadi, *Al-kaysānīya*, 312–22.

when al-Kaysāniyya had dissolved, would become an integral part of Shīʿī doctrinal tradition.[37]

The many groups that made up the Kaysāniyya movement in the second/eighth century were, according to the heresiographers, distinguished by various more or less 'extreme' views.[38] The movement gradually lost adherents, however, and in the fourth/tenth century it seems to be extinct. As Capezzone states, however, some notions that first appeared among the Kaysāniyya were taken up and developed by the larger Shiʿite community. Anthony specifies this by arguing that, in particular, the three notions of *rajʿa* (the return of the dead or hidden imam), *ghayba* (the occultation of the imam) and *badāʾ* (God's occasional change of mind owing to changed circumstances) survived the Kaysāniyya and were included in the doctrines of the Imamiyya branch in modified forms.[39] We will come across some of these concepts again in Chapter 10.

Summary

The movement of al-Mukhtār and the development of the Kaysāniyya are prime examples of the process of mythmaking, at least as the historical sources describe them. Al-Mukhtār in several ways is connected to the deceased ʿAlī: through his association with Ibn al-Ḥanafiyya, through his avenging the death of al-Ḥusayn and through the 'discovery' of a chair that was said to have belonged to ʿAlī and to be the bearer of supernatural powers. The eschatological implications of his movement are obvious, including expectations of the return of ʿAlī. In the words of McCutcheon quoted in Chapter 2, the story of al-Mukhtār is an account of mythmaking as 'a means of creating authority' by removing ʿAlī, his family and artefacts that have belonged to him 'from human history and hence from the realm of human doings'. Furthermore, in the reception of the chair of ʿAlī among some of his followers we see an interesting – though short-lived – example of the collective effervescence that

[37] Capezzone, 'Kaysāniyya'. As we have seen in Chapter 1, however, contrary to Capezzone, Anthony finds such ideas already among the forerunners of the Kaysāniyya, the Saba'iyya movement (*The Caliph*, 195–225).

[38] On these and their various beliefs, see al-Qadi, *Al-kaysānīya*, parts 3–5; Anthony, 'Kaysāniya'; Bayhom-Daou, 'Abū Hāshim'; Tucker, *Mahdis*.

[39] Anthony, 'Kaysāniya'.

Durkheim and later also Collins talked about. Thus, although al-Mukthār was severely criticised by people around him – even by dedicated Shiʿites such as Rifāʿa b. Shaddād, one of the leaders of the Tawwābūn[40] – many accepted his claims and enthusiastically stood by him.

Among the Kaysāniyya the ideas of the sons of ʿAlī – especially Ibn al-Ḥanafiyya – as his rightful successors lived on. Within this group, the idea of the imam and his eschatological return was further developed, and in the same environment several concepts and ideas that later became important in Shiʿism first originated.

Although the Karbala story is not prominent in the movements of al-Mukhtār and later on among the Kaysāniyya, they are important for the emergence of the context within which the battle of Karbala developed into a myth. As we will see in the following chapters, the story about the battle could not have developed as it did without the ideas about the imam, the dualist world-view and the eschatological vistas that first originated with these movements.

[40] On Rifāʿa's break with al-Mukhtār, see Al-Balādhurī, *Ansāb*, vol. VI, 400. Al-Ṭabari (II, 654, 659) relates how he fought and was killed on the side of al-Mukhtār's enemies, though still adhering to his Shiʿite conviction.

10

The Contest over the Imams in Early Shiʿism

Introduction

The Karbala story, needless to say, did not develop in isolation. It was one of several factors in the creation of a Twelver Shiʿite world-view. The story contributed to this world-view and at the same time drew input from it. In this chapter, I will attempt to give a brief survey of the evolution of Shiʿism from the second/eighth and up to the end of the fourth/tenth centuries: in other words, from the emergence of a strong Umayyad power in Damascus up to the era of the Buyids in Baghdad. The focus will be on the branch of Shiʿism that later became the Twelvers (the Rāfiḍīs and the Imamis), but since this development often took place in opposition to other Shiʿite groups, I will touch on these other groups as well. The chapter is based entirely on research performed by other scholars, and aims at locating the development of the Karbala story, which will be discussed in the following chapter, in its proper context.

The First Post-Karbala Imams

The use of the term 'Shiʿism' for the two or three centuries following the death of al-Ḥusayn may obscure the fact that the movement was in no way unified, but rather divided among numerous groups with different ideas on political, theological and legal matters.[1] Fundamental to all Shiʿites was the belief that ʿAlī was the legatee (*waṣī*) of the Prophet Muḥammad. The latter,

[1] See e.g. Watt, *Formative Period*, 54–7; van Ess, *Theologie*, vol. I, 233–4; Amir-Moezzi and Jambet, *Shiʿi Islam*, 19; Haider, *Shīʿī Islam*, 84–5.

according to Shiʿite historiography, had publicly designated ʿAlī as his successor at a place called Ghadīr Khumm on the way back from the so-called Farewell Pilgrimage.[2] An issue that functioned as an early watershed between various Shiʿite groups, though, was the implications of this belief. Since ʿAlī was the rightful successor of the Prophet, what attitude was one to take towards those caliphs who, rather than recognising this, had snatched the office of leadership of the community from ʿAlī? The three first caliphs, Abū Bakr, ʿUmar, and of course Uthmān, were indeed regarded as usurpers by all Shiʿites; the question under discussion was, however, whether these men were also to be counted as unbelievers because of what they had done, and whether it was correct to reject them as legitimate leaders. Those who refused to accept the first three caliphs were called Rāfiḍīs (from Ar. *rafḍ*, 'rejection'). Patricia Crone traced the idea of dissociation (*barāʾa*) from these caliphs back to the revolt of al-Mukhtār, and it is clearly found in texts from the turn of the second/eighth century, for example in a poem by the Kaysānī poet Kuthayyir ʿAzza, whom we encountered in Chapter 9.[3] The first time the term 'Rāfiḍa' is used as a designation for a group with these ideas is usually associated with the rebellion of Zayd b. ʿAlī in 122/740 (on which see below). On being prompted by some of his followers, Zayd refused to denounce Abū Bakr and ʿUmar as caliphs, which caused the companions to leave him and choose his nephew Jaʿfar as their imam. It is said that Zayd named the group *al-rāfiḍa*, though here the name refers to their abandonment of him.[4] Nevertheless, 'Rāfiḍī' soon became the appellation for those who refused to recognise Abū Bakr and ʿUmar as legitimate caliphs and declared them to be infidels. At the end of her discussion on the meaning of the Rāfiḍī position, Crone succinctly summarises the situation of Shiʿism in the decades after the turn of the century:

> In the course of the Umayyad period, Shīʿism thus came to exist in two different forms, one expressing a greater degree of alienation than the other. According to the one, the community had remained rightly guided until the first civil war, when the ʿUthmānī majority went astray but many followed

[2] For a study of the traditions – both Sunni and Shiʿite – concerning this event, see Dakake, *Charismatic Community*, 33–48.

[3] Crone, *Political Thought*, 73–4. Kuthayyir's poem is found in *Dīwān*, 490.

[4] Al-Ṭabarī, *Taʾrīkh*, II, 1,699–700. As van Ess argues, however, this story is probably 'an etiological legend with a Zaydī tendency', and perhaps stems from Abū Mikhnaf (*Theologie*, vol. I, 311).

> ʿAlī. According to the other, practically the entire community had gone astray the moment the Prophet died, only a tiny number of Companions remaining faithful to ʿAlī until he finally became caliph.[5]

The former group are often called 'soft' or 'weak' Shiʿites, the latter 'hard' or 'strong'.[6]

Another issue closely related to that of *rafḍ* was incessantly contested among the Shīʿites: the identity, nature and function of the imam. These were questions that particularly came to the surface when one imam had died, and the community had to decide what to do next. The struggle over who was the legitimate imam was one of the main factors that formed the branches of Shiʿism that survive today, as well as many of the numerous groups that did not last.[7] When surveying the development of Shiʿism and the debates over the figure of the imam in the second/eighth to fourth/tenth centuries, it is useful to highlight three major historical events that contributed to the fragmentation into the three still-extant divisions of Shiʿism, the Zaydi, the Ismaili and the Imami (or Twelver) branches.[8] This model is of course a great simplification of a very complex historical reality, but it serves well as a skeleton framework that can be fleshed out with other, perhaps less conspicuous processes.

The first historical incident is the above-mentioned insurrection against the Umayyads in 122/740 by one of al-Ḥusayn's grandsons, Zayd b. ʿAlī b. al-Ḥusayn. The aversion to Umayyad rule was widespread, but especially pronounced among Shiʿites, and it led to numerous rebellions against the ruling dynasty.[9] In spite of the instigations of their followers, however, many of the Shiʿite leaders kept a quiescent attitude towards the Umayyads. We have seen how ʿAlī's third son, Ibn al-Ḥanafiyya, remained in Medina and did not join al-Mukhtār's insurrection. The same is true of his nephew, al-Ḥusayn's son ʿAlī Zayn al-ʿĀbidīn (d. c. 94–5/712–13), the only male survivor of al-Ḥusayn's family at Karbala, who is counted as the fourth imam by the Twelvers. Zayn

[5] Crone, *Political Thought*, 74–5.
[6] van Ess, *Theologie*, vol. I, 252; Crone, *Political Thought*, 72 and *passim*.
[7] Kohlberg, 'From Imāmiyya to Ithnā-ʿAshariyya'; 'Early Attestations'.
[8] In this, I have followed Haider, *Shīʿī Islam*, 85–99.
[9] On this, see Hodgson, *Venture*, vol. I, 241–72, an important source for Haider's description, and Kennedy, *Prophet*, 94–101. The Shiʿite involvement in the political turmoil and their numerous rebellions in the Umayyad and early Abbasid period are succinctly described in Newman, *Twelver Shiism*, 19–31. See also the discussion about Arab chauvinism of the Umayyads in Chapter 9.

al-ʿĀbidīn is said to have spent all his life after Karbala in prayer and weeping over the disaster that befell his father and the suffering of the family of the Prophet.[10] Two of the sons of Zayn al-ʿĀbidīn, Abū Jaʿfar al-Bāqir (the fifth Twelver imam, d. c. 117/735)[11] and his younger half-brother Zayd, took opposite positions on the question of political activism. While al-Bāqir followed the quietist road of his father, Zayd was politically more active and for that reason gained the following of many Shiʿites who regarded him as the true imam (though, as we have seen, some abandoned him because of his soft position on the first two caliphs). Zayd was imprisoned, then later released but kept under surveillance by the Umayyad caliph Hishām b. ʿAbd al-Malik and his governor in Kufa. Nonetheless he was persuaded by his Kufan followers to raise an army and prepare for an insurrection, but before he had time to gather a strong enough force, the Umayyads were able to quench the rebellion and kill him.[12]

Out of this event, the Zaydi branch of Shiʿism emerged. Like all Shiʿites, the Zaydis believed that the legitimate leadership belonged to the family of the Prophet, but they defined this family much more widely than most other Shiʿites, so that any descendant of ʿAlī could aspire to the role of imam. Beyond that, Muslim heresiographers picture early Zaydism as a movement with several subdivisions, the two most important being the Batrīs and the Jārūdīs (named after their presumed founders).[13] The Batrīs are described as soft Shīʿites, while the Jārūdīs leant more towards the Rāfiḍī position. The general idea of the Batrīs was that a less worthy candidate could be deemed a legitimate ruler as long as his regime was just, even if a more worthy candidate existed at the time. Unlike other Shiʿites, the Batrīs furthermore held the view that knowledge about legal and religious matters was not confined to the imam, but could be found in the Muslim community as a whole. The Jārūdīs, on the other hand, held the first caliphs and their companions to be unbelievers because they had stolen the authority from ʿAlī and his sons. On several other issues, too, they were more radical than the Batrīs, and they were closer to those Shiʿite groups who were called Imamis and who later developed into the Twelvers.[14]

[10] On him, see Kohlberg, 'Zayn al-ʿĀbidīn', and on his participation at Karbala, see above, Chapter 3.

[11] On him, see Chapter 3.

[12] On this event, see al-Ṭabarī, *Taʾrīkh*, II, 1,667–88, 1,698–717; Madelung, 'Zayd'.

[13] So also Crone, *Political Thought*, 100–5.

[14] While modern scholars often follow the traditional image and picture these movements as contemporaneous (so e.g. Crone, *Political Thought*, 100–5), Haider argues that Batrism developed

We have already seen that Zayd's half-brother Abū Jaʿfar al-Bāqir (the purported originator of one of the versions of the Karbala story discussed in Chapter 3) stayed aloof from any political involvement with other Shiʿite groups. By the time Zayd instigated his rebellion, al-Bāqir had already died.[15] Like Zayd, al-Bāqir also had a substantial number of followers for whom he was the rightful imam. He was known for his erudition – a quality indicated by his sobriquet *bāqir al-ʿilm*, 'the one who splits knowledge open' – and a large number of Shiʿite hadiths trace their origin to him. His son Jaʿfar al-Ṣādiq, 'the truth-speaker' (d. 148/765), regarded as the sixth imam in the Twelver genealogy, followed in the quietist footsteps of his father.[16] Both were recognised as eminent scholars by Sunnis as well as Shiʿites.

With these two figures, the foundations of Imami Shiʿism were laid. Shiʿite law has its roots in their time, and so do many of the basic tenets of Imami Shiʿite theology.[17] One of these is the concept of *naṣṣ*, the idea that an imam must be designated by his father. Thus, the Imamis differ from the Zaydis in that they limit the legitimate imamate to the single blood line from ʿAlī and his union with Fāṭima (the passage from al-Ḥasan to his brother al-Ḥusayn excepted). Another important notion that originated at this time was that of a specific, esoteric knowledge, *ʿilm*, given directly by God and transferred from father to son through this designation. A third concept is *taqiyya* ('keeping the secret'), the idea that it is necessary, even mandatory, for true disciples of the imam to hide their Shiʿite persuasion – and in particular, the secret knowledge received from the imam – from malevolent outsiders in order to protect the imam and the Shiʿite community from persecution.[18] Furthermore, the notion of God's protection of the imam from error and sin (*ʿiṣma*), central for the development of the imam's role as a religious authority, developed in the second half of the second/eighth century. An important contributor to

into Jārūdism, the former being dominant in the late second/eighth century and the latter in the third/ninth century. Later again, Zaydism turned back into a 'softer' version of Shiʿism (*Origins*, 189–214; *Shīʿī Islam*, 105–12). Furthermore, Haider (*Shīʿī Islam*, 109–12) shows that the idea of Zaydi militance (so e.g. Crone, *Political Thought*, 107–9) must be nuanced.

[15] Amir-Moezzi, *Divine Guide*, 64; Newman, *Twelver Shiism*, 24.

[16] Modarressi, *Crisis*, 6–8.

[17] Lalani, *Early Shīʿī Thought*, 76–95; Amir-Moezzi and Jambet, *Shiʿi Islam*, 30; Crone, *Political Thought*, 110–11.

[18] Hodgson, 'Early Shīʿa', 8–13; Amir-Moezzi and Jambet, *Shiʿi Islam*, 30.

this aspect of imamology was the famous theologian Hishām b. al-Ḥakam (d. c. 179/795–6).[19]

Political turmoil continued right through the second/eighth century. In 132/750 the Abbasids overthrew the Umayyad dynasty in the name of the family of the Prophet.[20] As Shiʿite discontent with the rulers – both Umayyads and Abbasids – seethed, many hoped that al-Bāqir or his son al-Ṣādiq would take the lead in a political revolution, that one of them would be *al-qāʾim*, 'the one who stands' or 'the one who raises up'.[21] In early Shiʿism, this concept is connected to that of the imam who was to restore true religion, justice and equity; it later came to be used synonymously with the term *al-mahdī*.[22] That the two imams refused to become involved in politics and even prohibited their followers from joining revolutionary movements caused many of them disappointment and led some of them to join Zaydi revolutionary movements. Others, however, reinterpreted the role of the imam in a quietist direction. In the words of Hossein Modarressi,

> they instead viewed him as the most learned man from among the descendants of the Prophet who was to teach people what was lawful and what was not and to exhort them to turn towards God. He was the one to distinguish truth from falsity, to protect the religion from being distorted and corrupted by the ignorant and misguided, and to reestablish whatever truth suffered distortion or corruption at their hands. He guarded the integrity of the religion: if the people added anything to it he would reject it, and if they omitted anything he would restore it. Society needed an Imām to whom they could refer problems they encountered in religious practice, an Imām who would act as the ultimate authority in explicating the law of God and the true meaning of the Qurʾān and the Prophetic tradition so that differences of opinion among the believers could be removed by following his instructions in every question.[23]

[19] On him, see e.g. van Ess, *Theologie*, vol. I, 349–82 (the concept of *ʿiṣma* is discussed on 377–9); Bayhom-Daou, 'Hishām b. al-Ḥakam', 78–9; Bennett, 'Hishām b. al-Ḥakam'.

[20] All introductions to early Islamic political history deal with this crucial event. For brief surveys with further references, see e.g. Berkey, *Formation*, 102–9; Crone, *Political Thought*, 87–98; Kennedy, *Prophet*, 112–20.

[21] For a background to this very old concept, see Halm, *Die islamische Gnosis*, 362–3, n. 77.

[22] On the use of the term *al-qāʾim* and its connection with the concept of *al-mahdī*, see Modarressi, *Crisis*, 6–12, 86–91, esp. 89, n. 194.

[23] Modarressi, *Crisis*, 8–9

To many Shiʿites, however, the imam's functions did not stop at his being the foremost interpreter of the divine law. They depicted him as semi-divine or even divine, the bearer of the divine light, the only one knowing the hidden meaning of the Qur'ān and capable of interpreting it correctly and the upholder of the entire cosmos, without whom the world would immediately collapse.[24] I will return later in what follows to the development of the idea of the cosmic Imam.

The Later Imams

The second crucial event in the early history of Shiʿism occurred at the death of Jaʿfar al-Ṣādiq in 148/765. Al-Ṣādiq's eldest son, Ismāʿīl, had predeceased him by two or three years. Many Shiʿites had placed their trust in him as the coming imam, and it was widely believed that his father had appointed him as the next imam. The central Shiʿite doctrine of *naṣṣ* was here at stake. The basic problem was that, if al-Ṣādiq had indeed designated Ismāʿīl, it was owing not to his own decision, but to God's pre-ordained choice, which could not be questioned or revoked. Now, with Ismāʿīl already dead, what were they to think? Several groups emerged with various solutions to this crisis of succession. One short-lived faction argued that Ismāʿīl had not in fact died, but continued to live in occultation (*ghayba*); others held that the imamate had been transferred to Ismāʿīl's son, Muḥammad.[25]

From the latter group, over the following centuries, the Ismaili branch of Shiʿism developed.[26] According to the few sources available, Muḥammad b. Ismāʿīl moved from Medina to Khūzistān in south-western Iran, and died there around 179/795–6. For the next hundred years, virtually nothing is known about the Ismailis. Only at the end of the third/ninth century do they show up in the historical records again. Haider argues that the crisis caused by the occultation of the last Twelver imam (see below) caused insecurity and confusion among the Imamis and caused many of them to convert to Ismailism (or Zaydism).[27] These conversions were aided by numerous Ismaili missionaries

[24] Modarressi, *Crisis*, 9–10.
[25] Haider, *Shīʿī Islam*, 90–4.
[26] For overviews of early Ismailism, see Crone, *Political Thought*, 197–218; Daftary, *The Ismāʿīlīs*, 87–136; Haider, *Shīʿī Islam*, 123–44.
[27] Haider, *Shīʿī Islam*, 125. See also below.

who were active at the time, and Crone went so far as to say that '[t]he founders of Ismailism were probably breakaway Imamis. Practically all the early missionaries were Imami Shīʿites by origin, as were many of their converts.'[28] The fascinating cosmology and imamology of Ismailism had been influenced by Gnostic and Neoplatonic ideas from early times, but this need not concern us in the present study. The Ismaili imam was regarded as a political as well as a religious leader, leading in the fourth/tenth century to the foundation of the Fatimid Ismaili empire in North Africa, causing great trouble to the Abbasid caliphs for the next couple of hundred years.[29]

The majority of Shiʿites, however, did not accept the imamate of Ismāʿīl or of his son after the death of Jaʿfar al-Ṣādiq. To them, al-Ṣādiq's second son, ʿAbdallāh, was the new imam. When he died, only a few weeks after his father, most instead accepted his brother Mūsā as imam with the sobriquet al-Kāẓim, 'the reserved one' (d. 183/799). This eventually became the Imami line of thought, and thus al-Kāẓim came to be regarded as the seventh imam by this group. The theological rationale behind this choice was the doctrine of *badāʾ*, which we first encountered when discussing the Kaysāniyya in Chapter 9 and which held that God could alter His own decisions in accordance with changing historical circumstances. In this case, it was said, God changed His first choice of Ismāʿīl because of his death and substituted Mūsā.[30] Following the death of Jaʿfar al-Ṣādiq, several rebellions occurred in the second half of the second/eighth century, many with Zaydi overtones, which made the Abbasid rulers increasingly suspicious of all Shiʿites, with the result that the caliph eventually imprisoned Mūsā and, according to some sources, had him murdered by poisoning.[31] Around the turn of the third/ninth century, a network of agents (*wakīl*s) for collecting funds for the Imami Shiʿite community was established. Though their primary function was to gather money, these agents also functioned as links between the later imams and the community.[32]

[28] Crone, Political Thought, 197.

[29] Daftary, *The Ismāʿīlīs*, 137–255; Haider, *Shīʿī Islam*, 127–31.

[30] Haider, *Shīʿī Islam*, 93–4.

[31] Modarressi, *Crisis*, 54–60; Newman, *Twelver Shiism*, 25–6; Amir-Moezzi and Jambet, *Shiʿi Islam*, 32–3.

[32] On the development of the network of *wakīls* in the third/ninth century, see Hayes, *Agents*, 28–41.

At the death of Mūsā al-Kāẓim, the Shiʿite community was divided once again as to who was his legitimate successor – or, indeed, whether he had a successor. One group believed that Mūsā had been the last imam, either because he had died or because he still lived in occultation, and was the *qāʾim* who would return – from death or from his occultation – and set things right. Others favoured his son Aḥmad as the new imam, but when Aḥmad was appointed governor of Kufa by the Abbasids, most pledged their loyalty to his brother ʿAlī, who as the eighth Twelver imam is known by the sobriquet al-Riḍā, 'the Chosen One' (d. 203/818). Of all the imams in the Imami genealogy after the death of al-Ḥusayn at Karbala, ʿAlī b. Mūsā was the only one who was politically involved, because the Abbasid caliph al-Maʾmūn in 201/817 appointed ʿAlī al-Riḍā his successor. One of several reasons for this unexpected step by the caliph was probably his wish to ease the mood of the Shiʿites, who had recently created a lot of trouble through various insurrections in Iraq. Yet the appointment outraged both the Abbasid family and many Shiʿites. The imam accepted the designation, perhaps hesitantly, and the caliph was saved from further embarrassment by ʿAlī al-Riḍā's death a few months later.[33] Still, al-Maʾmūn and his immediate successors were relatively lenient towards the Shiʿites.

It seems that Muḥammad, the son of ʿAlī al-Riḍā, was generally accepted as imam by the Imami community, and he came to receive the sobriquet al-Jawād, 'the generous' (d. 220/835). But the problem of what an imam really was made painfully real, as Muḥammad was only around seven years old when his father died. In human terms, he could not possibly have had the legal and theological knowledge required by an imam, who was supposed to lead his subjects. The solution eventually accepted by the great majority of Imamis, Modarressi writes, was that

> one could be given the perfect knowledge of the *sharīʿa* and be appointed by God as the Imām even as a child in much the same way that Christ and John the Baptist were, according to the Qurʾān, prophets from their childhood.[34]

[33] For discussions and explanations from various perspectives of al-Maʾmūn's move and ʿAlī al-Riḍā's response, see e.g. Amir-Moezzi, *Divine Guide*, 63–4; Crone, *Political Thought*, 93; Newman, *Formative Period*, 2–4; *Twelver Shiism*, 26–7; Kennedy, *Prophet*, 138–9.

[34] Modarressi, *Crisis*, 33, referring to Qur. 19:12, 29–30.

This idea was an important step in promoting the image of the imam as a cosmic figure in possession of 'the divine light', and not just an eminent scholar or a political leader as many Shiʿites had perceived him to be (and which continued to be the Zaydi position). Al-Jawād was only twenty-five at his death, and his son ʿAlī, called al-Hādī, 'the guide' (d. 254/868), was also under-age when he succeeded his father. In his lifetime, the Abbasid caliph al-Mutawakkil (r. 847–61) came to power, and began pursuing a fiercely anti-Shiʿite policy. As we will see in Chapter 11, he had the grave of al-Ḥusayn at Karbala demolished, and he confined imam al-Hādī to house arrest in the new capital and military camp, Samarra. Al-Hādī's son, the eleventh imam, al-Ḥasan (d. 260/874), was also kept in confinement at Samarra, and thus was called al-ʿAskarī, 'of the military'.

These two factors – the young age of the ninth and the tenth imams, together with the imprisonment of the tenth and the eleventh – made it difficult for the Shiʿite community to keep contact with their imams and had the effect of increasing the importance of the religious scholars, as well as the *wakīls*, the network of financial agents of the imams mentioned above.[35]

Esoteric Theology

Before moving on to the third major historical event that contributed to the formation of Shiʿism, it is necessary to step back a little and look at the development of Shiʿite esoteric theology during the second/eighth and early third/ninth centuries. A rudimentary grasp of this kind of theology is necessary for an understanding not only of the image of the imam as a figure elevated far above ordinary humanity, but also of the world-view of Imami Shiʿism, which is the main driving force for the development of the Karbala story into a foundational myth. I base this section on the research of Mohammad Ali Amir-Moezzi, one of the contemporary scholars who have delved the deepest into the esoteric theology of early Shiʿism.[36] The main sources for his argument

[35] Crone, *Political Thought*, 116; Amir-Moezzi and Jambet, *Shi'i Islam*, 34–5. On the period of the last three 'historical' imams, see Hayes, *Agents*, 42–51.

[36] While details of Amir-Moezzi's research have at times been criticised (see below), as far as I am aware, his general methodology has only been critically assessed by K. D. Crow ('Shi'i Spirituality'), a critique which prompted Amir-Moezzi to reply in his brief article 'On Spirituality', his most thorough methodological statement so far. See also Gleave, 'Recent Research' for a comparison between different modes of conducting research on this subject.

are the collections of Shiʿite hadiths from the late third/ninth and early fourth/tenth centuries that will be discussed below. He argues, however, that the ideas expressed there are much earlier.[37]

Shiʿite esoteric theology, Amir-Moezzi argues, began to develop around the time of the imams al-Bāqir and al-Ṣādiq, with the appropriation and adaptation of similar ideas from various religious traditions in Late Antiquity.[38] In Chapter 4, I presented a short overview of early Shiʿite cosmology, with special reference to the concept of the divine covenant. There we saw that, according to the esoteric theology of the imams, the creation of human beings came about in stages, each new phase less subtle and more material than the previous one. From the very beginning, humanity is seen as divided between those who have pledged their *walāya* to the Prophet and the imams and those who have not; this division in turn is a consequence of the primeval cosmic conflict between the good and the evil powers of the universe. Amir-Moezzi uses the metaphor of a horizontal axis, which

> articulates the fight between two dualistic views of the world – illustrated by two opposing poles, imam and enemy, intelligence and ignorance, people of the right and people of the left, imams of justice and imams of violence – and it thus encapsulates the universal and perpetual struggle between the armies of supreme intelligence and ignorance.[39]

There is, however, also another kind of duality which is central in early Shiʿite theology, Amir-Moezzi argues: the duality between the manifest (*ẓāhir*) and the hidden (*bāṭin*). Thus, according to the sources, on one level, God is hidden and unknowable, but on another level, He reveals Himself. The foremost of all divine manifestations is the cosmic Imam (with capital 'I'), and knowledge of him is true knowledge of what can be known about God.[40] As with God, the Imam has a hidden and a manifest level: the cosmic, metaphysical Imam and the historical imams, respectively. On the 'historical' level, the imams

[37] Amir-Moezzi, 'On Spirituality', 111–12. Here, Amir-Moezzi bases his argument on previous scholarship without providing any detailed references. See also the discussion on the sources for the dualist Shiʿite cosmology in Chapter 4 above.

[38] For a thorough study that supports the argument for a pre-Islamic origin of the esoteric theology, see Asatryan and Burns, 'Ghulāt'.

[39] Amir-Moezzi, 'Early Shīʿī Theology', 88.

[40] On this notion, see Amir-Moezzi, *Spirituality*, Ch. 3.

and the prophets represent the hidden and apparent aspects, respectively. The prophets' mission is to preach the word of God to everyone, but each prophet throughout the history of humanity, from Adam to Muḥammad, has been accompanied by one or more imams whose mission it is to disclose and explain the esoteric meaning of the divine Word that the prophets proclaim. Hence, there exists also within the revelation itself a manifest and a hidden level, the former proclaimed by the prophets and available to everyone, and the latter only capable of being apprehended through the hermeneutical interpretation (*ta'wīl*) that the imams disclose to their initiate disciples:

> Thus, the prophet is said to be the messenger of the 'exoteric religion' – *islām* in the terminology of Shīʿism. At the same time, the imam or *walī* is the messenger of the esoteric religion, the initiator of the secret spiritual religion, *īmān*.[41]

Amir-Moezzi illustrates this duality with a vertical axis on which the lower pole represents the manifest aspects of religion and the upper pole the esoteric ones which are only reached through ascent from one lower level of knowledge to the next, through initiation by the imams and their secret teachings. The initiate is of course prohibited from disclosing the secret teachings of the imams; in situations of distress, the practice of *taqiyya*, 'preserving the secret', must be maintained.

As we will see below, from the fourth/tenth century onwards, a rationalist theology gradually came to prevail over the non-rational, esoteric trend. Biographies of the imams and heresiographers from this time onward refer to Shiʿites who entertained such esoteric ideas as *ghulāt* (sg. *ghālin*), 'extremists', and they make a clear distinction between *ghulūw*, 'extremism', and moderate Shiʿism.[42] Modern scholars, however, differ in their opinions on how to understand the position of these ideas in early Shiʿism. Some adhere to the division

[41] Amir-Moezzi, 'Early Shīʿī Theology', 86.

[42] A term which roughly corresponds to *ghulāt* is *mufawwiḍa*, 'delegationists', in that they argued that God had delegated certain powers to the imams. Other terms are also used to describe more or less 'extreme' positions regarding the imam. Adherents of the opposite position, which does not ascribe supernatural qualities to the imams, are called *muqaṣṣira*, 'shortcomers'. All these designations are of course nicknames given by opponents of the various groups. On the problems when they are used in modern academic studies and the difficulty in finding alternative terms, see Hayes, 'Review of *Controversies*', 518.

of the heresiographies. Thus, Wilferd Madelung argues that '[t]he *ghulāt* came to form a permanent wing in the Imāmiyya, but always remained ideologically separate from the moderate main body'.[43] Others maintain that there were originally no strict boundaries between *ghulāt* and moderate Imamis. In fact several scholars, including Amir-Moezzi in many of his works, maintain that the imams themselves entertained and taught these doctrines. Amir-Moezzi argues that the hadiths of the imams contain numerous traditions with a content that was not supposed to be known except to a small, initiated group of people. He identifies several circles of increasingly esoteric instruction centred around the imams. In the case of Jaʿfar al-Ṣādiq, eminent proto-Sunni theologians such as Abū Ḥanīfa and Mālik b. Anas (eponymous founders of two of the Sunni law schools), among others, occupied an outer circle of disciples who were taught matters of general Islamic law. Great Shiʿite theologians such as Hishām b. al-Ḥakam were in an intermediate circle, while only the closest initiates, such as Abū al-Khaṭṭāb, were allowed into the innermost circle, where Shiʿite theology and cosmology was communicated of a kind that was not supposed to be spread beyond that circle.[44] So, according to Amir-Moezzi, what are generally regarded as the imams' interdictions against 'extreme' thoughts and their curses against the disciples who publicly expressed them have been misunderstood. In reality,

> the imam's curse, when sincere and not a strategic manoeuvre, was not due to *what* the followers said, but *because* they said it, in other words, because they betrayed the rule, standard for all esoteric traditions of an initiatory nature, namely to dissimulate or keep the secret (*taqiyya*, *kitmān*, *khabʾ*).
> [...]
> The distinction between 'moderate' and 'extremist' Shiʿism appears to be artificial in terms of the early period unless one considers the imams themselves to be 'extremist', which would be at odds with the entire corpus and their sayings.[45]

[43] Madelung, 'Theology: Introduction', 458, and see also his 'Early Imāmī Theology as Reflected in the Kitāb al-kāfī of al-Kulaynī'. Crone (*Political Thought*, 80–4, 112–18) and Modarressi (*Crisis*, 9–10, 35–7) make the same distinction, but cf. Asatryan's critique of Modarressi's position in *Controversies*, 48–9, n. 21.

[44] Amir-Moezzi and Jambet, *Shīʿī Islam*, 30–1.

[45] Amir-Moezzi, *Spirituality*, 219–20, italics in the original. His article 'Les Imams' is entirely devoted to this issue. For a similar opinion, see Asatryan, *Controversies*, esp. Ch. 2.

Amir-Moezzi furthermore argues that, though the imams themselves also used the concept of *ghulāt*, it had a much more limited meaning for them than for the later heresiographers. The imams used this term to indicate people who shared their esoteric world-view, but who interpreted this to mean that they did not need to observe the law. Some of these regarded the law as unnecessary for those who had attained the esoteric level of knowledge; others thought religious duties and prohibitions to be code words standing for the imams and their enemies respectively.[46] The imams reacted strongly against such attitudes. Thus, according to them, it was antinomianism that constituted the real extremism, not belief in the divinity of the imam and other esoteric doctrines.[47]

Only in the fourth/tenth century, with the increasing influence of rationalist theology and the need to accommodate to society at large, were such ideas moved to the sectarian garbage bin. At this point it was claimed that they had never been part of the ideology of the imams and their moderate companions.[48] However, in spite of this later denunciation of the esoteric theology, it is important in that much of it was incorporated in later Imami Shiʿism, as we will see below.

The Occultation of the Twelfth Imam

To return once more to the historical overview. The third and final historical event of fundamental importance for the shaping of Shiʿism – in this case, the Imami or Twelver branch – was the crisis that followed the demise of the eleventh imam, al-Ḥasan al-ʿAskarī, in 260/874. The predicament was so dire that the Shiʿite literature of the period calls this era *al-ḥayra*, 'the Perplexity' or 'the Confusion'.[49] The death of al-ʿAskarī was unexpected, as he was still quite young (probably in his late twenties[50]), and he apparently died without leaving a son to succeed him. How was one to deal with this difficult situation? Many

[46] Dakake, *Charismatic Community*, 129–30. (Dakake does not share Amir-Moezzi's view about the *ghulāt*, however.) See also Asatryan, *Controversies*, 157–61; Asatryan, 'Wine'.

[47] Amir-Moezzi, 'Les Imams'.

[48] Amir-Moezzi forcefully argues along these lines in many of his works. See e.g. the articles reprinted in *Spirituality*, esp. 216–23; 'Les Imams'. See also Asatryan, *Controversies*, 163–6.

[49] For this term and its periodisation, see Hayes, *Agents*, 80, n. 1. The following section is based on Modarressi, *Crisis*, 77–105 and Haider, *Shīʿī Islam*, 94–8. Hayes discusses the period from the perspective of the development of the institution of four deputies (see below) (*Agents*, 80–119). All three treat this difficult period of Imami Shiʿism in much greater detail with numerous references.

[50] Halm, "Askarī'.

among those who believed that al-ʿAskarī had died without an heir defected to the Ismaili, and to a less extent also to the Zaydi forms of Shiʿism. Those who remained were fragmented into several groups. Some said that the imamate had ended with al-ʿAskarī; others that he had not died but lived in occultation (*ghayba*) and would return as *al-qāʾim*, the leader of an insurrection against the evil powers; another large group accepted his brother Jaʿfar as the new imam.

A minority, however, maintained that al-ʿAskarī in fact had a son (possibly still unborn at the time of his father's death) whom he had appointed as the succeeding imam. This, even though the presumed new imam was a minor, was the line of thought that ultimately prevailed. The boy's name was said to be Muḥammad; as the twelfth imam, he received the epithet al-Mahdī, 'the [divinely] guided'. It was made known that he was kept in hiding to save him from persecution by the Abbasids, and that he could only be reached through his deputies (*safīrs*). The period from the death of al-ʿAskarī to the death of the fourth and last deputy in 329/941 is called the minor occultation (*al-ghayba al-ṣughrā*). During these roughly seventy years, the deputies acted on behalf of the imam; they collected funding for him, received questions sent him from Believers, and returned written replies ostensibly given by him.[51] After the death of the fourth and last deputy in 329/941, the imam could not be reached at all: now the period of the greater occultation (*al-ghayba al-kubrā*) commenced.

Historians of early Shiʿism generally regard the early to mid-fourth/tenth century as a kind of turning point for Twelver Shiʿism. The disappearance of the twelfth imam caused great confusion among the Shiʿites, as we have seen. The gravity of the situation is well-described by Modarressi when he writes:

> Numerous references in the reports attest to a universal uncertainty about this question and to widespread conversions from the 'True Doctrine'. Some reports even suggest that the greater portion of the [Imami] community converted during these periods of uncertainty, as they quote earlier Imāms as predicting that the majority (according to some, up to two-thirds) of those who followed the truth would turn to other doctrines. The reports also speak of severe hostility and mistrust among the Shīʿites ...[52]

[51] On this period, see Newman, *Formative Period*, Ch. 2, and Hayes, *Agents*, Chs 4–6.
[52] Modarressi, *Crisis*, 98.

These problems were one of the main factors in the compilation of a number of works on hadiths of the imams, about the nature of the imamship and the occultation, as well as on matters of law and other aspects of theology – all of great import because the Believers themselves could not get in touch with the imam. Thus, throughout the century, important works were assembled by scholars, most of whom had their bases in the Shiʿite centres of Qom and Rayy in Iran. Some of the most prominent among these were Aḥmad b. Muḥammad al-Barqī (d. c. 280/894), al-Ṣaffār al-Qummī (d. 290/902–3), Muḥammad b. Yaʿqūb al-Kulaynī (d. 329/940), Ibn Abī Zaynab al-Nuʿmānī (d. 360/970–1), Ibn Qūluwayh (d. c. 369/979–80) and Ibn Bābawayh (or Bābūye, d. 381/991–2).[53] Many works by these scholars contained hadiths on various subjects, while others were collections of traditions on specific themes, such as al-Nuʿmānī's *Kitāb al-ghayba* ('The Book of the Occultation') and *Kāmil al-ziyārāt* ('The Complete Book of the Pilgrimages [to the Tombs of the Imams]') by Ibn Qūluwayh. These works, especially the earlier ones but to some extent also the later, mainly adhered to the old 'gnostic, initiatory, and mystical doctrines' discussed above.[54]

The efforts of the traditionists who compiled these works, as well as the scholars who interpreted and commented on them, were fruitful. In the decades following the death of al-ʿAskarī and throughout the fourth/tenth century, they resulted in the consolidation of an Imami Shiʿite identity. Two ideas that had old roots soon gained strength, and eventually were firmly established: the first, that the number of imams was set at twelve; the second, that the world is in constant need of an imam, or it will immediately perish. Together, these two notions paved the way for the idea that the twelfth imam is alive and lives in occultation, and the name Twelvers began to be used as a synonym for Imamis.[55]

Yet in many respects the theological tradition of the hadith compilations now became contested. The old traditions about the esoteric–exoteric duality discussed above – probably the dominant theology at least since the first half of the second/eighth century – were now strongly opposed by the rationalist

[53] On these scholars, see Newman, *Formative Period*; *Twelver Shiism*, Chs 2–3.

[54] Besides references given above, see also Newman, *Formative Period*, 97–8.

[55] This summary draws on Haider, *Shīʿī Islam*, 97. For more comprehensive discussions of this theological development, see Kohlberg, 'From Imāmiyya to Ithnā-ʿAshariyya'; Amir-Moezzi, *Divine Guide*, 99–105; Newman, *Twelver Shiism*, 36–60.

Shiʿite theology. The latter was influenced by rationalist currents in non-Shiʿite forms of Islam, and gained strength in Baghdad at this time. The rationalist trend in Shiʿism was not new, but had previously been overshadowed by the traditional views; now, as the rationalist influence increased, the old tradition was regarded as 'deviant and heretical'; furthermore, in contrast to the political quietism of the older theology, the new rationalism actively sought to engage in the politics of the state.[56] Once the Shiʿite Buyid dynasty had established their power over the Abbasid caliphate with the conquest of Baghdad in 334/945 and allowed Shiʿite theology, legal sciences and ritual practices to develop, the political situation in fact turned in favour of the Shiʿites.[57] The reaction from the non-Shiʿites was not long in coming. Riots between Shiʿites and non-Shiʿites were frequent, and as the power of the Buyids began to decline in the first decades of the fifth/eleventh century, the Abbasid caliph al-Qādir (r. 381–421/991–1031) took a definite stand against the Shiʿites. He made the veneration of the companions of the Prophet and of the first four caliphs obligatory for all Muslims. This, according to Hugh Kennedy, marks the first explicit and positive definition of Sunnism:

> Hitherto, the supporters of the Sunna had largely been defined by their opposition to the claims of the Twelver Shīʿīs; now, there was a body of positive belief which had to be accepted by anyone claiming to be a Sunnī. Like the Twelver doctrines developed during the previous century, it was exclusive; the acceptance of the veneration of the first four caliphs meant rejecting the claims of the Twelvers that ʿAlī had been unjustly deprived of the caliphate. It was no longer possible to be simply a Muslim; one was either a Sunnī or a Shīī [*sic*].[58]

Altogether, the Buyids were in power for about one century before the advent to power of the Sunni Seljuk dynasty – but that is beyond the scope of the present study.[59]

[56] Amir-Moezzi and Jambet, *Shiʿi Islam*, 106–7.
[57] A survey of the Buyids is provided by Kennedy, *Prophet*, Ch. 9. See also Baker, *Sectarianism*, for a slightly different interpretation of religio-political events and their consequences.
[58] Kennedy, *Prophet*, 229. But cf. Baker, *Sectarianism*, who de-emphasises the idea of the Buyid period as one of sectarian conflicts.
[59] On the Seljuks, see Hodgson, *Venture*, vol. II, 42–55, and see Index.

But in spite of the dominance of the rationalist theology from the end of the fourth/tenth century, old ideas and traditions continued to live. In an article focusing on the theological reorientation regarding the then-current notion of the *ghayba*, Saïd Amir Arjomand writes that

> theological rationalization is imposed on a nonrational – in this case, chiliastic – layer of belief. The superimposed rational layer contains the older one in both the senses of preserving it and placing it in quarantine. But both layers continue to coexist.[60]

Besides, there were always pockets of traditionalists who refused to accept rationalist methods and ideas, and at times the influence of these groups increased.[61] Thus, while the struggle between traditional and rationalist theologies endured, much of the basic thinking of the pre-*ghayba* era has continued to live until this day, though often under different guises. The hierarchical esoteric notion of revelation and knowledge is certainly found in contemporary theology, but it is perhaps the good–evil dualism that is most obvious, as can be seen in modern-day Iranian revolutionary and post-revolutionary discourse.[62]

Conclusion: The Search for a Myth

The history of Shiʿism before the occultation, as we have seen, is complex and at times confused – just like the history of non-Shiʿite Islam during the same time. Groups gather and split up, individuals change their loyalties, and ideas and institutions are formed and abandoned. In short, what we see here is a process of social formation in which the Shiʿites were trying to figure out what it meant to be loyal to the family of the Prophet. The foregoing survey has made clear, however, that this struggle did not result in the formation of one single Shiʿite identity, but rather of several, and that, in the ever-new circumstances brought about by the religio-political turmoil, these identities kept changing.

One problem for the study of history so far back in time is that we seldom get a glimpse of how 'ordinary people' perceived their situation. This is true also of Shiʿism in the second to fourth/eighth to tenth centuries. There are

60 Arjomand, 'Consolation of Theology', 568.
61 See e.g. Newman, *Twelver Shiism*, Ch. 5.
62 On modern Shiʿite esoterism, see e.g. Enayat, *Political Thought*, 21–3; on the cosmic struggle between good and evil in modern Iran, see e.g. Amanat, *Apocalyptic Islam*, Chs 2 and 9.

very few, if any, sources that reveal why people in general joined this group rather than that, or how they understood ideas and doctrines pronounced by their religious leaders, whether these leaders were the imams themselves or their disciples. What we have is the statements of these leaders, often in very cryptic forms which must have been totally incomprehensible to most of their subjects, and which, furthermore, were to a large extent reserved only for the initiated elite.

On a more general level, Jack Tannous has brilliantly argued that the absolute majority of the population in the region that is today called the Middle East were illiterate in Late Antiquity and the early Middle Ages – though the rate of literacy must have been slightly higher in the cities than in the countryside. Even fewer were what he calls 'theologically literate', that is, having an understanding of the theological content of the religious tradition to which they belonged and to some extent being able to participate in discussions about it.[63] Tannous works mainly with the Christian population, but he touches on early Islam as well, and his conclusions are, *mutatis mutandis*, true also of the Shiʿite population at the time. To be sure, early Islamic theological culture was to a large extent oral and aural; poems, books and various traditions – such as hadiths – were often transmitted by recitation and hearing rather than by reading.[64]

Through his studies of hadiths, their transmission and the derivation of legal rulings through them, Najam Haider has demonstrated that there was a clear Imami Shiʿite identity in relation to non-Shiʿite and Zaydi forms of Islam already at the beginning of the second/eighth century, at least in Kufa.[65] Doubtless, one way for the body of ordinary people to manifest their loyalty to the ʿAlīds was to follow the injunctions of the imams and their close disciples. As I have mentioned in Chapter 2, behaviour – ritual and other – is a very strong marker of identity; yet performance does not suffice to maintain a viable identity in the long run. A narrative which places the Believers in a context, explains the world to them and gives their behaviour meaning – in other words, a myth – is also necessary. On the rare occasions on which the

[63] Tannous, *Making*, Ch. 1, and see Index *s.v.* 'literacy'.
[64] Schoeler, *Genesis*.
[65] Haider, *Origins*, Ch. 9, which is a summary of the results of his study throughout the book.

concept of myth has been applied in research on early Shiʿism, as we saw in Chapter 2, it has mainly been used for narratives dealing with humanity from a pre- or post-historical perspective and limited to creation myths and eschatological myths.[66] Moreover, these myths are found only in fragmented form, often deliberately dispersed in the collections of hadiths in order to make them difficult to retrieve, so as to conceal their esoteric content from all but the initiated 'inner circle' of the imams, as Amir-Moezzi argues.[67] Hence, it must be assumed that the hadiths themselves, as well as their esoteric content, were inaccessible to 'ordinary people'.

Instead, I would suggest (perhaps unsurprisingly) that what helped disseminate a Shiʿite world-view to people who were not among the closest initiates were stories – stories narrated by preachers and professional storytellers,[68] who were able to expound them and make them meaningful to people in the context in which they lived. I furthermore suggest that it is possible to see the turbulent situation during the first three or four centuries of Shiʿite history, including the so-called *ḥayra*, the 'perplexity' that followed the death of the eleventh imam, as a contest over narratives. At the bottom of all this, and common to them all, was of course loyalty to the family of the Prophet, the assertion of ʿAlī's right to succeed the Prophet, and the idea that all those who had not accepted that order were guilty of betrayal. This basic myth was moulded and adapted to suit the various political, social and economic circumstances in which Shiʿites lived. It became the various stories of Zaydism, Ismailism and, eventually, Twelver Shiʿism. Among Imamis, then, the narrative of the twelve imams, the occultation of al-Mahdī and his return as the *qāʾim* finally prevailed and became the founding myth of the movement. In this narrative, the imams and their dealings are moved outside human history in the sense that their historical lives are given cosmological significance. Thus, the stories about the imams are neither strictly pre- nor post-historical but extra-historical. This can be seen in the biographical collections of hadiths about the twelve imams, the first of which were probably compiled in the first decades

[66] Dakake, *Charismatic Community*, see Index *s.v.* 'creation myths'; Vilozny, *Constructing a World View*, Ch. 2.

[67] Amir-Moezzi, *Divine Guide*, 5–6; Amir-Moezzi and Jambet, *Shiʿi Islam*, 12–13.

[68] The Arabic term is *quṣṣāṣ*, sg. *qāṣṣ*.

of the fourth/tenth century, studied by Matthew Pierce.[69] Pierce argues that 'there is good reason to resist the urge to cast these works as either "scholarly" (thus elite, and read by a few) or "popular" (and therefore widespread among the masses)'.[70] The narratives about the imams were an important factor in the building of Twelver Shiʿite identity; Pierce writes, further, that '[t]welver Shiʿism coalesced around these shared stories, and the systems of meaning embedded have continued ramifications in Shiʿa communities today'.[71]

Still, we must remember that stories about the imams existed long before the biographies of the Twelve. One of these is the story of the killing of al-Ḥusayn at Karbala, which has been the main study of this book. To this story, and to the developing image of the imam himself, I will return in the following chapter.

[69] Pierce, *Twelve Infallible Men*, 19–25.
[70] Pierce, *Twelve Infallible Men*, 39.
[71] Pierce, *Twelve Infallible Men*, 41.

11

Al-Ḥusayn among the Imams

Introduction

In the previous two chapters we saw how the Imami image of the imam developed from the movement of al-Mukhtār and the Kaysāniyya in the late first/seventh and early second/eighth centuries to the consolidation of the Twelver branch of Shiʿism after the occultation in the fourth/tenth century. For the Kaysāniyya (or at least some of them), there were four imams: ʿAlī and his three sons. Many of them thought that of these four, Ibn al-Ḥanafiyya, the last, was not dead, but had gone into occultation, to return one day as leader of a revolution against evil. It was also with the Kaysāniyya that some important theological concepts first saw the light which were later to be developed and become integrated in mainstream Shiʿite theology.

Although all Shiʿites agreed that ʿAlī had been the rightful successor of the Prophet as the leader (*imām*) of the community, they came to differ on how this legacy was passed on after the death of ʿAlī, to whom, and what the role and function of this leader were. Soon – to simplify matters a little – three views of the role and function of the imam developed. On the one hand, the imam was seen as the political leader, alive and active among his followers, who could lead the faithful in revolution against the rulers when necessary. This was basically the position of the Zaydis; to them, the lineage of the imam was of secondary importance, so long as he descended from ʿAlī. A second idea, held by, among others, the Ismailis, was an imam of a more esoteric, but still politically active nature, whose imamship was bequeathed from father to son. This imam was the manifestation of a cosmic principle and was also a political leader to his subjects. The third notion was held by the Imamis, the branch of Shiʿism that is the main concern of the present study. Their imam was the legal expert who did not engage in politics after the Karbala tragedy, but whose mission was to explain the true, but hidden meaning of the divine Word and lead his followers on the right path. To be capable of having this function, the imam must necessarily be shielded from the possibility of committing any kind of mistake. The imamate, including the esoteric knowledge that it involved, was passed down from father to son; the previous imam had to appoint his successor. On a deeper level, to which only the initiated adherent had access, this last kind of imam was a manifestation of the cosmic Imam, the supreme intellect of divine order without whom the world would immediately perish. Between him and his followers on the one hand, and the cosmic principle of ignorance with its armies on the other, there is a great and constant battle going on. The twelfth imam, the Mahdi or the *qāʾim*, remains in occultation, but one day will return and, together with his faithful, defeat the evil powers of the universe.

The question that will be discussed in this chapter is the role that al-Ḥusayn and the story of the Karbala tragedy played in this development. Like Chapter 10, this chapter primarily builds on previous research. The purpose is not to give a complete description of the development of the Karbala story, but rather to highlight a few factors in the process of its mythification. Each of these factors needs to be further discussed and developed in future studies, which, however, I leave for others to conduct.

Textual and Oral Transmission of the Karbala Story

Although most of the written accounts of the Karbala affair are lost to us, it is evident that several such texts did exist and circulated in the latter half of the second/eighth and the third/ninth century. These texts were originally lecture notes written down by teachers and transmitted by them or by their students (what Gregor Schoeler and others call *hypomnēmata*, as opposed to 'published' books, *syngrammata*).[1] As we saw in Chapter 2, many of these were later incorporated as sections of larger works of history or prosopography (for example al-Balādhurī's *Ansāb al-Ashrāf* and Ibn Saʿd's *Kitāb al-Tabaqāt*),[2]

[1] Schoeler, *Genesis*, 21 and Index *s.vv.* '*hypomnēma*' and '*syngramma*'; *The Oral and the Written*, 46. See also Günther, '*Maqātil* Literature', 197–9 for a slightly more detailed categorisation.

[2] Al-Balādhurī, *Ansāb*, vol. II, 334–43; vol. III, 368–426; Ibn Saʿd, *Ṭabaqāt*, vol. VI, 421–60.

and it is mainly fragments that are preserved within compositions like the larger historical works. From what is available to us, it seems that the fragments of the Karbala accounts are predominantly based on Abū Mikhnaf's version.

In the previous chapter, we saw that the majority of the population in the region were illiterate. Thus, it is unlikely that many Shiʿites were able to read these accounts of the Karbala drama. Quite apart from the widespread illiteracy, the texts would have been hard to get hold of. Books were of course copied by hand, and thus existed in very limited numbers and were expensive. Nonetheless, as we will see throughout this chapter, the Karbala story was obviously well-known to Shiʿites in general. The credit for spreading the knowledge about al-Ḥusayn's death must be given to the more or less professional storytellers and preachers,[3] and the mourners,[4] all of whom were active in mosques and sacred sites, at gatherings in homes and at various other important events.[5] So, for example, we read in the story of the Tawwābūn that they brought with them three storytellers, whose role was to incite and inspire the fighters, presumably by telling the story of al-Ḥusayn in an emotional way.[6] There is, of course, no way of establishing the historicity of this, but whether it is true or not, the idea was there that relating the tragic story would stir the fighters to braver deeds. Another example of the Karbala story being retold is found in a hadith ascribed to the sixth imam Jaʿfar al-Ṣādiq, related by Ibn Qūluwayh in his *Kāmil al-ziyarāt* (see below). Here, the imam talks to one of his followers about the merits of visiting the grave of al-Ḥusayn, and describes how pilgrims at the grave meet reciters, storytellers, wailers, and reciters of elegies.[7] As Mohammad Ali Amir-Moezzi has indicated, however, the imams frowned on the storytellers because they did not control the quality of the hadiths as strictly as they thought necessary.[8] Still, in my view it is safe

[3] In Arabic *quṣṣāṣ*, sg. *qāṣṣ*.

[4] In Arabic *nāʾiḥūn*, sg. *nāʾiḥ*.

[5] On the various functions and political importance of storytelling (*qaṣaṣ*), see Pellat, 'Ḳaṣṣ'; Athamina, 'Al-Qasas'. On the mourners, see Ayoub, *Redemptive Suffering*, 153–4.

[6] Al-Ṭabarī, *Taʾrīkh*, II, 559.

[7] '... *fa-min bayna qārīʾin yaqraʾu wa-qāṣṣin yaquṣṣu wa-nādibin yandubu wa-qāʾilin yaqūlu al-marāthī*' (Ibn Qūluwayh, Kāmil, 539).

[8] Amir-Moezzi, *Divine Guide*, 25. This critique, however, mainly concerns the transmission of hadiths. It was probably a different thing when it came to the stories of the imams. The imams, furthermore, were by no means the only ones who criticised the *quṣṣāṣ* (Pedersen, 'Criticism'; Berkey, *Popular Preaching*, 22–35).

to assume that they had an important function in transmitting the story of the death of al-Ḥusayn to the illiterate majority of the people. The problem, of course, is that we cannot know what the oral performances of the Karbala story were like in these days. What did the storytellers say, and how did they say it? How did their versions of the story conform to the early and later written versions? And so on.

Nevertheless, we can be sure that there was a constant mutual influence between the oral and the written versions, then as today.[9] In fact, although I have not analysed the earliest versions of the Karbala story from this perspective, even a cursory reading reveals clear traces of the kind of adaptations that go on in the process of oral transmission even between the three versions of Abū Jaʿfar, Ibn ʿAbd al-Raḥmān and Abū Mikhnaf, analysed in Chapter 3. Such traces are found both between the two short versions and, especially, between those two and the long one by Abū Mikhnaf. In her famous study on the creation of the story about the Prophet Muḥammad, *Meccan Trade and the Rise of Islam*, Patricia Crone indicated three characteristics of orality that shine through in the written tradition and that can be applied to the transmission of the Karbala story as well:[10] (1) contradictions (in the case of the Karbala story, for example, the temporal and spatial location of Muslim b. ʿAqīl's fight, the role and function of al-Ḥurr, and the poking with a cane in the mouth of al-Ḥusayn's severed head);[11] (2) 'the tendency for apparently independent accounts to collapse into variations on a common theme'[12] (thus, all the accounts of al-Ḥusayn distributing water to his adversaries while they, by contrast, stop him and his followers from getting water can be said to belong to a common theme of distributing and withholding water in Abū Mikhnaf's account, a theme which has important theological implications);[13] (3) the addition of details and information (the extremely detailed account of the battle itself and of the killing of al-Ḥusayn that Abū Mikhnaf gives, as compared to the laconic descriptions of the two shorter ones, is perhaps the

9 Recent scholarship on oral transmission has established that such transmission, in order to be faithful to the tradition, needs a textual basis. See Shoemaker, *Creating the Qur'an*, 180–7, and Index *s.vv.* 'oral cultures' and 'oral tradition'.

10 Crone, *Meccan Trade*, 217–24. See also Kelber, *Oral*, 64–80.

11 Ayoub (*Redemptive Suffering*, 125) mentions the same characteristic in later Shiʿite hadiths.

12 Crone, *Meccan Trade*, 219.

13 On this theme, see Hylén, 'Ḥusayn, the Mediator', 176–84 and *passim*.

prime example). The biblical scholar Werner Kelber gives another list of traits of oral transmission when he writes: 'Oral usability prompts the linguistic conduct that prefers type over character, action over tranquillity, extravagance over ordinariness, confrontation over harmony, and formularity over fortuity.'[14] Most, if not all, of these features can be found in the early accounts of the Karbala event.[15]

That the Karbala story was well-known can also be gathered from the character of the two early collection of hadiths about the twelve imams, the *Ithbāt al-waṣiyya* ('Establishment of the Inheritance'), attributed to al-Masʿūdī (d. 345/956),[16] and *Dalāʾil al-imāma* ('Proofs of the Imamate'), ascribed to al-Ṭabarī 'the lesser' (d. 310/923).[17] While the accounts about al-Ḥusayn in these biographies are relatively brief, they often allude to the fuller story and seem to presuppose that it is already known to readers. Thus, the first tradition in which al-Ḥusayn's journey to Iraq is mentioned in the *Ithbāt al-waṣiyya* begins:

> When al-Ḥusayn decided to leave for Iraq – after the people of Kufa had written to him, and he had sent Muslim b. ʿAqīl in advance and his affair turned out the way it did[18] – and he intended to go, Umm Salama sent a message to him, 'I admonish you by God, my master, not to leave.'[19]

There then follows a conversation between Umm Salama (a former wife of the Prophet Muḥammad[20]) and al-Ḥusayn, where she tells him that the Prophet predicted his death in Iraq and has given her a small container of soil. Al-Ḥusayn miraculously shows her his future grave, and Umm Salama mixes the soil she has received from the Prophet with that of the grave. This conversation is not

14 Kelber, *Oral*, 71.
15 The search for traces of oral transmission in Abū Mikhnaf's version of the Karbala story, as well as other stories in early Islamic historiography, is to my knowledge an almost totally neglected field of research. Here, I think, historians of early Islam have a lot to learn from New Testament studies.
16 Al-Masʿūdī, *Ithbāt* (the chapter about al-Ḥusayn is found on pp. 164–9).
17 Al-Ṭabarī, *Dalāʾil* (the chapter about al-Ḥusayn is found on pp. 71–9). Note that, despite their common names and even dates of death, this al-Ṭabarī is not the same as the famous historian and Qurʾan commentator that I have used as a source in the previous chapters in this book. See Pierce, *Twelve Infallible Men*, 23–5.
18 '... *wa-kāna min amrihi mā kāna*'.
19 Al-Masʿūdī, *Ithbāt*, 165.
20 On her, see Roded, 'Umm Salama Hind'; Dakake, *Charismatic Community*, 216.

mentioned in the old versions of the story analysed in Chapter 3, and it must be a rather late addition to the story (again, pointing to parallel oral and written transmission). What is most interesting in the present context, however, is that the reader (or listener) is supposed to know the basic plot of the story. With the exception of this hadith, the letters from the Kufans to al-Ḥusayn and Muslim's fatal journey to Kufa are not mentioned in the account of the *Ithbāt* at all, yet these details are only alluded to here. Later in the account, various episodes surrounding the battle are related, but nothing that is similar to the narrative found in the versions analysed in Chapter 3. The same is true of the *Dalāʾil*, which, like the *Ithbāt*, relates several hadiths about the miraculous deeds of al-Ḥusayn before, during and after the battle, but very little about the battle itself.

Thus, it is evident that readers of these two collections of hadiths knew the Karbala story well, and that the purpose of these collections was not to relate the drama of the killing of al-Ḥusayn, but rather, as their titles indicate, to provide proofs that he was an imam. In other words, unlike later biographies of the imams, the *Dalāʾil* and the *Ithbāt* are more focused on raising al-Ḥusayn to a position of a sacred person with traits and powers above ordinary humanity than on the Karbala event. This can be seen from his miraculous deeds and the supernatural events surrounding the battle (which are to some extent also found in later biographies, but are less conspicuous among the details of the longer narratives). So, for example, he has foreknowledge of his death; he quenches the thirst of his followers by miraculously producing water from his thumb; he alone is able to stand against, and kill, hundreds of enemies; he declines support from the angels in the battle; and after his death, his severed head speaks. In an interesting hadith in the *Ithbāt*, we are told that al-Ḥusayn, before the battle begins, bequeaths all the esoteric knowledge that pertains to the prophets and the imams to his son ʿAlī, who is to become the fourth imam.[21]

Another category of early sources which treat the Karbala story in a referential rather than narrative way, and which straddle the border between oral and written transmission, is Shiʿite poetry. From very early on, poetry was composed to commemorate the tragedy of the killing of al-Ḥusayn.

[21] Al-Masʿūdī, *Ithbāt*, 168.

This literary genre has been studied by several authors, and it is sufficient here to point to its existence and importance for early Shiʿite piety.[22] According to Ayoub, in most of this poetry, al-Ḥusayn is not described as a great hero. Rather, he writes, the imam and his family's suffering are highlighted, as this 'is meant to evoke sorrow, not the spirit of heroism, in the mind of the faithful'.[23] In this sense, the message and function of the poetry differs from that of the two early hadith collections mentioned above. Ayoub furthermore discusses poetry that raises al-Ḥusayn to a position above ordinary humanity. He shows that already in the second/eighth century, we can 'discern the rapid growth of the idea of the cosmic significance of Ḥusayn's death in poetry no less than in prose'.[24] In the earliest poetry, the cosmic significance of his death is mainly pictured through the grief of earth, heaven and the animals.[25] But the theme went on to develop, presumably with the growth of esoteric theology discussed in Chapter 10. Thus, the fourth/tenth-century Iraqi poet al-Zāhī (d. 352/963) wrote:

> I will not forget al-Ḥusayn at Karbala
> thirsty and lonely among the enemies,
> Prostrating in prayer, kissing the ground, while above him
> sharp swords bowing and prostrating.
> He searches for water, and though the Euphrates is close
> and he can see the water, it is far from him.
> O you sons of treachery, whom did you kill? By my life
> you killed him through whom all existence subsists.[26]

[22] See e.g. Ayoub, *Redemptive Suffering*, 158–76; Clarke, 'Elegy', 13–17. Some of the poems analysed by Ayoub belong to a later period than the one discussed in the present study. Another important study, though not dealing exclusively with poetry about al-Ḥusayn, is *La poésie šiʿite* by Taïeb El-Achèche [al-ʿAshshāsh], and the collection of such poetry in his *Dīwān*. One of several existing collections of Shiʿite poetry about al-Ḥusayn from earliest times until recently is Shubbār, *Adab al-Ṭaff*.

[23] Ayoub, *Redemptive Suffering*, 159.

[24] Ayoub, *Redemptive Suffering*, 167.

[25] See e.g. a poem by ʿAbdallāh b. ʿAwf (d. after 65/685) reconstructed by al-ʿAshshāsh [El-Achèche] in his *Dīwān*, 259–61, particularly verses 26–8, and another by Sulaymān b. Qatta in al-ʿAshshāsh [El-Achèche], *Dīwān*, 282–5, lines 7, 7′ and 14.

[26] Shubbār, *Adab al-Ṭaff*, vol. II, 53; the last verse is based on Ayoub's translation (*Redemptive Suffering*, 168).

In this poem, al-Ḥusayn is not merely the suffering imam at Karbala but also, in the last verse, a manifestation of the cosmic Imam (with capital 'I').[27] His death has significance for the whole universe. In the following section we will see how this idea affected Shiʿite eschatology at the time.[28]

Final Vengeance

I have previously described Shiʿite cosmogony as it is related in the early sources. We saw that from the very beginning, indeed in the fundamentals of Shiʿite cosmology as it is pictured in the hadiths from the imams, a constant struggle is in progress between the good and the evil powers of the universe.[29] This battle will continue until the end of the world, and is historically manifested in various ways. Several events in the history of Shiʿism are examples of this struggle, the most important being the usurping of the rightful authority of the family of the Prophet after the latter's death, and the Karbala tragedy. Shiʿite eschatology, then, must be seen in connection with its cosmogony and with the present historical situation, as Amir-Moezzi argues.[30] The Karbala event, in other words, was not regarded as an isolated happening; rather, it epitomised the ongoing cosmic drama, and perhaps was the culmination of the injustices experienced by the Shiʿites.[31]

The end, however, will bring revenge for the wrongs to which the true Believers fell victim. It is not possible here to give a full picture of Shiʿite eschatology; only some aspects that pertain directly to al-Ḥusayn's death at Karbala will be dealt with.[32] The return of the Mahdi or the *qāʾim* who will restore

[27] See also the similar expression already in the poem by the Kaysānī poet al-Sayyid al-Ḥimyarī (d. 173/789 or 179/795), who talked of Ibn al-Ḥanafiyya as the 'pole of existence' (*quṭb al-wujūd*) (*Dīwān*, 144, poem 35, line 2).

[28] Other textual evidence of al-Ḥusayn's superhuman qualities is also found, as we have seen. So, for example, his foreknowledge about his death is a common theme in the biographies and other texts. An interesting matter is the existence of texts expressing the idea that although he died corporeally, he did not do so in a spiritual sense. Such texts are translated and discussed by several modern scholars, e.g. Ayoub, *Redemptive Suffering*, 248–9; Halm, *Die islamische Gnosis*, 268–74; Asatryan, *Controversies*, 29–31. For other ideas about the supernatural qualities of al-Ḥusayn see also Crow, 'Death'.

[29] See above, Chapters 4 and 10.

[30] Amir-Moezzi, 'Eschatology'; *Spirituality*, 428.

[31] Pierce, *Twelve Infallible Men*, 56, 70–3.

[32] The following paragraphs are based on the comprehensive studies of Amir-Moezzi (esp. *Divine Guide*, 115–23; 'Eschatology'; *Spirituality*, 403–29) and Ayoub (*Redemptive Suffering*, 216–29), where they have attempted to systematise the many, often inconsistent early traditions on the

justice and faith is the centre of Shiʿite eschatology. A major event at the end is the final war between the *qāʾim* and his followers on the one hand and the forces of evil on the other, a war in which the enemies will be utterly defeated. An important reason for the battle is the avenging of the death of al-Ḥusayn and all other injustices that have befallen the true Shiʿite Believers, and the restoration of authority to the family of the Prophet.[33] In one hadith ascribed to imam Jaʿfar al-Ṣādiq, depicting a scene from heaven just after the Karbala battle, we read:

> When the affair of al-Ḥusayn turned out as it did, the angels cried loudly before God and said, 'This has been done to al-Ḥusayn, your beloved friend and the son of your Prophet.' Then God presented to them the shadow of the *qāʾim*, and said, 'With this one I will avenge that.'[34]

Here, the angels infer that God has allowed his beloved al-Ḥusayn to be killed unavenged; but God replies by showing the shadow (*ẓill*) of the future *qāʾim* (because he is not yet born and exists only in the world of shadows at this time[35]), assuring the angels that through the *qāʾim* He will avenge al-Ḥusayn. Vengeance for the death of al-Ḥusayn, who represents the whole family of the Prophet, will strike all who did not side with him, including all Muslims excepting a small minority who were loyal to the imams.[36] As we have seen, the fear of being counted as unfaithful and thus struck by God's punishment was already the driving force behind the Tawwābūn's initiative.[37]

A number of hadiths, furthermore, report the return to life in this world (*al-rajʿa* or *al-karra*) of some of the great persons from history, in many cases including al-Ḥusayn himself, in order to support the *qāʾim* in the final battle.[38] This is in some cases called 'the special resurrection' – in contrast to 'the general resurrection' of all human beings that will occur later. One person who, it is

subject into a coherent picture. The former scholar studies early Shiʿite eschatology at large, while the latter focuses on traditions about al-Ḥusayn in this drama. Ayoub partly draws on later sources than Amir-Moezzi. Crow's briefer study ('Death', esp. 93–101) also uses many slightly later sources. See also Sachedina, *Islamic Messianism*, 150–79.

33 Amir-Moezzi, *Divine Guide*, 118–20; 'Eschatology'.
34 Al-Kulaynī, *Al-kāfī*, vol. I, 296, Bāb 173, no. 6.
35 See Amir-Moezzi, *Divine Guide*, 224, n. 637.
36 Amir-Moezzi, *Divine Guide*, 119.
37 See above, Chapters 5–8.
38 Amir-Moezzi, *Spirituality*, 406–7; 'Eschatology'.

said in some hadiths, will return together with al-Ḥusayn is the prophet Ismāʿīl (Ishmael), mentioned in Qur. 19:54: 'And remember in the Book Ishmael: Surely he was true to the promise, and he was a messenger, a prophet.' In a hadith related by Ibn Qūluwayh (d. 369/979–80), a follower of imam Jaʿfar al-Ṣādiq asks the imam who this prophet was. The imam replies that the Ismāʿīl mentioned in this verse is not the son of Abraham, but a later prophet, the son of Ḥizqīl (Ezekiel). When he preached to his people, they caught him, tortured him gruesomely and killed him. God then sent the angel of chastisement to punish the people, but when the angel asked Ismāʿīl what kind of punishment he wanted them to have, he replied that he had no need of that. Rather, he said to God:

> 'You promised al-Ḥusayn that he would return to the world so that he could take revenge on those who did the same to him. My desire, O Lord, is that You let me return to the world so that I can avenge myself on those who did this to me, just as al-Ḥusayn will return.' God then promised Ismāʿīl b. Ḥizqīl that He would do that, and so he will return together with al-Ḥusayn.[39]

These examples show that vengeance for the injustices suffered by al-Ḥusayn and those loyal to him and his cause is a major contributor to the final battle. The restoration of justice, however, is only one aspect of the war and of the re-establishment of true Islam. This major renewal of the whole universe at the end of time has a host of additional dimensions, such as the bringing back of the (now lost) original version of the Qur'an, and the initiation of all the followers of the Mahdi into its hidden meaning.[40]

Placing the Karbala story and its implications in the eschatological perspective widens the argument developed by Matthew Pierce on the basis of the biographies of the imams that he has studied. Pierce maintains that the death of al-Ḥusayn at Karbala was not seen in isolation in these texts, but rather as one of many instances of the suffering of the family of the Prophet. He further argues that, unlike the death of Jesus in Christianity, the death of al-Ḥusayn was not unique: all the imams and the prophets had to suffer. The biographies, he writes,

[39] Ibn Qūluwayh, *Kāmil*, 139, Bāb 19, no. 3.

[40] I will not go further into these reasons, as this is not essential for the present study. Amir-Moezzi develops them in *Divine Guide*, 119–20 and in 'Eschatology'.

> regularly emphasised the ontological similarity between the imams and the prophets. Al-Husayn was unique only in how starkly his life displayed the realities and qualities that all imams faced and displayed. Devotion to al-Husayn was also a symbol of devotion to the entire family of the Prophet and to the Prophet himself.[41]

The example of the prophet Ismāʿīl, discussed above, provides an additional illustration for Pierce's argument from another source. Karbala is but one instance – though perhaps the most conspicuous – of the constant battle between the good and evil forces of the universe: the battle which has hitherto resulted in the defeat of the good, but which in the end will bring victory for the cosmic Imam and his followers.

Different genres of early Shiʿite literature, however, varied in their focus. While the earliest biographical collections of hadiths, such as the *Dalāʾil* and the *Ithbāt* discussed above, attempted to homogenise the images of the imams and lift their suffering to the same level, the suffering, death and avenging of al-Ḥusayn were clearly emphasised in other genres, such as poetry and texts about pilgrimages to the tombs of the imams (to be discussed below).[42] Again, it is almost unthinkable that people in general knew about the cosmology as it was depicted in the early sources, except to the extent that it was 'transposed' into narratives related by the storytellers and others, and thus popularised. Since no such stories are preserved in text, it is difficult to know how, or to what extent, people in general were able to see the larger cosmological picture and relate the death of al-Ḥusayn to it. The earliest Shiʿite version preserved – the account attributed to imam al-Bāqir, analysed in Chapter 3 – simply ends at the death of al-Ḥusayn and the return of the remnants of his family to Medina. There are no forward-looking or hopeful passages there.[43] In Abū Mikhnaf's account a few decades later, the pessimistic panorama for the Muslim community at large is there: the divine covenant, as we saw in Chapter 4, is broken. Those individuals who were faithful to al-Ḥusayn can, however, count on God's satisfaction and eternal

41 Pierce, *Twelve Infallible Men*, 70.
42 I owe this insight to George Warner.
43 The same is true of the version of Ibn ʿAbd al-Raḥmān, but as we have seen he was probably not a Shiʿite, so it is not to be expected.

reward in the hereafter. But in this version, which is also fairly early, it is still individuals who will benefit from their loyalty to al-Ḥusayn, rather than the restoration of the entire cosmos, that is in focus. In this world, evil prevails; nothing is said about a total eschatological restoration. Placing the Karbala drama in a cosmic framework replaces this gloomy future for the suffering ones with a glorious one. This is what the biographers, poets and theologians did, and although we can only speculate, my view is that this is just what the storytellers must have done in one way or another when relating the story to the Shiʿite populace. In this way, the story became something more than just a tragedy about the death of the grandson of the Prophet Muḥammad. It was removed from human history and developed into a narrative which gave the Shiʿites and their sufferings under various illegitimate authorities a place in the cosmic drama – a drama that will one day end in triumph for those who are now oppressed.

Ritual

In Chapter 2 we saw that ritual has always been one of the most important aspects in creating and affirming group identity, more so than theology; and this is as true of early Islam as of other contexts.[44] Furthermore, the most effective way to make a myth out of a narrative is to ritualise it. In this section, I will briefly discuss some of the early rituals connected to the death of al-Ḥusayn. I will argue that these rituals were crucial factors in the process of elevating the Karbala story to the level of myth.

It seems that from very early on, gatherings of the faithful were held where the Karbala story was retold and expounded by storytellers of various kinds, as mentioned above. Probably, elegiac poetry (*marthiyya*) was also recited at these sessions. No real studies have been made of these rituals, however, probably owing to the scarcity of source material, and I will not go deeper into the subject here.[45]

[44] Haider, *Origins*, 215–30, esp. Conclusion, pp. 229–30. For non-Islamic contexts, see e.g. Penn, *Kissing Christians*; Kraemer, *Jewish Eating*, esp. 1–86.

[45] Günther, '*Maqātil* Literature', 194. While several studies have been made of early Shiʿite *marthiyya* as literature and as expressions of a Shiʿite sentiment, very little is written about the ritual context in which it was recited. The only studies I have found that briefly touch on this issue are Clarke, 'Elegy', 13–21 and Pierce, *Twelve Infallible Men*, 59–62.

In Chapter 10 we saw that it was only once the Shiʿite Buyids had gained control in the middle of the fourth/tenth century that rituals publicly commemorating certain events central to the Shiʿites were allowed. Among these rituals was public mourning on the tenth of Muḥarram, the death day of al-Ḥusayn. While the earliest records of such mourning commemorating the Karbala tragedy come from this time (I will return to these below), pilgrimages to the grave of al-Ḥusayn are much earlier, and I will try to trace some early signs of this ritual. But first it is necessary to say a few words about weeping as an expression of grief for the tragedy of Karbala.

Weeping

Shedding tears was, from very early on, one of the most important means of expressing one's loyalty to al-Ḥusayn and the family of the Prophet. Weeping was the prime means of manifesting the sorrow over the sufferings of the *ahl al-bayt* and the loss of their rightful political and religious authority. As we have seen, the Karbala drama became 'the most tragic illustration of Shiʿism's dualistic vision of the world'.[46] Weeping for al-Ḥusayn, however, cannot be called a ritual in itself, as it was normally performed within a larger ritual context, such as listening to the story about his death or to elegiac poetry, or visiting his grave or taking part in a commemorative public mourning ritual. In this very short section, I will say just a few words about ritual weeping as a force in the social formation of Shiʿism up to the age of the Buyids.[47]

In Chapter 2, we saw that, according to the Durkheimian tradition of ritual analysis, collective expressions of emotions are a very forceful factor in building and maintaining group identities, and that such 'collective effervescence' is often brought about through ritual. These emotions charge symbols (such as the *ahl al-bayt*, the Karbala story and the grave of al-Ḥusayn) with meaning. In my view, this is just what happens when Shiʿites gather and weep together – in historical times as well as today – over the injustices that have befallen the prophets and the imams and their faithful. In early Shiʿism, then, weeping over the Karbala tragedy became a means of expressing a shared

[46] Amir-Moezzi and Jambet, *Shiʿi Islam*, 25.

[47] Ayoub treats the subject of weeping in early Shiʿism in a rather descriptive religio-historical way (*Redemptive Suffering*, 142–7). Pierce provides important theoretical perspectives on the functions of lamenting the sufferings of the *ahl al-bayt* (*Twelve Infallible Men*, 54–67).

solidarity with the sacred persons in past and present, and also of identifying with others who shared the same sentiment. It thus, furthermore, became a platform for a certain morality, which functioned as a litmus test for discerning who was part of the group and who was not.

In the earliest prose texts – in the accounts of the Karbala event and the story of the Tawwābūn – as well as in early poetry, we everywhere find people weeping over the death of al-Ḥusayn. There are many traditions from the imams about the merits of weeping for him and the rewards promised to the person who causes other people to weep. In the biographical collections of hadiths mentioned above, all imams weep; most of all, the fourth imam, ʿAlī b. al-Ḥusayn, called al-Sajjād, 'the prostrator', known for his constant weeping over the death of his father and the sufferings of the *ahl al-bayt*.[48] The *Kāmil al-ziyārāt*, the mid-fourth/tenth-century collection of hadiths about pilgrimages by Ibn Qūluwayh, has several chapters of hadiths about the entirety of creation, the animals, the angels and the jinn lamenting and weeping for al-Ḥusayn.[49] The following hadith from *Kāmil al-ziyārāt*, ascribed to the sixth imam al-Ṣādiq, illustrates that there were not only humans in the group of mourners. Angels who were prepared to help al-Ḥusayn in the battle, but were not allowed to do so, weep at his grave after his death:

> Four thousand angels descended intending to fight with al-Ḥusayn b. ʿAlī, but they were not allowed to fight. They returned to ask for permission [again], but when they descended al-Ḥusayn had been killed. They remain at his grave with matted and dust-covered hair, weeping until the day of judgement. Their leader is an angel called Al-Manṣūr.[50]

Besides being testimony to the angels' participation in the grief for al-Ḥusayn, this hadith shows that his grave is a place for mourning, and it thus becomes an object of visitation. It is to this ritual, the pilgrimage to the grave of al-Ḥusayn, that we now turn.

[48] On this, see Pierce, *Twelve Infallible Men*, 54–7.
[49] Ibn Qūluwayh, *Kāmil*, 165–200, Bāb 26–31.
[50] Ibn Qūluwayh, *Kāmil*, 171–2, Bāb 27, no. 2.

Ziyāra

Visits to graves, *ziyārāt al-qubūr*, as we saw in Chapter 7, formed an ancient custom that continued into the new movement that eventually came to be called Islam.[51] Such visits could be made in order to honour a saint and ask for personal benefits and blessings, or to pray on behalf of the deceased, to relieve him or her of the dullness or the tortures of the grave. While the first kind was often frowned on by Sunni theologians, visiting the dead to ease the tortures of the grave and ask for God's forgiveness was normally accepted.[52] Among Shiʿites, however, visits to the graves of the imams as a means of expressing one's loyalty to the family of the Prophet and to ask them for blessings of various kinds soon became not only accepted, but enjoined; to pray for God's forgiveness for them was, of course, by contrast totally wrong, given their elevated position. (The only exception I have encountered to this pattern of behaviour at the grave of an imam is the Tawwābūn's visit to the grave of al-Ḥusayn, discussed in Chapters 7 and 8.)[53] As we will see, in later pilgrimage guides, neglecting to perform pilgrimages to the graves of the imams could result in divine punishment, while the rewards for such visits were enormous.[54]

Here, I refer only to al-Ḥusayn's grave at Karbala as a site for pilgrimages. There are also other places where his severed head was supposed to have been buried – Damascus, Ascalon, Cairo. The traditions about al-Ḥusayn's head, however, seem to be later, and will not be discussed here.[55]

Although the *ziyāra* to the grave of al-Ḥusayn soon became one of the most important practices in Shiʿism, records from the second/eighth century of visits there are extremely scarce and only in passing report that this or that person was at the grave, often without describing any rituals such as praying or weeping performed at the site. There are a large number of *ḥadīth*s ascribed to the imams al-Bāqir and, especially, al-Sādiq about the importance of visiting Karbala. As Amir-Moezzi argues, however, the authenticity of such traditions

[51] Besides references in Chapter 7, see also Meri, 'Etiquette', 263–5.
[52] Halevi, *Muhammad's Grave*, 20–32, 226–33; Meri, 'Ziyāra'.
[53] For the case of ʿUbaydallāh b. al-Ḥurr al-Juʿfī, see below.
[54] Meri, 'Ziyāra'.
[55] The traditions concerning al-Ḥusayn's head and the pilgrimages to its supposed burial sites have been dealt with in Talmon-Heller, *Sacred Place*. See also Meri, *Cult*, 191–5.

and their *isnāds* must be regarded as unreliable until the contrary is proven – a task which seems very difficult, considering the state of the sources and the methods for interpreting them.[56] In what follows, I will discuss the most important references to visits to Karbala in the historiographical works, as well as in a few early Shiʿite poems often mentioned by scholars. I do not claim that the list is complete. I treat them in chronological order, ending the section by relating a few *ḥadīths* about pilgrimage to al-Ḥusayn's grave, to give an impression of the development of the *ziyāra* in the first centuries.[57]

Sources indicating that the survivors of al-Ḥusayn's family visited his grave on their way from Damascus to Medina on the fortieth day of his death are late and will not be reckoned with in the present study.[58] The visit of the Tawwābūn to the grave is often given as an example of a very early – if not the first – *ziyāra*.[59] Selby concludes, however, that there are important differences between the description of the stopover of the Tawwābūn at the grave and later *ziyāra*s and other Shiʿite rituals. In my view, and as I have indicated in my analysis in Chapter 7, the description of the Tawwābūn's visit cannot be regarded as a *ziyāra* in the sense that the concept is used later, even if it foreshadowed the rituals that were gradually 'Shiʿitised' as the decades went by.

Moreover, the Tawwābūn's visit to al-Ḥusayn's grave in 65/684 is not the earliest such journey related by Abū Mikhnaf. According to him, the Kufan nobleman and 'poet-rebel'[60] ʿUbaydallāh b. al-Ḥurr went there soon after the battle. Abū Mikhnaf relates that al-Ḥusayn had met Ibn al-Ḥurr before the battle and asked for his support; his request was declined, however.[61] Later, when he heard of the death of al-Ḥusayn, Ibn al-Ḥurr deeply regretted his decision. He had a verbal exchange with Ibn Ziyād, the governor of Kufa, and then, Abū Mikhnaf says, 'he set off and came to Karbala. He looked at the places where people were slain and he and his followers sought God's

[56] Amir-Moezzi, 'On Spirituality', 110–11.

[57] More comprehensive studies of early pilgrimage literature are Selby, 'Ḥusayn's Dirt'; Warner, 'One Thousand *ḥijaj*'. Hussain, 'Mourning of History', contains some interesting references but is less critical.

[58] See Selby, 'Ḥusayn's Dirt', 11–14.

[59] Selby, 'Ḥusayn's Dirt', 20–4, with further references.

[60] The expression is that of Kanazi, who gives a comprehensive but quite uncritical biography of Ibn al-Ḥurr in his book *Umayyad Poet-Rebel*.

[61] Al-Ṭabarī, *Ta'rīkh*, II, 305–6.

forgiveness for them.'[62] Al-Ṭabarī has added a poem ascribed to Ibn al-Ḥurr about his visit to the grave: he regrets not having taken part in the battle on the side of al-Ḥusayn, and says:

> I stood at their graves and their field of death
> My heart almost burst, and my eyes shed tears.[63]

This is one of the earliest recorded visits to the grave, and here we see the motif of regret for the failure to support al-Ḥusayn, as well as the plea to God to forgive al-Ḥusayn and his dead companions from their sins. As far as we know, however, Ibn al-Ḥurr probably did not identify as a Shiʿite.[64] His visit (if indeed it did occur) can therefore hardly be labelled a *ziyāra* in the later, Shiʿite sense.

Two other early poets who were clearly Shiʿites and who mention visits to Karbala in their poems are ʿUqba b. ʿAmr al-Sahmī (d. probably early second/eighth century) and Sulaymān b. Qatta (d. 126/743–4). The two were thus contemporaries, and it has been discussed which one of them was the first to produce an elegy for al-Ḥusayn.[65] ʿUqba begins his poem by talking of a visit to Karbala:

> I passed by the grave of Ḥusayn in Karbala
> and on it my tears flowed copiously.[66]

Similarly, Sulaymān begins his elegy by describing the ruins of the desert camp of Muḥammad's family at al-Ṭaff that he visits.[67] These poems, then, might be regarded as early testimonies of visits to Karbala.[68] It must be kept

[62] Al-Ṭabarī, *Taʾrīkh*, II, 389 (in this chapter, as throughout the book, translations from al-Ṭabarī are taken from, or at least heavily dependent on, the SUNY translation, *History of al-Ṭabarī*). This is, in fact, the only time the toponym Karbala is mentioned in Abū Mikhnaf's account. According to Ibn Aʿtham this incident occurred only a few days after the battle (*Futūḥ*, ed. Shīrī, vol. VI, 272).

[63] Al-Ṭabarī, *Taʾrīkh*, II, 389.

[64] Kanazi and al-Juʿfī, *Umayyad Poet-Rebel*, 40–8; Rotter, *Bürgerkrieg*, 219–21; but cf. El-Achèche, *La poésie šiʿite*, 158–60.

[65] See Ayoub, *Redemptive Suffering*, 160, 279, n. 44. On these poets, see El-Achèche, *La poésie šiʿite*, 140 and 181–4.

[66] Shubbār, *Adab al-Ṭaff*, 52, trans. by Ayoub in *Redemptive Suffering*, 161. Al-ʿAshshāsh has a slightly different order of the verses, and places this one as number two (*Dīwān*, 240).

[67] Al-ʿAshshāsh, *Dīwān*, 282–5. El-Acheche (*La poésie šiʿite*, 182–4) discusses the problems with the provenance of this poem and the order of verses. Ayoub (*Redemptive Suffering*, 167) follows the sequence of verses of Shubbār (*Adab al-Ṭaff*, 54).

[68] So Ayoub, *Redemptive Suffering*, 161, 167.

in mind, however, that they follow the *qaṣīda* form of Arabic poetry, which traditionally begins by recounting the deserted camp of the loved one. Thus, the descriptions of the visit at Karbala in the two poems do not necessarily mean that the poets were there. They could just have been following the literary conventions, opening their poems in the traditional manner.

Several scholars have mentioned what they take to be a pilgrimage to Karbala in connection with the death of Zayd b. ʿAlī, the grandson of al-Ḥusayn, in 122/740.[69] The context is the failed insurrection that led to Zayd's death, mentioned in the previous chapter. Interestingly, scholars taking this as an example of an early *ziyāra* only refer to the historian Ibn al-Athīr (d. 630/1233), who relates how Zayd's son Yaḥyā left Kufa and went to Karbala when his father was killed and buried. But Ibn al-ʿAthīr does not describe this visit as a pilgrimage. All he says is that, when the Umayyad governor of Kufa discovered the site of the body of Zayd, 'his son Yaḥyā travelled to Karbala and stopped at Nīnawā at [the house of] Sābiq, the *mawlā* of Bishr b. ʿAbd al-Malik b. Bishr'.[70] Nothing is mentioned about Yaḥyā stopping at the grave of al-Ḥusayn or performing any rituals there; it is, rather, an account of his attempt to get away from Kufa and hide from the governor's soldiers. That Yaḥyā's stop at Karbala had very little to do with al-Ḥusayn's grave becomes clear if Ibn al-Athīr's account is compared with the two more detailed versions of the same event in al-Ṭabarī's *Ta'rīkh*.[71]

Perhaps more important as testimony to the significance of al-Ḥusayn's grave in Karbala is an anecdote related by al-Ṭabarī about the famous ʿAbbāsid caliph Hārūn al-Rashīd (r. 170–93/786–809). According to this tradition, al-Rashīd's grandmother, Umm Mūsā, had appointed a certain Ibn Abī Dāwūd to take care of the grave of al-Ḥusayn, giving him an allowance of thirty dirhams per month for this.[72] Umm Mūsā was the wife of the second Abbasid caliph al-Manṣūr (r. 136–58/754–75). The report thus seems to indicate that she appointed a guardian of the grave sometime in the second quarter of the

[69] See e.g. Calmard, 'Culte', 611, n. 171; Honigmann, 'Karbalā''.

[70] Ibn al-Athīr, *Kāmil*, vol. IV, 455. The Nīnawā mentioned here was a village as well as a district in the *sawād* of Kufa; Karbala, which apparently was situated close to the village of Nīnawā, belonged to this district (Yāqūt, *Buldān*, vol. V, 339; Streck, 'Nīnawā'; see also al-Ṭabarī, *Ta'rīkh*, II, 287, 307).

[71] Al-Ṭabarī, *Ta'rīkh*, II, 1,710, 1,713–14.

[72] Al-Ṭabarī, *Ta'rīkh*, III, 752.

second/third quarter of the eighth century. If this is correct, then at least by this time the grave had some kind of religious significance and, presumably, pilgrimages were made to it. The information is not supported by other sources, however, so it can hardly by itself be regarded as a trustworthy testimony.[73]

The Imami traditionist Abū ʿAmr Muḥammad al-Kashshī (d. 367/978)[74] relates a tradition about the 'extremist' (*ghālin*) al-Mufaḍḍal b. ʿUmar al-Juʿfī (d. before 184/799),[75] in which he and two of his contemporaries made a *ziyāra* to Karbala. The purpose of al-Kashshī's mention is not to discuss the visit to al-Ḥusayn's grave, but probably to demonstrate al-Mufaḍḍal's extremism, as he abstained from performing the morning prayer when his two companions prayed.[76] It is significant, however, in that it recounts an intentional *ziyāra* to the grave of al-Ḥusayn sometime in the late third/eighth century. Again, the information is not corroborated by other sources, and it is of course difficult to know what to make of information related in a work written about two hundred years after the event it describes.

So far as I know, the first mention of the tomb of al-Ḥusayn as a structure of buildings is in connection with the infamous destruction of the site by the caliph al-Mutawakkil (r. 232–47/847–61) in 236/850–1. Al-Ṭabarī writes:

> In this year, al-Mutawakkil ordered the grave of al-Ḥusayn b. ʿAlī and the residences and palaces surrounding it be destroyed. The site of his grave was to be ploughed, sown, and irrigated, and people were to be prevented from visiting it. It is reported that an agent of the chief of security police announced in the area: 'Whomever we find near al-Ḥusayn's grave after three days we shall send to the prison.' People fled and refrained from going to the grave. The place was ploughed, and the area around it was sown.[77]

Here we are on much safer historical ground than with the previous examples. Al-Mutawakkil's reign occurred in the lifetime of al-Ṭabarī

[73] For other instances of early Abbasid dealings with the grave see Selby, 'Ḥusayn's Dirt', 44–5.

[74] This is the date given by Takim ('Kaššī'), but cf. Madelung, 'Al-Kashshī'.

[75] On him, see Asatryan, 'Mofażżal'.

[76] Al-Kashshī, *Rijāl*, 275–6. See also Modarressi, *Crisis*, 35, n. 101. On antinomianism, and in particular the abandonment of prayer as a mark of the *ghulāt*, see Amir-Moezzi, 'Les Imams', 19–20; and see also Asatryan, *Controversies*, 157–61.

[77] Al-Ṭabarī, *Taʾrīkh*, III, 1,407. On al-Mutawakkil and his politics in general, see Kennedy, 'al-Mutawakkil'.

(224–314/839–923).[78] Although the latter was only about eight years old when the caliph came to power, he met and got information from people who had first-hand experience of the ruler and the events that occurred during his time in power.[79] Furthermore, unlike the isolated anecdotes related above, the account of the destruction of the grave is placed in the well-known context of al-Mutawakkil's anti-Shiʿite politics. Abū al-Faraj al-Iṣfahānī, to take only one example, also mentions this episode in an account that is probably independent of al-Ṭabarī.[80] If this report relates a historical event – which I think it does – the natural conclusion is that the grave of al-Ḥusayn at Karbala would have become a site of pilgrimage well before al-Mutawakkil's reign. We read that not only the grave, but also 'the residences and palaces' (*al-manāzil wa-l-dūr*), are to be destroyed, buildings which must have been erected over many years preceding their destruction. Moreover, that people were to be prevented from going there makes it clear that visiting the grave was by now an established custom. This, then, implies that there was much activity at the grave, at least in the first half of the third/ninth century.[81]

Hadiths about visits to the grave of al-Ḥusayn are preserved from the late third/ninth century, if not before. Such hadiths are either embedded among traditions about other legal matters, or in books dedicated to pilgrimage to the graves of the imams. As George Warner has indicated, however, there seem to have existed a number of works on *ziyāra* that were written throughout that century but which are now lost.[82] The earliest extant collection of hadiths – a collection that, among other subjects, has several chapters on visits to the grave of al-Ḥusayn – is *al-Kāfī*, compiled by Muḥammad b. Yaʿqūb al-Kulaynī (d. 329/940–1). The first hadith in the chapter concerning the merits of

[78] Al-Ṭabarī himself was apparently not sure of exactly when he was born; see Rosenthal's introduction in al-Ṭabarī, *History*, 11.

[79] For an assessment of al-Ṭabarī's historical writing in this time, see Kraemer's foreword to al-Ṭabarī, *History*, vol. XXXIV, xiv–xxii.

[80] Al-Iṣfahānī, *Maqātil*, 478–9.

[81] An analysis of several sources on al-Mutawakkil's destruction of al-Ḥusayn's grave is found in Selby, 'Ḥusayn's Dirt', 45–51. See also Newman, *Twelver Shiism*, 55, n. 70.

[82] Warner, 'One Thousand *ḥijaj*', 417, referring to Āqā Buzurg al-Ṭihrānī, *Al-dharīʿa*, vol. XX, 316–26. The earliest reference to such a text that I have been able to detect in Āqā Buzurg's list is *Mazār amīr al-muʾminīn* by Muʿāwiya b. ʿAmmār al-Duhnī (d. 175/791–2), the son of the transmitter of the Karbala story from al-Bāqir (see Chapter 3) (*Al-dharīʿa*, vol. XX, 321). This book seems to have dealt with visits to the grave of ʿAlī (or perhaps the Prophet Muḥammad) rather than al-Ḥusayn, however (see Modarressi, *Tradition*, 331–2).

visiting the grave of al-Ḥusayn begins with the speaker Bashīr al-Dahhān, a disciple of the sixth Imam, al-Ṣādiq (here called Abū ʿAbdallāh):

> I said to Abū ʿAbdallāh, 'Sometimes I missed the *ḥajj*, and performed the pilgrimage rituals at the tomb of al-Husayn.'[83] He answered, 'Well done, O Bashīr! Whichever believer comes to the grave of al-Ḥusayn, with the knowledge of [al-Ḥusayn's] rights, on a day other than the day of the Eid, God counts it for him as twenty accepted and pleasing *ḥajj*s and *ʿumra*s, and twenty *ḥajj*s and *ʿumra*s together with a God-sent prophet or a just imam. And whoever goes to him on the day of the Eid, God counts it for him as one hundred *ḥajj*s, one hundred *ʿumra*s, and one hundred expeditions with a God-sent prophet or a just imam.' I said to him, 'How can I reach such a situation?' He looked at me as if he were irritated and said to me, 'O Bashir, when the believer comes to the grave of al-Ḥusayn on the day of ʿArafat, performs the major ablution in the Euphrates and then goes to him, for every step [he takes], God counts him a *ḥajj* with all its rituals.' As far as I know he also said, 'And an expedition.'[84]

In other words, a visit to the grave of al-Ḥusayn on a normal day equates to twenty pilgrimages to Mecca; and a *ziyāra* to al-Ḥusayn's grave during the Eid of the *ḥajj* is worth a hundred Meccan pilgrimages – and in addition to that, the participation of a hundred martial expeditions in the company of a prophet or an Imam. Moreover, for someone visiting the grave on the day of ʿArafat, the most important day of the *ḥajj* to Mecca, performing the ablutions in the Euphrates and then approaching the grave, every step will count as a complete *ḥajj*, perhaps even as a martial expedition.

Such extravagant statements about the worth of visiting the grave at Karbala are even more predominant in later collections exclusively dedicated to *ziyāra* hadiths. I end this section by referring to the earliest extant 'pilgrimage manual' by one of the students of al-Kulaynī, Jaʿfar b. Muḥammad al-Qummī, known as Ibn Qūluwayh (d. c. 369/979–80).[85] His *Kāmil al-ziyārāt* contains traditions about pilgrimages to the graves of the Prophet and the imams, the great

[83] *...fa-uʿarrifu ʿinda qabr al-Ḥusayn.*

[84] *Wa-la aʿlamuhu ilā qāla, 'Wa-ghazwatan'.* Al-Kulaynī, Al-kāfī, vol. IV, 334, Bāb 360, no. 1.

[85] Newman, *Twelver Shiism*, 60–2; Warner, 'One Thousand *ḥijaj*', 417. On Ibn Qūluwayh, see also Ansari, *L'imamat*, 62–4.

majority of which deal with the visit to al-Ḥusayn's grave.[86] Warner highlights two categories of traditions in this and other books of the same kind: the *ziyāra* litanies, and the *faḍāʾil* traditions. The first group consists of traditions which prescribe in detail the rituals of the visit: what to recite, the posture to hold, and how to position oneself at the grave when making this or that recitation.[87] The great weight of correct performance at the grave is illustrated by the fact that, by the time of Ibn Qūluwayh, the word *ziyāra* was used not only for the act of the pilgrimage, but also for the litany recited during the visit to the grave.[88]

The other category of traditions is the *faḍāʾil* traditions, which recount the merits of the grave at Karbala and the rewards given to those who make the *ziyāra* there.[89] We have already seen an example taken from Kulaynī's *al-Kāfī*. Ibn Qūluwayh also has a chapter with traditions that equate the *ziyāra* to Karbala to twenty, fifty or even a thousand pilgrimages to Kaʿba in Mecca;[90] another chapter is devoted to traditions equating a visit to al-Ḥusayn's grave to a visit to God on His throne.[91] The pilgrim to al-Ḥusayn will receive benefits even in this life, as we can see from the following tradition, where a certain ʿAbdallāh b. Hilāl asks the sixth Imam:

> 'May I be made your ransom, what is the least [reward] for the visitor at the grave of al-Ḥusayn?' He replied, 'O ʿAbdallāh, the least that he will get is that God protects him and his family until he returns to his family [from the pilgrimage], and when Judgement Day comes, God will be his protector.'[92]

Hence the benefits obtained by the believer who visits the grave are enormous, both in the present life and in the hereafter.[93] Yet the Shiʿite scholars of the

[86] Newman, *Twelver Shiism*, 61; Sindawi, 'Visit', 231, n. 8. An English translation of Ibn Qūluwayh's *Kāmil* is available online under the title *Kamiluz Ziyaraat*.

[87] Warner, 'One Thousand *ḥijaj*', 418–19, 428–33. This, for example, is the content of the longest chapter of the *Kāmil* (358–424, Bāb 79).

[88] Warner, 'One Thousand *ḥijaj*', 428–9.

[89] Warner, 'One Thousand *ḥijaj*', 419, 421–8. Selby discusses the Shiʿite *faḍāʾil* traditions in relation to the Sunni ones ('Ḥusayn's Dirt', 59–75).

[90] Ibn Qūluwayh, *Kāmil*, 302–7, Bāb 66.

[91] Ibn Qūluwayh, *Kāmil*, 278–82, Bāb 59. Warner points out, however, that such hadiths were normally regarded as exaggerations that were not taken literally even by Twelver Shiʿite jurists ('One Thousand *ḥijaj*', 424, n. 35).

[92] Ibn Qūluwayh, *Kāmil*, 255, Bāb 49, no. 6.

[93] 29 chapters, almost 100 pages (about one-sixth of the book), are devoted to the rewards of the pilgrim (*Kāmil*, 252–355, Bābs 49–77).

fourth/tenth and fifth/eleventh centuries were ambivalent about the question of whether the *ziyāra* to the grave of al-Ḥusayn and the other imams should be considered juridically obligatory, like the *ḥajj* to Mecca.[94]

By this time at least, the physical site of the grave itself had attained hallowed status. Clay from the site was supposed to have healing effects. This is illustrated in the only hadith about the grave of al-Ḥusayn that is extant in the earliest collection of Shiʿi hadiths partly preserved until today, the *Kitāb al-maḥāsin* by Aḥmad b. Muḥammad al-Barqī (d. c. 280/894). In what is left of the original work (probably only something like one-sixth or one-seventh of the original collection),[95] virtually nothing is said about pilgrimage to the grave of al-Ḥusayn. The one reference to the grave is found in a section on food, the subsection on honey, where a companion of the fifth imam, Abū Jaʿfar al-Bāqir, says:

> A woman gave me some yarn and said, 'Present this at Mecca so that it is sewn into the Kiswa of the Kaʿba.'[96] He said, 'I disliked presenting it to the guardians [of the Kaʿba], since I knew them. So, when I travelled to Medina, I went to Abū Jaʿfar and said to him, "May I be made your ransom, a woman gave me yarn." I told him about the words of the woman and my aversion to presenting the yarn to the guardians. He replied, "Buy honey and saffron [for the price of it] and take some soil from the grave of al-Ḥusayn, mix it with rainwater and put some of the honey and saffron in it. Then distribute it among the Shiʿa so that they may heal their sick with it."'[97]

This hadith is interesting in several respects. First, it shows that, by the late third/ninth century at least, the grave of al-Ḥusayn was compared to the Kaʿba in favour of the former (though, of course, already in a later addition to the story of the Tawwābūn the Black Stone of the Kaʿba is associated with the grave, as we saw in Chapter 7). The woman wants her yarn to be stitched into the textile cover of the Kaʿba, presumably in order to gain some divine benefit. The Imam advises his disciple to sell the yarn instead, to buy

[94] Warner, 'One Thousand *ḥijaj*', 424–8.

[95] This is Newman's estimate (*Formative Period*, 52). According to Vilozny (*Constructing a World View*, 27), eleven out of around ninety sub-books are still extant. On al-Barqī and the *Kitāb al-Maḥāsin*, see Newman, *Formative Period*, Ch. 4; Vilozny, *Constructing a World View*, Ch. 1.

[96] The *kiswa* is the textile cover of the Kaʿba (Munt, 'Kaʿba').

[97] Al-Barqī, *al-Maḥāsin*, vol. II, 301, no. 636.

honey and saffron with the proceeds, and to mix it with soil from the grave of al-Ḥusayn, that it may be consumed by sick Shiʿites for healing purposes.[98] In other words, by this time the grave was also considered to have supernatural healing qualities.

Parker Selby has analysed the *isnād*s of the traditions in Ibn Qūluwayh's *Kāmil* in an MA thesis and has found that two important sources of his are the Kufans al-Ḥasan b. ʿAlī b. al-Faḍḍāl (d. 224/838–9) and al-Ḥusayn b. Saʿīd al-Ahwāzī (whose exact date of death is unknown, but who was probably contemporary with al-Ḥasan b. ʿAlī).[99] Both are well-attested in Shiʿite and Sunni biographical works, and both are significant in this context because they are said to have written two of the earliest *ziyāra* manuals, none of which is extant today. Their prominence as sources for Ibn Qūluwayh rightly leads Selby to conclude that 'we can confidently push the practice of *ziyāra* to Ḥusayn and other imams' tombs in the early ninth century during the reign of the ʿAbbāsid caliph al-Ma'mūn (198–218/813–33) or possibly earlier'.[100] The historical traditions discussed above, especially that of caliph al-Mutawakkil's destruction of the tomb in 236/850–1, point in the same direction, as Selby has also argued.[101]

Public Mourning Rituals

The Shiʿite ritual probably best known by non-Shiʿites is the public mourning rituals commemorating the death of al-Ḥusayn and mourning for him. Compared to the rituals discussed above, however, these manifestations are probably quite late; they did not develop, at least not on a larger scale, until Buyid times. Several medieval Muslim historians give an account of the mourning celebrations in Baghdad in the year 352/963. The earliest of them, Ibn al-Jawzī (d. 597/1201), writes:

> On the tenth of Muḥarram, the markets in Baghdad were closed and all business was suspended. The butchers ceased their slaughtering [and the cooks did not cook]. People did not cease to ask for a drink of water. Tents were

[98] See also Bursi, 'Scents of Space', 218.
[99] Selby, 'Ḥusayn's Dirt', 39–43.
[100] Selby, 'Ḥusayn's Dirt', 43.
[101] Selby, 'Ḥusayn's Dirt', 44–51.

> pitched in the markets and draped with felt covers. The women wandered through the market with their hair hanging loose, slapping their faces, and lamentations for al-Ḥusayn could be heard.[102]

The younger contemporary historian, Ibn al-Athīr (d. 1233), also mentions this event, but introduces his short account by writing that the Buyid ruler Muʿizz al-Dawla commanded that the markets close for the occasion. He furthermore adds that the Sunnis could not prevent these demonstrations because of the large number of Shiʿites and the support they had from the authorities.[103] A few decades later, the famous scholar Abū Rayḥān al-Bīrūnī (d. c. 442/1050) mentions that, on the day of ʿĀshūrā', when al-Ḥusayn was killed at Karbala, Shiʿites lament and weep in public in cities like Baghdad and other places, and make pilgrimages to Karbala.[104] By the end of the fourth/tenth century, then, we see the embryo of what came to develop into the large passion plays of the Safavid era. Such public manifestations, of course, encountered opposition from the non-Shiʿite population: anti-Shiʿite riots erupted, and counter-celebrations soon developed.[105] Christine Baker, however, argues that since both Ibn Jawzī and Ibn al-Athīr were staunch Sunnis, and furthermore wrote their histories retrospectively in a Sunni environment, their descriptions of the events in fourth/tenth-century Baghdad must be nuanced. Sources contemporary with the Buyids do not mention sectarian violence at all, she maintains.[106] Whether these rituals led to clashes or not, the testimonies of Ibn al-Jawzī and Ibn al-Athīr are the earliest we have about public mourning for al-Ḥusayn.

Ehsan Yarshater traced a pre-Islamic background to the later passion plays to the old Persian tales 'Memorial of Zarer' and the tragedy of Siyāvush. While a Mesopotamian or Egyptian background cannot be ruled out, he argued, these two Persian traditions – especially the one about Siyāvush – show so many similarities to the later passion plays about al-Ḥusayn that they must

[102] Ibn al-Jawzī, *Al-muntaẓam*, vol. XIV, 150. According to the text I have used, the words in brackets are not found in the manuscript used by the editors. I have relied heavily on the translation in Halm, *Shiʿa Islam*, 43.

[103] Ibn al-Athīr, *Kāmil*, vol. VII, 279. Calmard has translated yet another account (which I have not seen) of the same event by Ibn Kathīr (d. 774/1373) ('Culte', 94).

[104] Al-Bīrūnī, *Āthār*, 329.

[105] Calmard, 'Culte', 98–100.

[106] Baker, *Sectarianism*, 84–8.

have had a profound influence on the latter.[107] But that is a subject which goes far beyond the scope of the present study.

Summary and Final Reflections

In this chapter I have attempted to map the development of the Karbala story and the image of al-Ḥusayn in the centuries following the Karbala event itself, up to the end of the fourth/tenth century. While developments like these are never as neatly linear as we would like them to be – with various groups holding different and often opposing views at the same time, both formal and informal leaders relapsing to a previous opinion, and so on – the general trend is clear: over these centuries, the original story of a skirmish, a small conventional fight, develops into a drama of a cosmic battle which has implications for all Believers. It thus becomes a real myth, a narrative which is foundational for the Shiʿite identity and world-view.

Two factors are particularly significant in this development. The first is the placing of the Karbala event in a cosmological context in which the suffering and death of al-Ḥusayn are not unique, though they form the prime instance of the constant struggle between the good and evil forces of the universe. The Karbala story, then, becomes a pattern for interpretation of the suffering of the individual. While the story itself has a bad ending – as do the lives of so many people in this world – Shiʿite eschatology promises that the faithful believer will one day triumph together with imam al-Ḥusayn. The second factor is the ritualisation of the Karbala story and the commemoration of the death of al-Ḥusayn, and the emotional support these rituals create for the world-view presented in the myth, and for solidarity within the group. The emotions engendered in the rituals, performed in company with other Believers, feed back into the myth and the world-view it paints, thus creating a feedback loop from the microcosm of the individual, via the mesocosm of the group, to the macrocosm depicted in Shiʿite theology, and back again, thus building and consolidating a Shiʿite identity.[108]

[107] Yarshater, 'Taʿziyeh'.
[108] See Figure 2.1 and the adjacent discussion.

12

Conclusion: Mythmaking and Identity in Early Shiʿism

I will begin this concluding chapter by returning to Russell McCutcheon, whose ideas about myth and mythmaking I reviewed in Chapter 2, where he encourages us to reconsider the concept of myth and regard it as 'the product and the means of creating authority by removing a claim, behavior, artifact or institution from human history and hence from the realm of human doings'.[1] Throughout this book, I have endeavoured to demonstrate how the story about the battle was already within a century 'removed from human history' and made into a conflict primarily located beyond this world. From a historical point of view, the battle of Karbala was hardly more than a skirmish, one among innumerable battles large and small between competing groups vying with one another in the religio-political turmoil that eventually came to consolidate as Islam. All scholars acknowledge, however, that the repercussions of the battle in the long run far outweighed its immediate consequences. Out of the oldest, brief accounts of this skirmish there eventually emerged the myth of a cosmic battle in which al-Ḥusayn and his followers are interpreted as representatives of the cosmic Imam and his armies, and their enemies as agents of the principle of Ignorance. The story thus developed into a narrative which became foundational to the Shiʿite world-view and identity.

Part I of the present book analyses the earliest available versions of the story about the battle. In Chapter 3, we saw how the two earliest versions – al-Bāqir's and Ibn ʿAbd al-Raḥmān's accounts from the first decades of the second/eighth century – are terse and sketchy; in those versions, the battle itself

[1] McCutcheon, 'Myth', 207.

is described in a few lines and the killing of al-Ḥusayn almost in passing. The battle and its prelude are furthermore described as merely human businesses; although various characters refer to God in oaths and prayers, He is not given an active role in the events. Towards the end of the same century, the story in the hands of Abū Mikhnaf had already developed into a long and detailed account in which God intervened in the battle in various ways. Abū Mikhnaf's version, moreover, has a clear theological agenda, discussed in Chapter 4. Abū Mikhnaf maintained that disloyalty to the family of the Prophet meant breaking the divine covenant. Though his account of the Karbala tragedy served as a pattern for almost all the later versions, his theological interpretation of the battle was never, however, accepted among Shiʿites, at least not in the form in which he presented it. Instead, an alternative dualist narrative about the divine covenant emerged among Shiʿites, according to which a cosmic battle has been going on since the creation of the first entities, and it seems that the Karbala event was at least beginning to be interpreted within this framework. While it is not possible to date these ideas with certainty, it is not improbable that they first emerged in the second/eighth century, that is, simultaneously with Abū Mikhnaf's writings. Thus, already less than a century after the Karbala event, the story was moved away from history and regarded in one way or another as a metaphysical struggle between Good and Evil.

Part II of the book (Chapters 5–8) is entirely devoted to the movement of the Tawwābūn ('the Penitents'), a few years after the Karbala event. I argue there that the traditions on which this story is based can be traced back to at least the beginning of the second/eighth century, but were subsequently overlaid and expanded by later additions. In the earliest layer of the story, ʿAlī is absent; it is al-Ḥusayn's consanguineous relation to the Prophet through Fāṭima that is emphasised. In this layer, furthermore, it is evident that many of the later Shiʿite ideas about the imam have not yet developed. Some of these, however, can be discerned in the later strata of the story, in which ʿAlī is also more visible. The story of the Tawwābūn furthermore indicates that among the earliest emotions associated with the Karbala drama was a profound sense of guilt for the failure to support al-Ḥusayn in his crisis, as well as a wish to repent in order to avert divine punishment for this sin. Here, we also see the rudiments of the ritual pilgrimage to the grave of al-Ḥusayn, an element that developed in the following centuries. Though the main narrative is related by Abū Mikhnaf, it seems to be corroborated in a very early poem by Aʿshā Hamdān from the end of the first/seventh century.

The first two parts of the book are based on close textual analyses, which provide results of relatively high probability. The chapters of Part III, especially Chapter 11, are of a more impressionistic character, more sweeping in their overviews and perhaps suggestive rather than probative. A kind of resolution to the Karbala event is found in the vengeance exacted by the rebellion of al-Mukhtār in 65–7/685–7, discussed in Chapter 9. In this story, al-Ḥusayn and his death play a minor role; among the ʿAlīds, it is ʿAlī himself and his son Ibn al-Ḥanafiyya who are in focus. But despite the modest role accorded the Karbala drama, the story of al-Mukhtār and its aftermath is important for my study because it is here that we find the embryo of later Shiʿite imamology, in which the imam is elevated into a figure above ordinary human beings – an important factor in the location of the Karbala story in a cosmic framework. This is especially apparent in the ideology of the Kaysāniyya movement that emerged during and after al-Mukhtār's insurrection. In the ideology of this movement, we see for the first time ideas like the occultation (*ghayba*) of the imam and the expectation that he will return to set the world right. The further development of competing ideologies of the imam is in turn crucial for an understanding of the elevation of the Karbala story into a myth of cosmic significance, and is the subject of Chapter 10. There and in Chapter 11, I endeavoured to show that the story and its trajectory cannot be understood in isolation, but must be considered within the social formation of Shiʿism as a whole. The significance of the emergence of the various rituals and the emotional effervescence connected to them, such as the re-telling of the story on various occasions, the weeping in response to hearing about and remembering the death of al-Ḥusayn, and the weeping also on the visits to his grave, cannot be underestimated in this context. At the same time, the creation of a cosmological context in which the Karbala story found a natural position as the principal representation of the cosmic struggle between good and evil transformed the apparent defeat of al-Ḥusayn into a glorious victory for all true Believers. Much of this cosmological framework must have been inaccessible to people in general, so my argument there is that the Karbala story popularised it, made the battle more concrete and tangible, although it was at the same time made clear that it was not only an earthly affair.

If grief can be said to be a prominent ethos of Shiʿism, however, it is secondary to *walāya*, love for and loyalty to the family of the Prophet. The grief expressed in the various rituals relating to the *ahl al-bayt* and their descendants is not, in the first place, a sorrowing for the death of al-Ḥusayn alone, but for the suffering of all in the family of the Prophet and, by extension, of all the Shiʿites, the true Believers. As the Karbala tragedy was gradually raised above the confines of human history, it came to be seen on the one hand as the prime example of the great betrayal of them, and on the other as the epitome of the cosmic battle between the good and evil forces in the universe that has been under way since creation and will continue until the end of time. Here, as in so many instances in the history of religions, an in-built tension is found between the free will of the individual to choose what is good or evil and the inevitability of events caused by divine predestination.

In this book I have attempted to highlight one factor in the social formation of early Shiʿism: the making of the story of al-Ḥusayn's death at Karbala in 61/680 into the myth of a cosmic battle. This study forms one piece in a giant mosaic. A more complete picture of the emergence of Shiʿism requires that it be seen in concert with previous research, but also that further investigations are made of the political, social and religious institutions at the time, of the contest for power in both theological and political terms, and of the life of the 'ordinary people' – without whom 'the people in power' would have no power at all.

The Karbala story is still developing. The many studies made of later versions of the story and their significance for Shiʿites in various historical contexts have made it abundantly clear that the rituals and drama commemorating the event, the iconography depicting it, and the social and political movements for which it has been a source of inspiration all testify to the continued importance of this story.[2]

[2] Only a few examples of studies of these phenomena can be given here. On rituals, see e.g. Chelkowski, 'Time Out of Memory'; Schubel, *Religious Performance*; on art, Flaskerud, *Visualizing Belief*; Marzolph, 'Visual Culture'; on socio-politics, Enayat, *Political Thought*, 181–94; Aghaie, *Martyrs of Karbala*; Amanat, *Apocalyptic Islam*, 4–6, 91–109.

Bibliography

Abbreviations

EI[1] = Houtsma, M. T. *et al.* (eds), *Encyclopaedia of Islam*, 1st edn (Leiden: Brill, 1916–36).

EI[2] = Bosworth, C. E. *et al.* (eds), *Encyclopaedia of Islam*, 2nd edn (Leiden: Brill, 1960–2002).

EI[3] = Fleet, Kate *et al.* (eds), *Encyclopaedia of Islam, three*, online edition (Leiden: Brill, 2007–).

EIr = *Encyclopaedia Iranica Online*, online edition (New York: Columbia University, 1996–).

EIsl = Madelung, Wilferd and Farhad Daftary (eds), *Encyclopaedia Islamica*, online edition (Leiden: Brill, 2008–).

EQ = McAuliffe, Jane Dammen (ed.), *Encyclopaedia of the Qur'ān* (Leiden: Brill, 2001–6).

Primary Sources and Secondary Literature

Ådna, Gerd Marie, '"O Son of the Two Sacrifices": Muhammad and the Formation of Sacrifice in Early Islam', PhD thesis (Bergen: University of Bergen, 2006).

Aghaie, Kamran Scot, *The Martyrs of Karbala: Shi'i Symbols and Rituals in Modern Iran* (Seattle: University of Washington Press, 2004).

Alexander, Scott C., 'Fear', in *EQ*.

Algar, Hamid, 'Čahārdah Maʿṣūm', in *EIr*.

Allison, Dale C., 'How to Marginalize the Traditional Criteria of Authenticity', in Tom Holmén and Stanley E. Porter (eds), *Handbook for the Study of the Historical Jesus* (Leiden: Brill, 2011), vol. I, 1–30.

Amanat, Abbas, *Apocalyptic Islam and Iranian Shi'ism* (London: I. B. Tauris, 2009).

Amir-Moezzi, Mohammad Ali, 'Cosmogony and Cosmology v. In Twelver Shiʿism', in *EIr*.

Amir-Moezzi, Mohammad Ali, *The Divine Guide in Early Shiʿism: The Sources of Esotericism in Islam* (Albany: State University of New York Press, 1994).

Amir-Moezzi, Mohammad Ali, 'Early Shīʿī Theology', in Sabine Schmidke (ed.), *The Oxford Handbook of Islamic Theology* (Oxford: Oxford University Press, 2016), 81–90.

Amir-Moezzi, Mohammad Ali, 'Eschatology iii. Imami Shiʿism', in *EIr*.

Amir-Moezzi, Mohammad Ali, 'Les Imams et les Ghulāt. Nouvelles réflexions sur les relations entre imamisme "modéré" et shiʿisme "extrémiste"', *Shii Studies Review*, 4, nos 1–2 (2020), 5–38.

Amir-Moezzi, Mohammad Ali, 'Muḥammad le paraclet et ʿAlī le messie: nouvelles remarques sur les origines de l'islam et de l'imamologie shiʿite', in Mohammad Ali Amir-Moezzi *et al.* (eds), *L'ésoterisme shiʿite. Ses racines et ses prolongements = Shiʿi Esotericism: Its Roots and Developments* (Turnhout: Brepols, 2016), 19–54.

Amir-Moezzi, Mohammad Ali, 'On Spirituality of Shiʿi Islam: A Reply to Prof. Karim Douglas Crow', *Studia Islamica*, 108, no. 1 (2013), 108–15.

Amir-Moezzi, Mohammad Ali, 'Reflections on the Expression *dīn ʿAlī*: The Origins of the Shiʿi Faith', in Farhad Daftary and Gurdofarid Miskinzoda (eds), *The Study of Shiʿi Islam: History, Theology and Law* (London: I. B. Tauris, 2014), 17–46.

Amir-Moezzi, Mohammad Ali, *The Silent Quran and the Speaking Quran: Scriptural Sources of Islam between History and Fervor* (New York: Columbia University Press, 2016).

Amir-Moezzi, Mohammad Ali, *The Spirituality of Shiʿi Islam: Beliefs and Practices* (London: I. B. Tauris, 2011).

Amir-Moezzi, Mohammad Ali and Guillaume Dye (eds), *Le Coran des historiens* (Paris: Les éditions du Cerf, 2019).

Amir-Moezzi, Mohammad Ali and Christian Jambet, *What is Shiʿi Islam?: An Introduction* (London: Routledge, 2018).

Ansari, Hassan, *L'imamat et l'Occultation selon l'imamisme: étude bibliographique et histoire des textes* (Leiden: Brill, 2017).

Anthony, Sean W., *The Caliph and the Heretic: Ibn Sabaʾ and the Origins of Shīʿism* (Leiden: Brill, 2012).

Anthony, Sean W., 'Kaysāniya', in *EIr*.

Anthony, Sean W., *Muhammad and the Empires of Faith: The Making of the Prophet of Islam* (Oakland, CA: University of California Press, 2020).

Āqā Buzurg al-Ṭihrānī, *Al-dharīʿa ilā taṣānīf al-shīʿa* (Beirut: Dār al-ʿAḍwāʾ, 1983).

Arjomand, Saïd Amir, 'The Consolation of Theology: Absence of the Imam and Transition from Chiliasm to Law in Shiʿism', *The Journal of Religion*, 76, no. 4 (1996), 548–71.

Arjomand, Saïd Amir, 'Islamic Apocalypticism in the Classic Period', in Bernard McGinn, John Joseph Collins and Stephen J. Stein (eds), *The Encyclopedia of Apocalypticism* (New York: Continuum, 1998), vol. II, 238–83.

Asatryan, Mushegh, *Controversies in Formative Shiʿi Islam: The Ghulat Muslims and their Beliefs* (London: I. B. Tauris in association with the Institute of Ismaili Studies, 2017).

Asatryan, Mushegh, 'Mofażżal al-Joʿfi', in *EIr*.

Asatryan, Mushegh, 'Of Wine, Sex, and Other Abominations: The Meanings of Antinomianism in Early Islamic Iraq', *Global Intellectual History* (2023). DOI: 10.1080/23801883.2022.2163911.

Asatryan, Mushegh and Dylan M. Burns, 'Is Ghulāt Religion Islamic Gnosticism? Religious Transmission in Late Antiquity', in Mohammad Ali Amir-Moezzi *et al.* (eds), *Shiʿi Esotericism: Its Roots and Developments* (Turnhout: Brepols, 2016), 55–86.

Aʿshā Hamdān, *Dīwān Aʿshā Hamdān wa-akhbāruhu*, ed. Ḥasan ʿĪsā Abū Yāsīn (Riyad: Dār al-ʿulūm, 1983).

Al-Aʿshā, Maymūn ibn Qays, *Gedichte von Abû Basîr Maimûn ibn Qais al-ʾAʿšâ: nebst Sammlungen von Stücken anderer Dichter des gleichen Beinamens und von al-Musayyab ibn ʿAlas*, ed. Rudolf Geyer (London: Luzac & Co., 1928).

Al-ʿAshshāsh, al-Ṭayyib, *Dīwān ashʿār al-tashayyuʿ ilā al-qarn al-thālith/al-tāsiʿ* (Beirut: Dār al-gharb al-islāmī, 1997).

Assmann, Jan, *Cultural Memory and Early Civilization: Writing, Remembrance, and Political Imagination* (Cambridge: Cambridge University Press, 2011).

Assmann, Jan, *Religion and Cultural Memory: Ten Studies* (Stanford: Stanford University Press, 2006).

Athamina, Khalil, 'Abū Mikhnaf', in *EI*³.

Athamina, Khalil, 'Al-Qasas: Its Emergence, Religious Origin and Its Socio-Political Impact on Early Muslim Society', *Studia Islamica*, no. 76 (1992), 53–74.

Ayoub, Mahmoud, *Redemptive Suffering in Islam: A Study of Devotional Aspects of ʿĀshūrāʾ in Twelver Shīʿism* (The Hague: Mouton, 1978).

Bahramian, Ali et al., 'Abū Mikhnaf', in *EIsl*.

Baker, Christine D., *Medieval Islamic Sectarianism* (Amsterdam: Arc Humanities Press, 2019).

Al-Balādhurī, Aḥmad b. Yaḥyā, *Ansāb al-Ashrāf*, ed. Suhayl Zakkār and Riyaḍ Ziriklī, 13 vols (Beirut: Dar al-Fikr, 1996).

Bar-Asher, Meir, *Scripture and Exegesis in Early Imāmī Shiism* (Leiden: Brill, 1999).

Al-Barqī, Aḥmad b. Muḥammad, *Kitāb al-maḥāsin*, ed. Mahdī Rajā'ī. 2 vols (Qum: al-Majmaʿ al-ʿālamī li-ahl al-bayt, 2011).

Bascom, William, 'The Forms of Folklore: Prose Narratives', in Alan Dundes (ed.), *Sacred Narratives: Readings in the Theory of Myth* (Berkeley, CA: University of California Press, 1984), 6–29.

Bayhom-Daou, Tamima, 'Abū Hāshim', in *EI*[3].

Bayhom-Daou, Tamima, 'Hishām b. al-Ḥakam (d. 179/795) and His Doctrine of the Imām's Knowledge', *Journal of Semitic Studies*, 48, no. 1 (2003), 71–108.

Bayhom-Daou, Tamima, 'The Imām's Knowledge and the Quran according to al-Faḍl b. Shādhān al-Nīsābūrī (d. 260 A.H./874 A.D.)', *Bulletin of the School of Oriental and African Studies*, 64, no. 2 (2001), 188–207.

Bennett, David, 'Hishām b. al-Ḥakam', in *EI*[3].

Berkey, Jonathan P., *The Formation of Islam: Religion and Society in the Near East, 600–1800* (Cambridge: Cambridge University Press, 2003).

Berkey, Jonathan P., *Popular Preaching and Religious Authority in the Medieval Islamic Near East* (Seattle: University of Washington Press, 2001).

Al-Bīrūnī, Abū Rayḥān, *Al-āthār al-bāqiya ʿan al-qurūn al-khāliya*, ed. Eduard Sachau (Leipzig, 1878).

Borrut, Antoine, 'Remembering Karbalā': The Construction of an Early Islamic Site of Memory', *Jerusalem Studies in Arabic and Islam*, 42 (2015), 249–82.

Böwering, Gerhard, 'Covenant', in *EQ*.

Böwering, Gerhard, 'Early Sufism between Persecution and Heresy', in Frederick De Jong and Bernd Radtke (eds), *Islamic Mysticism Contested: Thirteen Centuries of Controversies and Polemics* (Leiden: Brill, 1999), 45–67.

Brock, Sebastian P., 'North Mesopotamia in the Late Seventh Century: Book XV of Johna Bar Penkāyē's *Rīš Mellē*', *Jerusalem Studies in Arabic and Islam*, 9 (1987), 51–75.

Buckley, Ron P., 'Muḥammad al-Bāqir', in *EI*[3].

Buhl, Frants, 'Alidernes stilling til de shiʿitiske bevægelser under umajjaderne', in *Øversigt over det kgl. Danske videskabernes selskabs forhandlinger* (Copenhagen: Danske Videnskabernes Selskab, 1910), 355–94.

Bursi, Adam, 'Scents of Space: Early Islamic Pilgrimage, Perfume, and Paradise', *Arabica*, 67, nos 2–3 (2020), 200–34.

Calmard, Jean, 'Le culte de l'Imām Ḥusayn: Etude sur la commémoration du Drame de Karbalā dans l'Iran pré-safavide', unpublished PhD thesis (University of Paris III: EHESS, 1975).

Calmard, Jean, 'Popular Literature under the Safavids', in Andrew J. Newman (ed.), *Society and culture in the Early Modern Middle East: Studies on Iran in the Safavid Period* (Leiden: Brill, 2003), 315–39.

Cameron, Averil, 'Late Antique Apocalyptic: A Context for the Qur'an?', in Hagit Amirav, Emmanouela Grypeou and Guy Stroumsa (eds), *Apocalypticism and Eschatology in Late Antiquity. Encounters in the Abrahamic Religions, 6th–8th Centuries* (Leuven: Peeters, 2017), 1–19.

Capezzone, Leonardo 'Kaysāniyya', in *EI*[3].

Chelkowski, Peter, J., 'Time Out of Memory: Ta'ziyeh, the Total Drama', *The Drama Review*, 49, no. 4 (2005), 15–27.

Clarke, Lynda, 'Elegy (*Marthīya*) on Ḥusayn: Arabic and Persian', *Al-Serat*, 12 (1986), 13–28.

Collins, Randall, *Interaction Ritual Chains* (Princeton, NJ: Princeton University Press, 2004).

Conrad, Lawrence I., 'Ibn A'tham and His History', *Al-'Uṣūr al-Wusṭā: The Journal of Middle East Medievalists*, 23 (2015), 87–125.

Cook, Michael, *Commanding Right and Forbidding Wrong in Islamic Thought* (Cambridge: Cambridge University Press, 2000).

Crone, Patricia, 'The Ancient Near East and Islam: The Case of Lot-Casting', in Hanna Siurua (ed.), *Islam, the Ancient Near East and Varieties of Godlessness: Collected Studies in Three Volumes* (Leiden: Brill, 2016), vol. III, 17–43.

Crone, Patricia, '*Mawālī* and the Prophet's Family: An Early Shī'ite View', in Monique Bernards and John Nawas (eds), *Patronate and Patronage in Early and Classical Islam* (Leiden: Brill, 2005), 167–94.

Crone, Patricia, *Meccan Trade and the Rise of Islam* (Princeton, NJ: Princeton University Press, 1987).

Crone, Patricia, *Medieval Islamic Political Thought* (Edinburgh: Edinburgh University Press, 2004).

Crone, Patricia, 'The Significance of Wooden Weapons in al-Mukhtār's Revolt and the 'Abbāsid Revolution', in Ian R. Netton (ed.), *Studies in Honour of Clifford Edmund Bosworth, vol. I: Hunter of the East: Arabic and Semitic Studies* (Leiden: Brill, 2000), 174–87.

Crone, Patricia and Michael Cook, *Hagarism: The Making of the Islamic World* (Cambridge: Cambridge University Press, 1977).

Crone, Patricia and Martin Hinds, *God's Caliph: Religious Authority in the First Centuries of Islam* (Cambridge: Cambridge University Press, 1986).

Cross, Frank Moore, 'Kinship and Covenant in Ancient Israel', in Frank Moore Cross (ed.), *From Epic to Canon: History and Literature in Ancient Israel* (Baltimore, MD: Johns Hopkins University Press, 1998), 3–21.

Crow, Karim Douglas, 'The Death of al-Ḥusayn b. ʿAlī and Early Shīʿī Views of the Imamate', *Al-Serat*, 12 (1986), 71–116.

Crow, Karim Douglas, 'Shiʿi Spirituality: A Response to Amir-Moezzi', *Journal of Shiʿa Islamic Studies*, 5, no. 3 (2012), 295–315.

Csapo, Eric, *Theories of Mythology* (Oxford: Blackwell, 2005).

Daftary, Farhad, *The Ismāʿīlīs: their history and doctrines*, 2nd edn (Cambridge: Cambridge University Press, 2007).

Dakake, Maria Massi, *The Charismatic Community: Shiʿite Identity in Early Islam* (New York: State University of New York Press, 2007).

Darnell, Robert C., 'The Idea of Divine Covenant in the Qur'ān', unpublished PhD thesis (University of Michigan, 1970).

Deacon, E. Lucy, 'The Curious Addition of Non-Religious Characters to The Martyrdom of Imam Husain', *Iranian Studies*, 54, nos 1–2 (2021), 193–220.

Denny, Frederick Mathewson, 'The Qur'ānic Vocabulary of Repentance: Orientations and Attitudes', *Journal of the American Academy of Religion*, 47, no. 4 (1980), 649–64.

Denny, Frederick Mathewson, 'Tawwābūn', in *EI*[2].

Al-Dhahabī, Muḥammad b. Aḥmad, *Mīzān al-iʿtidāl*, ed. ʿAlī Muḥammad Muʿawwaḍ and ʿĀdil Aḥmad ʿAbd al-Mawjūd (Beirut: Dār al-kutub al-ʿilmiyya, 1995).

Al-Dīnawarī, Abū Ḥanīfa, *Al-akhbār al-ṭiwāl*, ed. Vladimir Guirgass and Ignace Kratchkovsky (Leiden: Brill, 1888–1912).

Dixon, Abd al-Ameer Abd, *The Umayyad Caliphate, 65–86/684–705 (A Political Study)* (London: Luzac, 1971).

Djaït, Hichem, 'Les Yamanites à Kūfa au Ier siècle de l'Hégire', *Journal of the Economic and Social History of the Orient*, 19, no. 2 (1976), 148–81.

Donner, Fred M., 'From Believers to Muslims: Confessional Self-Identity in the Early Islamic Community', *Al-Abhath: Journal of the Center for Arab and Middle East Studies*, 50–1 (2003), 9–53.

Donner, Fred M., *Muhammad and the Believers at the Origins of Islam* (Cambridge, MA: Belknap Press of Harvard University Press, 2010).

Donner, Fred M., *Narratives of Islamic Origins: The Beginnings of Islamic Historical Writing* (Princeton, NJ: Darwin Press, 1998).

Droge, Arthur J., *The Qur'ān: A New Annotated Translation* (Sheffield: Equinox, 2013).

Durkheim, Émile, *The Elementary Forms of Religious Life* (New York: Free Press, 1995).

Ebstein, Michael, 'Covenant (Religious) Pre-eternal', in *EI*[3].

Ebstein, Michael, '"In Truth You are the Polytheist!": Mythic Elements in Ibn Ibn al-ʿArabī's Teachings on the Divine Names', *Intellectual History of the Islamicate World*, 6, no. 3 (2018), 359–87.

El-Achèche, Taïeb [al-ʿAshshāsh, al-Ṭayyib], *La poésie šiʿite des origines au IIIe siècle de l'Hégire* (Damascus: Presses de l'Ifpo, 2003).

El-Hawary, Hassan Mohammed, 'The Most Ancient Islamic Monument Known Dated A.H. 31 (A.D. 652) from the Time of the Third Calif ʿUthman', *Journal of the Royal Asiatic Society*, 62, no. 2 (1930), 321–33.

Enayat, Hamid, *Modern Islamic Political Thought: The Response of the Shīʿī and Sunnī Muslims to the Twentieth Century* (London: Macmillan, 1982).

van Ess, Josef, *Theologie und Gesellschaft im 2. und 3. Jahrhundert Hidschra: eine Geschichte des religiösen Denkens im frühen Islam* (Berlin: de Gruyter, 1991–7).

Firestone, Reuven, 'Is There a Notion of "Divine Election" in the Qur'ān?', in Gabriel S. Reynolds (ed.), *Perspectives on the Qur'ān. The Qur'ān in Its Historical Context 2* (London: Routledge, 2011), 51–67.

Firestone, Reuven, 'The Qur'ān and the Bible: Some Modern Studies of Their Relationship', in John C. Reeves (ed.), *Bible and Qur'ān: Essays in Scriptural Intertextuality* (Atlanta: Society for Biblical Literature, 2003), 1–22.

Firestone, Reuven, 'Shekhinah', in *EQ*.

Fishbein, Michael, 'The Life of al-Mukhtār b. Abī ʿUbayd in Some Early Arabic Historians', unpublished PhD thesis (Los Angeles: University of California, 1988).

Flaskerud, Ingvild, *Visualizing Belief and Piety in Iranian Shiism* (London: Bloomsbury, 2012).

Gilliot, Claude, 'Mythe, récit, histoire du salut dans le commentaire coranique de Tabari', *Journal Asiatique*, 282, no. 2 (1994), 237–70.

Gleave, Robert, 'Recent Research into the History of Early Shiʿism', *History Compass*, 7, no. 6 (2009), 1,593–605.

Görke, Andreas and Gregor Schoeler, *Die ältesten Berichte über das Leben Muhammads: das Korpus ʿUrwa ibn az-Zubair* (Princeton, NJ: Darwin Press, 2008).

Görke, Andreas and Gregor Schoeler, 'Reconstructing the Earliest Sīra Texts: The Hiǧra in the Corpus of ʿUrwa b. al-Zubayr', *Der Islam*, 82, no. 2 (2005), 209–20.

Görke, Andreas, Harald Motzki and Gregor Schoeler, 'First Century Sources for the Life of Muhammad? A Debate', *Der Islam*, 89, nos 1–2 (2012), 2–59.

Günther, Sebastian, 'Abū l-Faraj al-Iṣfahānī', in *EI*[3].

Günther, Sebastian, '*Maqātil* Literature in Medieval Islam', *Journal of Arabic Literature*, 25, no. 3 (1994), 192–212.

Günther, Sebastian, '"... *nor have I learned it from any book of theirs*". Abu l-Faraj al-Iṣfahānī: a Medieval Arabic Author at Work', in Rainer Brunner *et al.* (eds), *Islamstudien ohne Ende: Festschrift für Werner Ende zum 65. Geburtstag* (Würtzburg: Ergon-Verlag, 2002), 139–53.

Gwynne, Rosalind Ward, *Logic, Rhetoric, and Legal Reasoning in the Qur'ān: God's Arguments* (New York: RoutledgeCurzon, 2004).

Hagemann, Hannah-Lena, *The Khārijtes in Early Islamic Historical Tradition: Heroes and Villains* (Edinburgh: Edinburgh University Press, 2021).

Hahn, Scott, 'Covenant in the Old and New Testaments: Some Current Research (1994–2004)', *Currents in Biblical Research*, 3, no. 2 (2005), 263–92.

Haider, Najam I., 'al-Mukhtār b. Abī ʿUbayd', in *EI*[3].

Haider, Najam I., *The Origins of the Shīʿa: Identity, Ritual, and Sacred Space in Eighth-Century Kūfa* (Cambridge: Cambridge University Press, 2011).

Haider, Najam I., *The Rebel and the Imam in Early Islam: Explorations in Muslim Historiography* (Cambridge: Cambridge University Press, 2019).

Haider, Najam I., *Shīʿī Islam: An Introduction* (Cambridge: Cambridge University Press, 2014).

Halevi, Leor, *Muhammad's Grave: Death Rites and the Making of Islam* (New York: Columbia University Press, 2007).

Halm, Heinz, ''Askarī, Abu Moḥammad', in *EIr*.

Halm, Heinz, *Die islamische Gnosis: die extreme Schia und die ʿAlawiten* (Zürich: Artemis Verlag, 1982).

Halm, Heinz, *Shiʿa Islam: From Religion to Revolution* (Princeton, NJ: Marcus Wiener, 1997).

Hawting, Gerald R., 'Al-Mukhtār b. Abī ʿUbayd al-Thaḳafī', in *EI*[2].

Hawting, Gerald R., *The First Dynasty of Islam: The Umayyad Caliphate AD 661–750*, 2nd edn (London: Routledge, 2000).

Hawting, Gerald R., 'The Tawwābūn, Atonement and ʿĀshūrā'', *Jerusalem Studies in Arabic and Islam*, 17 (1994), 166–81.

Hayes, Edmund, *Agents of the Hidden Imam: Forging Twelver Shi'ism, 850–950 CE* (Cambridge: Cambridge University Press, 2022).

Hayes, Edmund, 'Review of *Controversies in Formative Shi'i Islam: The Ghulat Muslims and Their Beliefs*. By Mushegh Asatryan', *Journal of the American Oriental Society*, 140, no. 2 (2021), 516–18.

Hodgson, Marshall G., 'How Did the Early Shīʿa Become Sectarian?', *Journal of the American Oriental Society*, 75 (1955), 1–13.

Hodgson, Marshall G., *The Venture of Islam: Conscience and History in a World Civilization*. 3 vols (Chicago: University of Chicago Press, 1974).

Honigmann, E., 'Karbalāʾ', in *EI*[2].

Howard, I. K. A., 'Husayn the Martyr: A Commentary on the Accounts of the Martyrdom in Arabic Sources', *Al-Serat*, 12 (1986), 124–42.

Howard, I. K. A., 'Translator's Foreword', in I. K. A. Howard (ed.), *The History of al-Ṭabarī*, vol. XIX (New York: State University of New York Press, 1990), ix–xvi.

Hoyland, Robert G., *In God's Path: The Arab Conquests and the Creation of an Islamic Empire* (Oxford: Oxford University Press, 2015).

Hoyland, Robert G., 'Writing the Biography of the Prophet Muhammad: Problems and Solutions', *History Compass*, 5, no. 2 (2007), 581–602.

Hughes, Aaron W. and Russell T. McCutcheon, *Religion in 50 Words: A Critical Vocabulary* (Abingdon: Routledge, 2022).

Humphreys, R. Stephen, *Islamic History: A Framework for Inquiry*, rev. edn (Princeton, NJ: Princeton University Press, 1991).

Humphreys, R. Stephen, 'Qur'ānic Myth and Narrative Structure in Early Islamic Historiography', in F. M. Clover and R. S. Humphreys (eds), *Tradition and Innovation in Late Antiquity* (Madison, WI: University of Wisconsin Press, 1989), 271–90.

Hussain, Ali J., 'A Developmental Analysis of Depictions of the Events of Karbalāʾ in Early Islamic History', unpublished PhD thesis (University of Chicago, 2001).

Hussain, Ali J., 'The Mourning of History and the History of Mourning: The Evolution of Ritual Commemoration of the Battle of Karbala', *Comparative Studies of South Asia, Africa and the Middle East*, 25, no. 1 (2005), 78–88.

Hylén, Torsten, 'Closed and Open Concepts of Religion: The Problem of Essentialism in Teaching about Religion', in Bengt-Ove Andreassen and James R. Lewis (eds), *Textbook Gods: Genre, Text and Teaching Religious Studies* (Sheffield: Equinox, 2014), 16–42.

Hylén, Torsten, 'The Date of the Story of the Tawwābūn', *Studia Islamica*, 112, no. 2 (2017), 175–205.

Hylén, Torsten, 'Emerging Patterns of Authority in Early Shīʿism: al-Mukhtār's Use of the Aesthetics of Persuasion', *Shii Studies Review*, 3, nos 1–2 (2019), 5–36.

Hylén, Torsten, '"The Hand of God is over their Hands" (Q. 48:10), On the Notion of Covenant in al-Ṭabarī's Account of Karbalā"', *Journal of Qur'anic Studies*, 18, no. 2 (2016), 58–88.

Hylén, Torsten, 'Ḥusayn, the Mediator: A Structural Analysis of the Karbala Drama according to Abū Jaʿfar Muḥammad b. Jarīr al-Ṭabarī (d. 310/923)', unpublished PhD thesis (Uppsala University, 2007).

Hylén, Torsten, 'Mukhtār and the *Mahdī*: A Critical Inquiry into the Sources', *DIN: Tidsskrift for religion og kultur*, no. 1 (2018), 138–57.

Hylén, Torsten, 'Myth, Ritual, and the Early Development of Shiite Identity', *Intellectual History of the Islamicate World*, 6, no. 3 (2018), 300–31.

Ibn al-Athīr, ʿIzz al-Dīn Abū al-Ḥasan, *Al-kāmil fī al-tārīkh*, ed. Muḥammad Yūsuf Daqqāq. 11 vols (Beirut: Dār al-kutub al-ʿilmiyya, 1987).

Ibn al-Jawzī, Abū al-Faraj, *Al-muntaẓam fī-l-ta'rīkh al-mulūk wa-l-umam*, ed. Muḥammad ʿAbd al-Qādir ʿAṭā and Muṣṭafā ʿAbd al-Qādir ʿAṭā. 20 vols (Beirut: Dār al-kutub al-ʿilmiyya, 1995).

Ibn al-Nadīm, Muḥammad ibn Isḥāq, *Kitāb al-Fihrist*, ed. Gustav Flügel, Johannes Roediger and August Müller. 2 vols (Leipzig: Vogel, 1871–2).

Ibn Aʿtham al-Kūfī, Ahmad, *Kitāb al-futūḥ* (Hyderabad: Maṭbaʿat Majlis Dā'irat al-maʿārif al-ʿuthmānīya, 1972).

Ibn Aʿtham al-Kūfī, Ahmad, *Kitāb al-futūḥ*, ed. ʿAlī Shīrī. 8+1 vols (Beirut: Dār al-aḍwā', 1991).

Ibn Ḥajar al-ʿAsqalānī, *Tahdhīb al-tahdhīb*. 12 vols (Hyderabad: Majlis dā'irat al-maʿārif al-niẓāmīya al-ka'ina, 1907–9).

Ibn Hishām, ʿAbd al-Malik, *Kitāb sīrat rasūl allāh*, ed. Ferdinand Wüstenfeld. 2 vols (Göttingen: Dieterichsche Univertitäts-Buchhandlung, 1858–9).

Ibn Qūluwayh, Jaʿfar ibn Muḥammad, *Kāmil al-ziyārāt*, ed. Jawād Qayyūmī al-Iṣfahānī. (Qum: Nashr al-Faqāha, 2003).

Ibn Qūluwayh, Jaʿfar ibn Muḥammad, *Kamiluz Ziyaraat (Merits and methods of visiting holy tombs)* (Karbala: The Holy Shrine of Imam Hussain (AS), 2013).

Ibn Saʿd, Abū ʿAbdallāh Muḥammad, *Kitāb al-ṭabaqāt al-kabīr*, ed. Eduard Sachau. 9 vols (Leiden: Brill, 1904–40).

Ibn Saʿd, Abū ʿAbdallāh Muḥammad, *Kitāb al-ṭabaqāt al-kabīr*, ed. ʿAlī Muḥammad ʿUmar. 11 vols (Cairo: Maktabat al-Khānjī, 2001).

Inloes, Amina, 'Joseph Campbell, Shi'ism, and the Karbala Narrative', *British Journal of Middle Eastern Studies* (2022). DOI: 10.1080/13530194.2022.2153799.

Al-Iṣfahānī, Abū al-Faraj, *Maqātil al-Ṭālibiyyīn*, ed. Sayyid Aḥmad Ṣaqr (Beirut: Mu'assasat al-a'lamī li-l-maṭbū'āt, 2018).

Izutsu, Toshihiko, *Ethico-Religious Concepts in the Qur'ān*, 2nd edn (Montreal and Kingston: McGill-Queen's University Press, 2002).

Jaffer, Tariq, 'Is There Covenant Theology in Islam?', in Majid Daneshgar and Walid Saleh (eds), *Islamic Studies Today: Essays in Honor of Andrew Rippin* (Leiden: Brill, 2016), 98–121.

Jaffer, Tariq, 'The Mu'tazila on Covenantal Theology: A Study of Individualist Approaches', *Oriens*, 49, nos 1–2 (2021), 131–71.

Jafri, Syed Husain Mohammad, *The Origins and Early Development of Shi'a Islam* (Oxford: Oxford University Press, 1979).

Kanazi, George J. and 'Ubaydallāh b. al-Ḥurr al-Ju'fī, *The Umayyad Poet-Rebel: 'Ubaydullāh ibn al-Ḥurr al-Ju'fī* (Wiesbaden: Harrassowitz, 2000).

Al-Kashshī, Muḥammad Ibn-Umar, *Rijāl al-Kashshī*, ed. Aḥmad al-Ḥusaynī (Karbala: Mu'assasat al-a'lamī li-'l-maṭbū'āt, n.d.).

Kazerouni, Jahangir and Ferial Salahshour, *Reverse Painting on Glass: Jahangir Kazerouni and Ferial Salahshour's Collection* (Tehran: Naẓarpub, 2008).

Kazimirski, A. de Biberstein, *Dictionnaire arabe–français*, repr. by Libraire de Liban, Beirut Edition (Paris: Maisonneuve, 1860).

Kelber, Werner H., *The Oral and the Written Gospel: The Hermeneutics of Speaking and Writing in the Synoptic Tradition, Mark, Paul, and Q* (Bloomington: Indiana University Press, 1997).

Kennedy, Hugh, 'al-Mutawakkil', in *EI*^{2}.

Kennedy, Hugh, *The Prophet and the Age of the Caliphates: The Islamic Near East from the Sixth to the Eleventh Century*, 4th edn (Abingdon: Routledge, 2022).

Kister, Meir Jacob, 'Khuzā'a', in *EI*^{2}.

Kister, Meir Jacob, 'Social and Religious Concepts of Authority in Islam', *Jerusalem Studies in Arabic and Islam*, 18 (1994), 84–127.

Kohlberg, Etan, 'A'maš, Abū Moḥammad', in *EIr*.

Kohlberg, Etan, 'Early Attestations of the Term "Ithnā 'Ashariyya"', *Jerusalem Studies in Arabic and Islam*, 24 (2000), 343–57.

Kohlberg, Etan, 'From Imāmiyya to Ithnā-'Ashariyya', *Bulletin of the School of Oriental and African Studies*, 39 (1976), 521–34.

Kohlberg, Etan, 'Some Imāmī Views on the Ṣaḥāba', *Jerusalem Studies in Arabic and Islam*, 5 (1984), 143–75.

Kohlberg, Etan, 'Zayn al-ʿĀbidīn', in *EI*[2].

Kraemer, David Charles, *Jewish Eating and Identity through the Ages* (London: Routledge, 2007).

Al-Kulaynī, Muḥammad b. Yaʿqūb, *Al-kāfī*, ed. ʿAlī Akbar Ghaffārī. 8 vols (Tehran: Dār kutub al-islāmiyya, 1986–7).

Kuthayyir ʿAzza, *Dīwān Kuthayyir ʿAzza*, ed. Iḥsān ʿAbbās (Beirut: Dār al-Thaqāfa, 1971).

Ladewig Petersen, Erling, *ʿAlī and Muʿāwiya in Early Arabic Tradition: Studies on the Genesis and Growth of Islamic Historical Writing until the End of the Ninth Century* (Copenhagen: Munksgaard, 1964).

Lalani, Arzina R., *Early Shīʿī Thought: The Teachings of Imām Muḥammad al-Bāqir* (London: Tauris, 2004).

Lammens, Henri, 'Al-Husain', in *EI*[1].

Landau-Tasseron, Ella, *The Religious Foundations of Political Allegiance: A Study of Bayʿa in Pre-modern Islam* (Washington, DC: Hudson Institute, 2010).

Lane, Edward W., *Arabic–English Lexicon*, rev. edn (Cambridge: Islamic Texts Society, 1984).

Leder, Stefan, 'The Literary Use of the *Khabar*: A Basic Form of Historical Writing', in A. Cameron and L. Conrad (eds), *The Byzantine and Islamic Near East. Vol. I, Problems in the Literary Source Material* (Princeton, NJ: Darwin, 1992), 277–315.

Lincoln, Bruce, *Theorizing Myth: Narrative, Ideology and Scholarship* (Chicago: University of Chicago Press, 1999).

Lindstedt, Ilkka, 'Al-Madāʾinī's *Kitāb al-Dawla* and the Death of Ibrāhīm al-Imām', in Ilkka Lindstedt, Jaakko Hämeen-Anttila, Raija Mattila and Robert Rollinger (eds), *Case Studies in Transmission* (Münster: Ugarit-Verlag, 2014), 103–30.

Lindstedt, Ilkka, 'Sources for the Biography of the Historian Ibn Aʿtham al-Kūfī', *Orientalia Lovaniensia Analecta*, 254 (2017), 299–309.

Lindstedt, Ilkka, 'Who is In, Who is Out? Early Muslim Identity through Epigraphy and Theory', *Jerusalem Studies in Arabic and Islam*, 46 (2019), 147–246.

Lucas, Scott C., 'Ibn Saʿd', in *EI*[3].

Lumbard, Joseph E. B., 'Covenant and Covenants in the Qur'an', *Journal of Qur'anic Studies*, 17, no. 2 (2015), 1–23.

Lumbard, Joseph E. B., 'Humanity in Covenant with God', in George Archer, Maria Massi Dakake and Daniel A. Madigan (eds), *Routledge Companion to the Qur'an* (London: Routledge, 2021), 58–68.

Mack, Burton L., 'On Redescribing Christian Origins', *Method & Theory in the Study of Religion*, 8, no. 3 (1996), 247–69.

Mack, Burton L., 'Social Formation', in Willi Braun and Russell T. McCutcheon (eds), *Guide to the Study of Religion* (London: Cassell, 2000), 283–96.

Mack, Burton L., *Who Wrote the New Testament?: The Making of the Christian Myth* (San Francisco, CA: HarperSan Francisco, 1995).

Madelung, Wilferd, "Alī b. Ḥosayn b. 'Alī b. Abī Ṭaleb', in *EIr*.

Madelung, Wilferd, 'Al-Kashshī', in *EI²*.

Madelung, Wilferd, 'Badā'', in *EIr*.

Madelung, Wilferd, 'Early Imāmī Theology as Reflected in the *Kitāb al-kāfī* of al-Kulaynī', in Farhad Daftary and Gurdofarid Miskinzoda (eds), *The Study of Shi'i Islam: History, Theology and Law* (London: I. B. Tauris, 2014), 465–74.

Madelung, Wilferd, 'Imāma', in *EI²*.

Madelung, Wilferd, "Iṣma', in *EI²*

Madelung, Wilferd, 'Shī'a', in *EI²*.

Madelung, Wilferd, *The Succession to Muḥammad: A Study of the Early Caliphate* (Cambridge: Cambridge University Press, 1997).

Madelung, Wilferd, 'Theology: Introduction', in Farhad Daftary and Gurdofarid Miskinzoda (eds), *The Study of Shi'i Islam: History, Theology and Law* (London: I. B. Tauris, 2014), 455–63.

Madelung, Wilferd, 'Zayd b. 'Alī b. al-Ḥusayn', in *EI²*.

Al-Majlisī, Muḥammad Bāqir, *Bihār al-anwār* (Beirut: Dār al-iḥyā' al-turāth al-'arabī, 1983).

Marshall, David, 'Punishment Stories', in *EQ*.

Marsham, Andrew, *Rituals of Islamic Monarchy: Accession and Succession in the First Muslim Empire* (Edinburgh: Edinburgh University Press, 2009).

Mårtensson, Ulrika, 'Discourse and Historical Analysis: The Case of al-Tabari's History of the Messengers and the Kings', *Journal of Islamic Studies*, 16, no. 3 (2005), 287–331.

Mårtensson, Ulrika, 'Ibn Isḥāq's and al-Ṭabarī's Historical Contexts for the Quran: Implications for Contemporary Research', in Sebastian Günther (ed.), *Knowledge and Education in Classical Islam* (Leiden: Brill, 2020), 315–53.

Mårtensson, Ulrika, *Tabari* (Oxford: Oxford University Press, 2009).

Mårtensson, Ulrika, 'The True New Testament: Sealing the Heart's Covenant in al-Tabarî's *Ta'rîkh al-Rusul wa'l-Mulûk*', unpublished PhD thesis (Uppsala University, 2001).

Marzolph, Ulrich, 'The Visual Culture of Iranian Twelver Shi'ism in the Qajar Period', *Shii Studies Review*, 3, nos 1–2 (2019), 133–86.

Al-Mas'ūdī, Abū al-Ḥasan, *Murūj al-dhahab*, ed. and trans. C. Barbier de Meynard and A. Pavet de Courteille. 9 vols (Paris, 1861–77).

Al-Mas'ūdī, Abū al-Ḥasan (attrib.), *Ithbāt al-waṣiya li-l-imām 'Alī ibn Abī Ṭālib* (Qum: Ansarian, 2005).

McCutcheon, Russell T., 'Myth', in Willi Braun and Russell T. McCutcheon (eds), *Guide to the Study of Religion* (London: Cassell, 2000), 190–208.

McLaren, Andrew G., 'Dating Ibn A'tham's History: Of Persian Manuscripts, Obscure Bibliographies, and Incomplete *Isnāds*', *al-'Uṣūr al-Wusṭā: The Bulletin of Middle East Medievalists*, 30 (2022), 183–234.

Meier, John P., *A Marginal Jew: Rethinking the Historical Jesus*. 5 vols (New Haven, CT: Yale University Press, 1991–2016).

Mendenhall, George E. and Gary A. Herion, 'Covenant', in Gary A. Herion, Astrid B. Beck and David Noel Freedman (eds), *Anchor Bible Dictionary* (New York: Doubleday, 1992).

Meri, Josef W., *The Cult of Saints among Muslims and Jews in Medieval Syria* (Oxford: Oxford University Press, 2002).

Meri, Josef W, 'The Etiquette of Devotion in the Islamic Cult of Saints', in James Howard-Johnston and Paul Anthony Hayward (eds), *The Cult of Saints in Late Antiquity and the Early Middle Ages* (Oxford: Oxford University Press, 1999), 263–86.

Meri, Josef W., 'Ziyāra: 1. In the Central and Eastern Arab Lands During the Premodern Period', in *EI*².

Metzger, Bruce M., 'Names for the Nameless in the New Testament; a Study in the Growth of Christian Tradition', in Bruce M. Metzger (ed.), *New Testament Studies: Philological, Versional, and Patristic* (Leiden: Brill, 1980), 23–45.

Al-Mizzī, Yūsuf b. al-Zakī, *Tahdhīb al-kamāl fī asmā' al-rijāl*, ed. Bashshār 'Awwād Ma'rūf. 35 vols (Beirut: Mu'assasat al-Risāla, 1983–92).

Modarressi, Hossein, *Crisis and Consolidation in the Formative Period of Shi'ite Islam: Abū Jaf'ar ibn Qiba al-Rāzī and his Contribution to Imamite Shi'ite Thought* (Princeton, NJ: Darwin Press, 1993).

Modarressi, Hossein, *Tradition and Survival: A Bibliographical Survey of Early Shī'ite Literature* (Oxford: Oneworld, 2003), Vol. 1.

Mortensen, Mette Bjerregaard, 'Sourate 20, Ṭā' Hā'', in Amir-Moezzi, Mohammad Ali and Guillaume Dye (eds), *Le Coran des historiens* (Paris: Les éditions du Cerf, 2019), vol. II, 765–98.

Motzki, Harald, with Nicolet Boekhoff-van der Voort and Sean Anthony, *Analysing Muslim Traditions: Studies in Legal, Exegetical and Maghāzī Ḥadīth* (Leiden: Brill, 2010).

Al-Mufīd, Muḥammad b. Muḥammad b. al-Nuʿmān, *Al-Irshād* (Beirut: Muʾassasat al-aʿlamī li-l-maṭbūʿāt, 1979).

Al-Mufīd, Muḥammad b. Muḥammad b. al-Nuʿmān, *Kitāb al-Irshād. The Book of Guidance into the Lives of the Twelve Imams*, trans. I. K. A. Howard (London: Muhammadi Trust, 1981).

Munt, Harry, 'Kaʿba', in *EI³*.

Neuwirth, Angelika, 'Myths and Legends in the Qurʾān', in *EQ*.

Newman, Andrew J., *The Formative Period of Twelver Shīʿism: Hadīth as Discourse Between Qum and Baghdad* (Richmond: Curzon, 2000).

Newman, Andrew J., *Twelver Shiism: Unity and Diversity in the Life of Islam, 632 to 1722* (Edinburgh: Edinburgh University Press, 2013).

Noth, Albrecht and Lawrence I. Conrad, *The Early Arabic Historical Tradition: A Source-Critical Study* (Princeton, NJ: Darwin, 1994).

Ohlander, Erik S., 'Fear of God (*taqwā*) in the Qurʾān: Some Notes on Semantic Shift and Thematic Context', *Journal of Semitic Studies*, 50, no. 1 (2005), 137–52.

Paden, William E., 'Before "The Sacred" Became Theological: Rereading the Durkheimian Legacy', *Method & Theory in the Study of Religion*, 3, no. 1 (1991), 10–23.

Pedersen, Johannes 'The Criticism of the Islamic Preacher', *Die Welt des Islams*, 2, no. 4 (1953), 215–31.

Pellat, Charles, 'Ḳaṣṣ', in *EI²*.

Penn, Michael Philip, *Kissing Christians: Ritual and Community in the Late Ancient Church* (Philadelphia: University of Pennsylvania Press, 2005).

Pierce, Matthew, *Twelve Infallible Men: The Imams and the Making of Shiʿism* (Cambridge, MA: Harvard University Press, 2016).

Pregill, Michael E., '"Turn in Repentance to Your Creator, Then Slay Yourselves": The Levitical Election, Atonement, and Secession in Early and Classical Islamic Exegesis', *Comparative Islamic Studies*, 6, no. 1/2 (2010), 101–50.

Al-Qadi, Wadad, *Al-kaysānīya fi-l-taʾrīkh wa-l-adab* (Beirut: Dār al-Thaqāfa, 1974).

Al-Qadi, Wadad, 'The Development of the Term *Ghulāt* in Muslim Literature with Special Reference to the Kaysāniyya', in Albert Dietrich (ed.), *Akten des VII. Kongresses für Arabistik und Islamwissenschaft: Göttingen, 15. bis 22. August 1974* (Göttingen: Vandenhoeck & Ruprecht, 1976), 295–319.

Al-Qummī, Saʿd b. ʿAbdallāh al-Ashʿarī, *Kitāb al-maqālāt wa-l-firaq*, ed. Muḥammad Jawād Mashkūr (Tehran, 1941).

Reeves, John C. (ed.), *Bible and Qur'ān: Essays in Scriptural Intertextuality* (Atlanta, GA: Society of Biblical Literature, 2003).

Reynolds, Gabriel Said and Amir Moghadam, 'Repentance in the Quran, Hadith, and Ibn Qudāma's *Kitāb al-Tawwābīn*', *Journal of the American Oriental Society*, 141, no. 2 (2021), 381–401.

Rippin, Andrew, 'Literary Analysis of Qur'ān, Tafsīr and Sīra: The Methodologies of John Wansbrough', in Richard C. Martin (ed.), *Approaches to Islam in Religious Studies* (Tucson: University of Arizona Press, 1985), 151–63.

Roberts, Joseph B., 'Early Islamic Historiography: Ideology and Methodology', unpublished PhD thesis (Ohio State University, 1986).

Robinson, Chase F., *Islamic Historiography* (Cambridge: Cambridge University Press, 2003).

Roded, Ruth, 'Umm Salama Hind', in *EI²*.

Rossner, Meredith and Mythily Meher, 'Emotions in Ritual Theories', in Jan E. Stets and Jonathan H. Turner (eds), *Handbook of the Sociology of Emotions*. (Dordrecht: Springer, 2014), vol. II, 199–220.

Rotter, Gernot, *Die Umayyaden und der zweite Bürgerkrieg (680–692)* (Wiesbaden: Deutsche Morgenländische Gesellschaft, 1982).

Rubin, Uri, 'Traditions in Transformation: The Ark of the Covenant and the Golden Calf in Biblical and Islamic Historiography', *Oriens*, 36 (2001), 196–214.

Sachedina, Abdulaziz, *Islamic Messianism: The Idea of Mahdism in Twelver Shīʿism* (Albany: State University of New York Press, 1981).

Al-Sayyid al-Ḥimyarī, *Dīwān al-Sayyid al-Ḥimyarī*, ed. Shākir Hādī Shukr (Qum: Manshūrāt al-maktaba al-ḥaydariyya, 2011).

Schoeler, Gregor, *The Biography of Muḥammad: Nature and Authenticity* (London: Routledge, 2011).

Schoeler, Gregor, *The Genesis of Literature in Islam: From the Aural to the Read* (Edinburgh: Edinburgh University Press, 2009).

Schoeler, Gregor, *The Oral and the Written in Early Islam* (London: Routledge, 2006).

Schöller, Marco, *The Living and the Dead in Islam: Studies in Arabic Epitaphs* (Wiesbaden: Harrassowitz, 2004).

Schubel, Vernon James, *Religious Performance in Contemporary Islam: Shiʿi Devotional Rituals in South Asia* (Columbia: University of South Carolina Press, 1993).

Seidensticker, Tilman, 'Aʿshā Hamdān', in *EI*[3].
Selby, Parker, 'Ḥusayn's Dirt: The Beginnings and Development of Šīʿī *Ziyāra* in the Early Islamic Period' (Ohio State University, 2017).
Sezgin, Fuat, *Geschichte des arabischen Schrifttums* (Leiden: Brill, 1967).
Sezgin, Ursula, *Abū Miḫnaf: Ein Beitrag zur Historiographie der umaiyadischen Zeit* (Leiden: Brill, 1971).
Shaban, M. A., *Islamic History: A New Interpretation* (Cambridge: Cambridge University Press, 1971).
Sharon, Moshe, 'Ahl al-Bayt – People of the House', *Jerusalem Studies in Arabic and Islam*, 8 (1986), 169–84.
Shoemaker, Stephen J., *Creating the Qur'an: A Historical-Critical Study* (Oakland: University of California Press, 2022).
Shoemaker, Stephen J., *The Death of a Prophet: The End of Muhammad's Life and the Beginnings of Islam* (Philadelphia: University of Pennsylvania Press, 2012).
Shoemaker, Stephen J., 'In Search of ʿUrwa's Sīra: Some Methodological Issues in the Quest for "Authenticity" in the Life of Muhammad', *Der Islam*, 85, no. 2 (2011), 257–344.
Shoshan, Boaz, *Poetics of Islamic Historiography: Deconstructing Ṭabarī's 'History'* (Leiden: Brill, 2004).
Shubbār, Jawād, *Adab al-Ṭaff aw shuʿarāʾ al-Ḥusayn min al-qarn al-awwal al-hijrī ḥatta al-qarn al-rābiʿ ʿashar* (Beirut: Muʾassasat al-aʿlamī li-ʾl-maṭbūʿāt, 1969).
Sindawi, Khalid A., 'Visit to the Tomb of al-Ḥusayn b. ʿAlī in Shiite Poetry: First to Fifth Centuries AH (8th–11th Centuries CE)', *Journal of Arabic Literature*, 37, no. 2 (2006), 230–58.
Sinding Jensen, Jeppe, 'Modern Myths and Mythologies', in Jeppe Sinding Jensen (ed.), *Myths and Mythologies: A Reader* (London: Equinox, 2009), 429–40.
Stetkevych, Jaroslav, *Muḥammad and the Golden Bough: Reconstructing Arabian Myth* (Bloomington: Indiana University Press, 1996).
Streck, M., 'Nīnawā', in *EI*[2].
Su, I-Wen, *The Shīʿī Past in the Great Book of the Songs: A New Perspective on the Kitāb al-Aghānī by Abū al-Faraj al-Iṣfahānī and Shīʿī Islam in the Tenth Century* (Piscataway, NJ: Gorgias Press, 2021).
Summers-Effler, Erika, 'Ritual Theory', in Jan E. Stets and Jonathan H. Turner (eds), *Handbook of the Sociology of Emotions* (New York: Springer, 2007), 135–54.
Al-Ṭabarī, Muḥammad b. Jarīr, *The History of al-Ṭabarī. Vol. I: General Introduction and From the Creation to the Flood*. trans. by Franz Rosenthal (Albany, NY: State University of New York Press, 1989).

Al-Ṭabarī, Muḥammad b. Jarīr, *The History of al-Ṭabarī. Vol. XIX: The Caliphate of Yazīd b. Muʿāwiyah*, trans. I. K. A. Howard (Albany: State University of New York Press, 1990).

Al-Ṭabarī, Muḥammad b. Jarīr, *The History of al-Ṭabarī. Vol. XX: The Collapse of Sufyānid Authority and the Coming of the Marwānids*, trans. G. R. Hawting (Albany: State University of New York Press, 1989).

Al-Ṭabarī, Muḥammad b. Jarīr, *The History of al-Ṭabarī. Vol. XXI: The Victory of the Marwānids*, trans. Michael Fishbein (Albany: State University of New York Press, 1990).

Al-Ṭabarī, Muḥammad b. Jarīr, *The History of al-Ṭabarī. Vol. XXXIV: Incipient Decline*, trans. Joel L. Kraemer (Albany: State University of New York Press, 1989).

Al-Ṭabarī, Muḥammad b. Jarīr, *Jāmiʿ al-bayān ʿan taʾwīl āy al-Qurʾān*, ed. Ṣidqī Ḥamīd al-ʿAttār. 15 vols (Beirut: Dār al-Fikr, 1995).

Al-Ṭabarī, Muḥammad b. Jarīr, *Tārīkh al-rusul wa-ʾl-mulūk*, ed. M. J. de Goeje *et al.* (Leiden: Brill, 1879–1901).

Al-Ṭabarī, Muḥammad b. Jarīr (attrib.), *Dalāʾil al-imāma* (Beirut: Muʾassasat al-aʿlamī li-l-maṭbūʿāt, 1988).

Takim, Liyakat 'Kaššī, Abu ʿAmr Moḥammad', in *EIr*.

Talmon-Heller, Daniella, *Sacred Place and Sacred Time in the Medieval Islamic Middle East: A Historical Perspective* (Edinburgh: Edinburgh University Press, 2020).

Tannous, Jack, *The Making of the Medieval Middle East: Religion, Society, and Simple Believers* (Princeton, NJ: Princeton University Press, 2018).

Tucker, William F., *Mahdis and Millenarians: Shīʿite Extremists in Early Muslim Iraq* (Cambridge: Cambridge University Press, 2008).

Tyan, Émile, 'Bayʿa', in *EI²*.

Urban, Elisabeth, 'The Early Islamic *Mawālī*: A Window onto Processes of Identity Construction and Social Change', unpublished PhD thesis (University of Chicago, 2012).

Veccia Vaglieri, Laura, 'Ḥusayn b. ʿAlī b. Abī Ṭālib', in *EI²*.

Vilozny, Roy, *Constructing a Worldview: Al-Barqī's Role in the Making of Early Shiite Faith* (Turnhout: Brepols, 2017).

Wansbrough, John, *Quranic Studies: Sources and Methods of Scriptural Interpretation* (Oxford: Oxford University Press, 1977).

Warner, George, 'One Thousand *ḥijaj*: Ritualization and the Margins of the Law in Early Twelver Shiʿi *ziyāra* Literature', *Journal of the American Oriental Society*, 142, no. 2 (2022), 415–34.

Watt, W. Montgomery, *The Formative Period of Islamic Thought* (Edinburgh: Edinburgh University Press, 1973).

Watt, W. Montgomery, 'Shi'ism under the Umayyads', *Journal of the Royal Asiatic Society*, 92, nos 3–4 (1960), 158–72.

Webb, Peter, 'al-Azd', in *EI*^{3}.

Webb, Peter, *Imagining the Arabs: Arab Identity and the Rise of Islam* (Edinburgh: Edinburgh University Press, 2016).

Webb, Peter, 'Poetry and the Early Islamic Historical Tradition: Poetry and Narratives of the Battle of Ṣiffīn', in Hugh Kennedy (ed.), *Warfare and Poetry in the Middle East.* (London: I. B. Tauris, 2013), 119–48.

Weiss, Bernard G., 'Covenant and Law in Islam', in Edwin R. Firmage, Bernard G. Weiss and John W. Welch (eds), *Religion and Law: Biblical-Judaic and Islamic Perspectives* (Winona Lake, IN: Eisenbrauns, 1990), 49–84.

Wellhausen, Julius, *The Religio-Political Factions in Early Islam* (Amsterdam: North-Holland Publishing Company, 1975).

Al-Yaʿqūbī, Ibn Wāḍiḥ, *Tārīkh*, ed. M. T. Houtsma, 2 vols (Leiden: Brill, 1883).

Al-Yaʿqūbī, Ibn Wāḍiḥ, *The Works of Ibn Wāḍiḥ al-Yaʿqūbī: An English Translation*, ed. Matthew S. Gordon *et al.*, 3 vols (Leiden: Brill, 2018).

Yāqūt, *Muʿjam al-Buldān*. 5 vols (Beirut: Dār Ṣādir, 1955–7).

Yarshater, Ehsan, 'Taʿziyeh and Pre-Islamic Mourning Rites in Islam', in Peter Chelkowski (ed.), *Taʿziyeh, Ritual and Drama in Iran* (New York: New York University Press, 1979), 88–94.

Index

Note: *f* indicates a figure, *t* indicates a table

EU Authorised Representative:
Easy Access System Europe Mustamäe tee 50, 10621 Tallinn, Estonia
gpsr.requests@easproject.com

Printed and bound by CPI Group (UK) Ltd, Croydon, CR0 4YY
07/10/2026
02229138-0013